Pivotal Moments

Pivotal Moments

How Educators Can Put
All Students
on the Path to College

Roberta Espinoza

Harvard Education Press
Cambridge, Massachusetts

Library of Congress Control Number 2011937500

Paperback ISBN: 978-1-61250-119-2
Library Edition ISBN: 978-1-61250-120-8

Published by Harvard Education Press,
an imprint of the Harvard Education Publishing Group

Harvard Education Press
8 Story Street
Cambridge, MA 02138

Cover Design: Sarah Henderson

The typefaces used in this book are Bembo and Scala Sans.

*This book is dedicated to all
the educators who go above and beyond
to nurture the academic talents
of low-income and minority students.*

CONTENTS

FOREWORD

I can imagine no more life-affirming Saturday morning ritual than the one practiced by a certain African American man I know of, a guidance counselor from a large Chicago high school. Throughout his long career, this gentleman pushed hard for the students in his charge to go on to higher education. Every September, a creditable number of that school's graduates left their familiar neighborhoods and set out on their college journeys.

He could have sat back on his laurels. Yet this wise man did not consider his job done. Every Saturday morning, he pulled his chair up next to the telephone and dialed his graduated seniors to check in with them. These were fatherly conversations, ranging from homesickness to homework, from professors to payments due. He listened, encouraged, lent a hand at times. Always, before hanging up, he'd say, "Talk to you next week."

If those first-generation college students went back to school after the Thanksgiving break, this veteran educator drew a deep, and provisional, breath of relief. He knew the odds from long experience: to thrive and persist in higher education requires sustained and heartfelt support far beyond what most such students receive.

Making college dreams come true for America's youth is a joint production, requiring all of us. Its work starts early and takes many years, often surfacing at the moments that we least expect and entailing actions that don't appear in job descriptions. It involves close observation and listening, skillful negotiation, persistent intervention. That work may demand more of us as educators than we imagine. And yet it is not more than we can do.

This conclusion sounds loud and clear in the stories that young people themselves tell, when asked what makes the difference as they find their precarious way, against the odds, to success in higher education.

And it also sounds in Roberta Espinoza's timely and important book, as she shows educators how to tell of reaching beyond their assignments to connect with students in what she aptly calls educational "Pivotal Moments."

Over the past decade, our nonprofit organization What Kids Can Do (WKCD) has spent countless hours with low-income students who would be the first generation in their families to go on to college and graduate school. In our *First in the Family* book series, college students at critical points in their journeys reflect on what helped them persist and advise those who would follow in their footsteps. In our *Hear Us Out* report and videos, high school students present striking evidence that they lacked college-going help until far too late in the game. Whatever point they had reached at the time they spoke to us, these students all agreed on one thing: an adult who offered an "arm around" at critical moments could provide the key to negotiating an unfamiliar process and culture that their own families could do little to unlock.

Our schools and colleges may already have structures designed to support students. We counsel them in their choices of academic pathways, arrange college visits, provide information about application requirements, advise families on financial aid, and more. We often believe that we are doing everything we can; some of us even hold back, convinced that doing "too much" for young people results in their inability to make it on their own.

"Don't be so sure," we hear low-income and first-generation-college students reply. When the young researchers for WKCD's *Hear Us Out* study surveyed close to 5,000 peers from nine comprehensive high schools in Washington state and Tennessee, they found a startling disconnect: almost a third of their respondents said they had never spoken with a school counselor about college. Although that percentage dropped to 12 percent by twelfth grade, 28 percent of seniors said they had completed their college applications mostly on their own. And three-quarters of those surveyed named their families as the chief source of college motivation and support—even when their parents and guardians had not attended college themselves.

In reality, as Roberta Espinoza makes clear, middle-class, college-educated school adults often find it difficult to step out of the beliefs and assumptions they take for granted. Their voices—reasonable, dutiful, professional—sound throughout the pages of this book. These educators take pains to fulfill their job descriptions, which already require an overload of difficult work constrained by budgets and policies beyond their control. Why, they ask implicitly, should they go beyond?

The answers only come when we look within and look around, watching closely for what the blinders of culture, class, and color may hide from view. I think of one comfortable suburban school district that buses in students from a nearby city as part of a desegregation initiative. In a senior year tradition, its high school invites each graduating senior to post a baby picture on a hallway display. But why, one teacher queried this year, were the faces all white? The omission was "nobody's fault," came the reply. "We sent the information home with everybody."

Faced with such rejoinders, Espinoza might argue, we must look harder, ask more, think deeper. What barriers—perhaps of culture, of resources, of unstated or unexamined "otherness"—kept those absent photos off that wall of honor? Likewise, whose responsibility is it to see that no one is left out when it comes to college access and success?

Story by story, Espinoza sets out and analyzes the poignant and powerful contrast between a hands-off "call me if you need me" approach and an "arm around" approach that goes beyond that—bordering on intrusion, if necessary, to raise a student's sights and move him or her forward. She also underlines the crucial role of timing: how early, and how often, these pivotal moments occur makes an enormous difference in the trajectory of success.

Some of the author's examples center on individuals: a single educator's sharp eye, persistent communication, trust-building, and sheer doggedness with a particular student. Others center on institutions: robust academic outreach programs for low-income and first-generation college students, combining ongoing and consistent advisement by peers and faculty with individualized tutoring support. Others involve outside players: nonprofit and community-based initiatives that step in with critical skills and mentoring. An intricate dynamic emerges among those people and institutions; its elements include knowing the student well, individual mentoring and advocacy, passing on crucial knowledge about how to navigate the higher education system, and fostering the academic skills the student needs. And driving that dynamic in every case, as Espinoza rightly sees, is hard-won trust.

The students in our charge—regardless of family income, race, or ethnicity—have no shortage of ambition or ability. If we are to support them on the path to a satisfying and productive life, each of us must continually look for the hidden stories behind the pictures posted in the hallway. We must ask the uncomfortable questions of ourselves and of others. We must step beyond "what's necessary," each, in our way, pulling our chairs up to the phone and dialing. When we do—and when we take the extra steps that follow—each one of us may be creating the pivotal moments that can change a student's life, and perhaps even the world.

Kathleen Cushman
What Kids Can Do, Inc.

ACKNOWLEDGMENTS

This project involved many people to whom I am extremely thankful. I am greatly indebted to the academic mentors who have supported my scholarship. In particular, I would like to thank Arlie Hochschild, Barrie Thorne, Danny Solórzano, and Daryl Smith.

I would also like to express my appreciation to all the scholars who have encouraged my research and provided thoughtful words of advice and guidance. I specifically thank Evelyn Nakano Glenn, Jerome Karabel, Annette Lareau, Hugh Mehan, Jeannie Oakes, Patricia Gándara, Gary Orfield, Rachel Moran, Ray Buriel, Gilda Ochoa, Jill Grigsby, Lynn Rapaport, Deb Smith, Jose Calderon, Miguel Tinker-Salas, Eva Valle, Mike Soldatenko, Maria Soldatenko, Frances Contreras, Robert Ream, Sal Oropesa, Michael Perez, Eileen Walsh, and Dana Collins.

I owe a debt of gratitude to two wonderful research assistants who provided help at various stages of this research. Special thanks to Cynthia Alcantar for spending countless hours recruiting and interviewing participants, and Monica de la Cruz for diligently transcribing interviews. I am also indebted to the numerous teachers, counselors, academic outreach professionals, school administrators, and students who graciously allowed me to visit their classrooms, observe their work with students, and interview them. Thank you for taking time out of your busy schedules to share your experiences, which gives this book its richness.

I am extraordinarily thankful to Will Perez for his unwavering support throughout the writing of this book. I am also grateful to my sister, Frances Espinoza, who paved the path for me to higher education as the first person in our family to go to college. Lastly, thank you to Caroline Chauncey, who recognized and patiently nurtured the potential in this manuscript from the very beginning and provided the necessary support to see this book to completion. It is an honor and a privilege to have this work published by Harvard Education Press.

INTRODUCTION

SOCIAL CLASS AND SCHOOL SUCCESS

Contradictions of the U.S. Educational System

M ost of us have experienced moments in our lives that have been pivotal in altering our life course. These pivotal moments significantly
change both the way we see the world and how we function within it. I
have experienced numerous pivotal moments in my life, many of which
took place in the school system. When I was in eighth grade, my English teacher invited me to participate in a program to visit local university
campuses. This was my first introduction to college in which I was given
concrete information about what it takes to get there. The college visits,
as well as the connections I developed with educators through the program, instilled in me a sense of possibility about going to college. Then in
college, one of my professors encouraged me to apply to an academic outreach program that introduced me to graduate school and doctoral studies. The program helped me gain valuable research experience, a keen
understanding of what doctoral studies entailed, and knowledge about
navigating the graduate school application process. These distinct moments in my education have allowed me to achieve academic success and
advance through the school system.

These experiences were pivotal because I was not the type of student
most educators would have expected to earn a doctorate and become a
university professor. In fact, decades of educational research suggest that
my social and economic background—a Latina, living in poverty, raised

in a single-parent household by my Mexican father, who had only a third-grade education—usually predicts otherwise. Although most people may view my success as the result of individual determination and hard work, recent studies argue that this assumption could not be further from the truth. I certainly did not reach this high level of academic achievement on my own. Rather, my educational success is the direct result of numerous educators who significantly helped me along the way. The relationships I formed with school-based college-educated adults allowed me to develop the academic skills needed to excel in school and navigate the educational system all the way up to the doctorate. Without key educational Pivotal Moments, I would not be in the privileged place I am today as an educator, teacher, researcher, scholar, and mentor. In this book, I explain why students from low-income and minority backgrounds, like my own, need significant academic interventions, and how efforts to provide them can help decrease national achievement gap trends.

Low-income minority students who overcome obstacles to achieve academic success usually encounter at least one college-educated adult in their schooling who takes the initiative to reach out to them and provide concrete academic guidance. When a relationship between an educator and a student becomes genuinely supportive, it can be pivotal in transforming the student's educational trajectory. This book introduces you to a diverse group of students who describe the impact educational Pivotal Moments had on their lives when they connected with a caring educator who played a critical role in their academic success. Their experiences highlight how the practices of Pivotal Moment educators—teachers, counselors, academic outreach professionals, and professors—become effective in helping students circumvent the barriers they encounter in attaining school success. I hope this book inspires educators to assess their own practices and informs their efforts to develop and implement new strategies for working with disadvantaged students.

INDIVIDUAL MERIT VERSUS EDUCATOR SUPPORT

Stories about disadvantaged students who are able to beat the odds and become academically successful abound in mainstream media outlets. Two years ago, in 2009, when I first began to conceptualize the project on which this book is based, I came across an article published in the *Los Angeles Times* about a high-achieving African American student named Khadijah Williams, who had overcome a lifetime of living in homeless shelters to gain admission to Harvard University. To explain her rise in the education system, the article highlighted her "individual drive and determination" to succeed. Her high test scores in the early part of her schooling testify to her innate abilities and raw academic talent. Upholding the ever prevalent American achievement ideology, Khadijah was doing well in school all on her own. It was not until tenth grade that she realized that if she wanted to go to college, she could not navigate that process alone. So she actively began to reach out to organizations such as Upward Bound, Higher Edge Los Angeles, Experience Berkeley, and South Central Scholars to find teachers, counselors, and college alumni networks that helped her enroll in summer community college classes, gave her access to computers and scholarship applications, and taught her about social networking.

It is quite common to find stories like Khadijah's in various television shows, magazine articles, and broadcast news features. The stories all follow a similar formula: a person's life accomplishments and outcomes are primarily connected to individual effort and talent such as being a hard worker or showing leadership potential.[1] Americans are much more comfortable recognizing the power of individual initiative than recognizing the power of social forces such as social class, race, ethnicity, or gender in shaping people's lives and experiences. Studies show that fewer than 20 percent of Americans see race, social class, or gender as having an impact on one's life opportunities.[2] Americans continue to affirm the American Dream: if you work hard and play by the rules, you will go as far as your given ability and initiative will take you.

There is no doubt that stories like Khadijah's are amazing. As a researcher, however, I question whether there is another part to her story—equally as important—that is missing. I wonder, Who helps these students figure out they need to reach out for assistance to navigate the educational system? Once they connect with others, who advises and mentors them? Does the mentoring they receive have lasting effects on their ability to adjust to and succeed at elite universities like Harvard? A closer examination of these success stories reveals they are incomplete, and yet they still manage to perpetuate the notion that individuals achieve educational success solely by virtue of their own initiative.

Khadijah's graduation from Harvard will undoubtedly confirm her ultimate success, but in the meantime, we need to fill in the part of these portraits that frequently get left out. In this book, I introduce a new framework called educational "Pivotal Moments" to explain exactly how and why low-income minority students successfully progress through the school system to gain access to higher education and, ultimately, upward socioeconomic mobility. I argue that academic success is hardly an individual affair but rather is the result of the formal and informal academic interventions of educators who foster meaningful relationships with students to transform their educational trajectories.

EDUCATIONAL PIVOTAL MOMENTS

The educational Pivotal Moment framework emerged from my previous work, which examined the educational experiences of minority female doctoral students from working-class backgrounds attending highly selective universities.[3] I wanted to learn from their experiences how, despite the odds, they reached the top of the educational ladder. As they shared the details of their academic pathways to graduate school, a distinct pattern emerged. Each had experienced at least one educational intervention that set her on the path to higher education. In interview after interview, I kept hearing that they had connected with an educator in a significant way that resulted in a turnaround moment that altered their educational trajectory. These academic interventions—what I came to call *educational Pivotal Moments*—had a lasting impact on them by transforming their social and psychological orientations toward academic achievement, augmenting the accumulation of college knowledge and relationship-building skills that facilitated school success.

An educational Pivotal Moment occurs when a college-educated adult, such as a teacher, counselor, academic outreach professional, or professor, makes a concerted effort to support and mentor a disadvantaged student in either an informal or an official role. Educational Pivotal Moments are characterized by a deep and trusting relationship with

4

an educator who provides guidance, information, advice, and emotional support. These interventions become significant and life changing because, through them, students gain hands-on knowledge about navigating the educational system and, for the first time, begin to develop the skills and behaviors that launch them on the path of academic success. In contrast, middle-class students usually do not require such an intervention because of the ongoing guidance and support they receive from their college-educated parents and other adults in their social networks who are intimately familiar with the educational system.

Educational Pivotal Moments are transformative events in which a student's educational trajectory is recalibrated, resulting in subsequent success and advancement in the school system. The educational Pivotal Moment framework offers a unique approach to understanding specifically how disadvantaged students are able to overcome the social class and racial or ethnic barriers they likely encounter in school. Examining the intensity and timing of educational Pivotal Moments can be particularly useful in understanding how students gain access to and persist in higher education. It provides insight into how students use the academic knowledge and skills they learn through these interventions to become proactive in using the educational system to attain social mobility. This book unpacks both the theory and the practice behind educational Pivotal Moments using extensive in-depth empirical research that includes over 100 hours of participant observation at high schools, academic outreach programs, and college events, 140 interviews with students, and 90 interviews with educators. I translate the theory of educational Pivotal Moments into concrete practices that K–16 educators can use to more effectively intervene in the lives of low-income minority students. I discuss how adults in schools and other student-serving organizations can be more intentional in their daily interactions with students to create interventions that will ultimately enhance the educational attainment levels of students from underrepresented backgrounds.

THE CONSEQUENCES OF SOCIAL CLASS

The major contradiction of education in the modern era is that it is both an avenue for upward mobility and the main social institution in which socioeconomic status is reinforced from one generation to the next.[4] Although school is ideologically viewed as the great equalizer that gives everyone, regardless of background, an opportunity for upward social mobility, the reality is that one's starting point, which is determined by social class origins, eventually plays a part in academic success or failure. Many scholars argue that schools require the cultural resources with which only middle-class students are endowed. In other words, only the culture of the dominant class is rewarded by the educational system.[5] As a result, students from the lower classes are unable to access the academic rewards that depend on the cultural capital that belongs to members of the upper classes, leaving disadvantaged students with little hope of achieving success. For students from lower-class and minority backgrounds, the promise of upward social mobility is an illusion unless someone (such as a Pivotal Moment educator) interrupts their downward educational trajectory.

To fully understand why students from low-income minority backgrounds need academic interventions to achieve school success, it is important to understand the powerful ways in which social class impacts children's daily lives. Growing up middle class in a safe neighborhood attending well-resourced, high-performing schools is vastly different from growing up in an impoverished neighborhood attending underfunded, low-performing schools. These two distinct environments have differential consequences for children's mental and physical health, including differences in nutrition, health care access to address medical needs, a decent place to live, and nurturing families to develop cognitive and non-cognitive skills, healthy self-concepts, and a desire to do well in school.

Unlike low-income children, most middle-class children arrive at school primed for learning. They are born to mothers who had consistent prenatal care, their own nutrition is adequate, they have visited doctors regularly to address physical problems, and, if applicable, vision problems have been corrected. Middle-class children are also very likely to have had safe areas to play, educational toys to play with, and caregivers who introduced them to the rudiments of literacy and numeracy. In contrast, low-income students are born to mothers who often do not have adequate prenatal care, a lack that leads to health problems during childhood. They have inadequate nutrition, come to school hungry, and lack medical and vision care, which impacts their ability to clearly see the content on the board at the front of the class. They may also have other health problems, such as toothaches or ear infections that interfere with their ability to concentrate in the classroom. Additionally, the toys low-income children play with are not likely to be the sort that will prepare them to succeed in school, and their parents instead may have turned to television as an affordable babysitter that occupies them for an average of four hours a day or more—time not spent reading.[6] Poor children are less likely than their middle-class peers to have many books in their homes, be read to by parents or caregivers, and observe adults in the household reading for enjoyment.[7] Because poor and low-income children lack the resources to become educationally prepared for school, they are dependent on the educational system and society to invest in them in areas where their parents simply cannot.

There is no question that society is stratified along social class lines. The possession of highly valued resources such as wealth, a prestigious job, a good education, and homeownership are not evenly distributed throughout society.[8] These resources are then passed on from one generation to the next, giving each subsequent generation an accumulation of them. For the middle class, this generational transfer creates an accumulation of wealth to solidify members' place in the social class structure. For the working class, this process holds no significance for upward social mobility. Nationally, only 25 percent of working-class students are able to move up the socioeconomic ladder by becoming college-educated, full-fledged members of the middle class.[9] The vast majority of working-class students will remain working class, and, ultimately, so will their children.

One of the best predictors of whether a child will one day graduate from college is whether her parents are college graduates.[10] Even before kindergarten, children of highly educated parents are much more likely to exhibit educational readiness skills such as knowing their letters, identifying colors, counting up to twenty, and being able to write their first names.[11] In particular, children of highly educated mothers continue to outperform children of less-educated mothers throughout their schooling years. By the time young people take the SAT examination for admission to college, the gap is dramatic—averaging a

150-point disparity between children of parents who are high school dropouts compared to those with parents who have a graduate degree.[12]

An important aspect of formal education is the cultural capital (knowing how educational processes work) and social capital (having access to important social networks) that are acquired while students earn a diploma and a college degree.[13] Instrumental educational knowledge—such as knowing the process of how to enter college, negotiate school bureaucracies, approach professors, and find financial aid resources—is vital for success in higher education. Scholarly work has emphasized the role of parents in providing this type of school knowledge to their children.[14] Working-class parents, with their relatively low levels of formal education, have far fewer of these important assets to pass on to their children. In addition, low-income youth have few adult individuals in their community who exemplify educational, occupational, and social success, and few peers who are supportive of educational achievement. It is not surprising, therefore, that most students who succeed in higher education come from households where one or both parents attended college and provide instrumental educational knowledge and skills.

GAINING ACCESS TO HIGHER EDUCATION

My extensive research on the educational paths of working-class minority students highlights that the educational experiences of students like Khadijah, much like my own, are an exception to the rule. Most students who share our social class or ethnic backgrounds (or both) do not make it through high school, nor find their way to college. Media stories constantly call our attention to the fact that one-third of students who enter our nation's high schools do not graduate. Of those who graduate, only 38 percent of low-income high school seniors go straight to college as compared to 81 percent of their high-income peers. Once enrolled in college, low-income students earn bachelor's degrees at a rate less than half that of high-income students—21 percent compared to 45 percent.[15]

The current national 44 percent college dropout rate is undoubtedly cause for national concern. Despite billions of dollars in financial aid and scores of government efforts, the college graduation rate for low-income Americans who are the first in their families to go to college has been falling drastically.[16] Research finds distressing signs that demographic factors such as gender, race, and parental education play large roles in determining a student's fate—no matter how smart or hardworking the particular student. Additionally, those from low-income families or parents who did not finish college, as well as African Americans, Hispanics, and males, are failing college at disproportionate rates compared with peers who have similar grades and test scores. Even when students from low-income families score high on early performance assessment exams (e.g., an eighth-grade math test), they are still 10 times less likely to complete college than their low-scoring peers from high-income families. Not only are these findings alarming, but also they illuminate the fact that being from a low-income family hinders college completion even for top-performing students. Thus, failing to open educational opportunities to all students will undoubtedly endanger the long-term health of our country.

THE ROLE OF SCHOOLS AND EDUCATORS

Low-income minority students encounter numerous structural barriers in the educational system (e.g., tracking, lower enrollment in Honors and Advanced Placement courses, inadequate access to academic guidance counselors, being taught by undercredentialed teachers, attending overcrowded and poorly maintained schools, etc.) that prevent them from gaining access to higher education. For this reason, the role of schools in preparing students for college needs to take center stage in the national dialogue about higher education access and attainment. If we recognize the country's urgent need for a large college-educated workforce, then we must figure out how schools and educators can play a more effective role in that effort. If low-income minority students are less likely to have parents to provide them with the school readiness and information that middle-class students receive, schools must be prepared to fill in that critical gap by training educators at all levels on effective practices to accomplish this goal.

Teachers, counselors, and other educators do far more than fulfill their formal roles to teach, enforce discipline, and organize class schedules. They often develop meaningful and multifaceted relationships with students. In fact, educators frequently find themselves acting as co-parents, mentors, advocates, and informal psychologists with students. Recent educational research has shown that for low-income minority students, success in school depends on opportunities to develop supportive relationships with key institutional agents. Patricia Gándara and her colleagues find that students who beat the odds and make it into four-year colleges usually encounter a college-educated adult who takes the initiative to encourage them—tell them they are smart and "can do it"—and provides the critical academic guidance to make it happen. The intervening adult who takes them under her wing is often a teacher, counselor, or someone associated with a special academic program. For low-income minority students, the advocate and mentor role educators can fulfill holds considerable transformative power. When educator-student relationships become genuinely supportive, they carry the potential to change a student's educational trajectory in extremely positive and enduring ways. Beyond mere support, educators can create a link to transfer instrumental educational knowledge to students—much as middle-class parents do with their children—to enhance their academic outcomes and produce an educational Pivotal Moment intervention.

ORGANIZATION OF THIS BOOK

Part I describes the educational Pivotal Moment framework and the impact Pivotal Moment interventions have on students' educational trajectories. Chapter 1 explains why low-income minority students need academic interventions by documenting some of the challenges and obstacles they face in their families, neighborhoods, and schools that hinder academic success. Chapter 2 elaborates on the characteristics of Pivotal Moment interventions, and explains how they occur in practice through the experiences of Blanca and Terry, two minority women who were the first in their family to graduate from college and subsequently enroll in doctoral studies. Chapters 3 and 4 discuss how the timing of Pivotal Moments impact students' long-term academic adjustment and success. These two chapters profile the narratives of low-income minority students at different points along the educational system to illustrate why academic interventions are more beneficial and produce better educational outcomes if they occur earlier. Carmen and Valerie, who experienced late Pivotal Moments, struggled to adjust to higher education settings because they had not developed the academic knowledge and skills needed to make a smooth transition. Whereas Dora and Brianna, who experienced early Pivotal Moments, did not have the same difficulties because they have acquired the necessary academic knowledge and skills to successfully transition to postsecondary education.

Part II showcases the practices of exemplary Pivotal Moment educators at the high school and college level. Although these educators face daunting institutional challenges in their schools, they still manage to effectively assist the low-income minority students they work with to become academically successful and prepare for college. Chapter 5 highlights the practices of various educators like Mr. Chang, a high school counselor who, despite his caseload of 560 students, has a personalized approach to working with students that builds trust—the foundational component of a Pivotal Moment. Chapter 6 describes the practices of several educators like Mr. Montes, a high school science teacher, who integrates information about college into his course curricula and actively mentors and advocates for students—another key element of a Pivotal Moment. Chapter 7 focuses on educators like Ms. Johnson, a high school counselor, who exemplify the third central component of a Pivotal Moment through her efficient transmission of academic knowledge and skills to her students to get them on path to college. I also compare and contrast the practices of educators who also work with low-income minority students but do not employ a Pivotal Moment approach.

Part III discusses the Pivotal Moment practices of academic outreach professionals. Chapter 8 profiles staff from government-funded academic support programs who do a phenomenal job building trust with students and providing mentoring and advocacy, but fall short in transmitting important academic knowledge that diminishes the potential of their efforts to become Pivotal Moments. Chapter 9 highlights a nonprofit academic outreach program called College Match that has institutionalized the educational Pivotal Moment approach. As a result, they have amassed an impressive success record in helping low-income minority students get accepted into highly selective college and universities.

Part IV translates the theory of educational Pivotal Moments into effective practice for all educators. Chapter 10 provides detailed recommendations about how to create Pivotal Moments for students and how schools can build institutional capacity to train their staff to become Pivotal Moment educators through professional development activities. I also stress the need to incorporate Pivotal Moment training into teacher preparation and credential programs, as well as coursework and practicum in counseling programs that train and license guidance counseling professionals. The conclusion chapter discusses the implications of Pivotal Moments for educational practice and for the long-term educational success of low-income and minority students. It draws attention to the role that schools, academic outreach programs, and nonprofit organizations should play in fostering early Pivotal Moments to place first-generation students on a path to college completion, graduate education, and subsequent social mobility.

AUDIENCE FOR THIS BOOK

This book has been written for K–16 educators of all types: teachers, administrators, guidance counselors, academic outreach professionals, university faculty, and higher education student affairs staff, among others. I hope the lessons learned from the educational Pivotal Moments captured in this book from both the student and the educator perspectives will give school personnel effective strategies to provide academic support to students as well as serve as an impetus for self-reflection on their own educational practices and interactions with students.

The goal of this book is not to criticize educators but rather to offer strategies to help them more effectively work with low-income and minority students. I encourage readers to carefully evaluate and implement new ways to improve their relationships with students in an effort to become Pivotal Moment educators. The transformative power educators have to positively alter a student's educational trajectory is exciting, on the one hand, but can be challenging, on the other. Nonetheless, given what is at stake for students and for the nation, I hope readers will embrace this challenge and work toward making a difference in the lives of disadvantaged students by providing the necessary academic preparation and support to ensure that they successfully access and complete higher education.

MOVING FORWARD

The most powerful determinants of a student's entrance into and success in higher education are her social class origin, racial or ethnic background, and gender. Children raised in middle-class homes with college-educated parents are more likely to acquire the skills and behaviors necessary to both navigate and excel in school. In contrast, children from working-class homes are not exposed to the knowledge that is compatible with academic success in school, placing them at a distinct disadvantage.

Some students from low-income and ethnic minority backgrounds, however, reach high levels of academic success, indicating that their social class and racial or ethnic background do not always predestine low achievement. For these students, something else comes into play, an often hidden variable that allows them to acquire information to navigate the educational system and counter the sorting process of school. The powerful hidden variable, which so often gets overlooked in a meritocratic system that places such great importance on individual merit, is the educational practitioners—teachers, counselors, academic outreach professionals, and professors—who make key academic interventions on behalf of disadvantaged students, interventions that I call educational Pivotal Moments.

An educational Pivotal Moment is a turnaround event, one in which a student's educational trajectory is positively reset in a new direction toward higher education. This book pays tribute to the overlooked efforts of exemplary educators and places their practices in the spotlight to explain how they occur and what makes them so transformative. In the chapters that follow, I present an analysis of Pivotal Moment educators, and tell the amazing stories of low-income minority students who experienced life changing educational Pivotal Moments.

PART I

Understanding Pivotal Moments

1

OVERCOMING DISADVANTAGES
IN SCHOOL
Why Students Need Pivotal Moments

Why do working-class children end up with working-class jobs as adults? For the past four decades, researchers have been trying to find an answer to this lingering question. Scholars have suggested that processes within educational systems—such as tracking, standardized testing, and the hidden curriculum—perpetuate the social class structure from one generation to the next.[1] Their work also highlights the role of school personnel as "gatekeepers" who screen and classify students according to perceived ability. The research characterizes schools as "factories" that determine the paths taken by students through the educational system based on arbitrary notions of academic aptitude.

Although it is important to focus on large-scale trends to develop effective policies that will reduce educational disparities, it is equally critical to recognize that educators also have the potential to disrupt school processes that reinforce social inequality. The informal roles educators play in the lives of disadvantaged students are often undervalued or overlooked. As a result, it is easy for educators themselves to disregard the various ways in which they proactively alter students' educational paths in extremely positive ways.[2] After all, it is often the tacit and imperceptible informal exchanges with educators that have the most enduring impact on low-income and minority students' school success and educational trajectories.

Interactions between educators and students build confidence, strengthen academic self-concepts, and instill the possibility of reaching future educational goals such as attending college—all of which arguably are life changing.

The purpose of this book, therefore, is not to beat up on educators as sorters and gatekeepers who reinforce inequality, but rather to remind them that they are life changers and to give them tools to be more effective in this important role. Educators can guide and mentor students in various formal and informal ways to enhance their overall academic achievement. Moreover, through academic interventions, educators can help low-income minority students circumvent school sorting to gain access to higher education. Instead of following the usual pattern of low achievement and lack of access to higher education, disadvantaged students who receive key support from educators can successfully navigate and advance in the educational system.

EDUCATORS AS GATEKEEPERS

Conventional thinking defines the various roles assumed by school personnel in a narrow range of formal and professional duties. Seldom in the public arena do we fully recognize that teachers, counselors, advisers, coaches, and other educators do far more than teach, organize class schedules, and supervise students. Educators also participate in the social networks of low-income and minority students and thus play a critical role in helping students choose a life path.

The multiple roles of educators, as well as the relationships between educators and students, are complex. For example, a teacher's explicit professional responsibilities are fairly straightforward: to develop students' literacy, provide academic content, and enforce discipline. However, teachers and other school personnel often operate far beyond their pedagogical function. In fact, especially if they work in low-income schools where students' basic needs are much greater than in more advantaged schools, educators frequently act as coparents, advocates, mentors, and informal psychologists. The advocate or mentor role that educators often assume is one of considerable transformative power in the lives of their students.[3] When educators embrace the role of advocate or mentor and become genuinely supportive, their actions carry the potential to transform students' educational opportunities in positive and lasting ways.

Educators can expose students to information and resources that their families and communities may lack as well as encourage students to take programs of study and academic courses to prepare them for the challenges of postsecondary education. They may also encourage students to participate in extracurricular activities that contribute to their academic and social development. Teachers and counselors can help students seek out and take advantage of opportunities that facilitate access to postsecondary education, such as applying for scholarships.[4] In particular, low-income and minority students rely on school personnel to transfer information about the education system, because their families and communities may not be familiar with postsecondary options.[5]

The Value of Informal Mentoring

Relationships with teachers and counselors often facilitate college planning for students.[6] Compared with minority students who matriculate into two-year community colleges, for example, minority students who matriculate into four-year universities usually have greater access to high school counselors who make sure they take the right classes and visit with college representatives.[7] Counselors' personal relationships with students also help provide the appropriate support for minority students' college planning.[8]

Through their interactions with students, educators can also help them learn more effectively, study efficiently, and perform well in the classroom.[9] Many teachers and counselors provide emotional support and exhibit loving parental behaviors towards their students.[10] In his book *Manufacturing Hope and Despair*, Ricardo Stanton-Salazar describes the case of Elena. After joining the cheerleading team, Elena developed a strong relationship with the team adviser, Ms. Rogers. After the relationship developed, Ms. Rogers became a critical part of Elena's success by monitoring her academic progress and stepping in as her advocate at school when needed.

Stanton-Salazar also describes a physics teacher who played casual basketball with his students to establish trust and initiate tutoring sessions during lunch or after school. Over time, students came to see this teacher as an approachable and reliable source of support. Like many others, this teacher had a fluid and expansive notion of his role as an educator. He intentionally imparted knowledge of physics in the context of sports, outside the formal classroom, between teacher and student. In this case, students gained much more than information about physics; they also added a valuable relationship with a college-educated adult to their social network.

Students and educators develop close relationships in many ways: through interactions outside normal academic or administrative routines, through participation in school organizations or clubs, and through involvement in sports teams. Relationships that produce measurable academic benefits for students have several key characteristics. They involve a high level of interaction, require a significant foundation of trust, and remain consistent over an extended period. The educator also often assumes multiple roles in the students' life both inside and outside school—roles that can include informal coparent, mentor, and advocate.[11] Through these relationships, students begin to acquire critical academic knowledge and skills that enable them to gradually and positively alter their academic paths. Students who participate in school sports, for example, typically develop strong relationships with their coaches, who provide academic advice on school matters, emotional support, and, in some cases, occasional financial assistance for school-related expenses. This type of support is a by-product of routine interactions between coaches and their athletes. Students with these intricate and multifaceted relationships with educators tend to be more involved in school organizations, extracurricular activities, and special academic programs. The development of close and complex relationships between students and educators often extends over several years.

Limits to Mentoring Opportunities

Opportunities for students to benefit from school relationships are limited in large high schools, because those schools are often organized around bureaucracy, hierarchy, and formal relationships.[12] The scope of teachers' and counselors' roles in college planning is limited. Schools with high student-to-counselor ratios are disproportionately populated by low-income and minority students.[13] These students face large counselor caseloads of one counselor to 740 or more students as well as restricted counselor time for college advising, resulting in disproportionately limited access to college counseling.[14] High student–counselor ratios often prohibit minority students from accessing information about college in their high schools, even though they are the only potential sources of such information.[15] Thus, most low-income minority students do not have elaborate and multifaceted supportive ties with educators to help them solve the wide array of educational challenges they face.[16]

The fortunate students who have these types of transformative relationships receive various forms of support from educators—support that usually goes beyond their official duties—because the educators have a personal concern about and emotional investment in them. When youths receive emotional support and intimate counsel from middle-class, college-educated adults, they can acquire highly valuable educational knowledge if it is properly transmitted to them. Educators, therefore, can play a fundamental role in the lives of low-income minority students, because trusting and caring relationships create the necessary conditions for the effective transfer of the information and skills needed for academic success. Educators who develop strong connections with low-income minority students who are severely disadvantaged in the school system have the highest potential to make a positive impact.[17] These forms of support can foster coping strategies such as problem-solving skills, interpersonal and networking adeptness, and the development of other instrumental behaviors that help low-income and minority students overcome institutional barriers and marginalizing forces to successfully advance in the school system.[18] Educators can, in many ways, compensate for the disadvantages faced by low-income minority students as a result of their socioeconomic and racial or ethnic backgrounds.

WHY LOW-INCOME AND MINORITY STUDENTS NEED PIVOTAL MOMENTS

Low-income and minority students face challenges in their daily lives that continually interfere with their academic performance as well as their ability to prepare for college. From an early age, they often assume household chores and take care of younger siblings because their parents work long hours in low-wage, physically demanding jobs. Such students can experience frequent financial hardships and live in poor housing conditions. Their low-income communities are often ridden with crime and violence, forcing them to worry constantly about their safety. They attend low-performing schools with limited resources, are taught by undercredentialed teachers, and are surrounded by negative peer influences. Those from immigrant backgrounds face the additional struggle of learning English proficiently at school and accessing the necessary courses to qualify for college admissions.

All these factors hinder low-income and minority students' ability to gain access to higher education. Additionally, because their parents and most people in their extended families have low levels of education, these students lack the information and guidance necessary to navigate the educational system. To put these socioeconomic and educational challenges into perspective, I have summarized the responses from the low-income minority students I interviewed for this research study.[19]

Socioeconomic Challenges

When I asked her to tell me about her childhood, Andrea, a high school senior, said that her parents always worked long hours when she was growing up. Most days, her mother did not get home until 9:00 p.m., and her dad, even later. Her mother worked as a seamstress in a clothing factory, and her dad was a hotel valet. In fact, many students I interviewed said they came home to empty houses after school because of their parents' hectic work schedules. One student stated that he and his sister had to grow up fast and learn quickly how to fend for themselves: "We were home alone when I was six [years old] and my sister was eight [years old], so we had to learn how to do everything ourselves. We had to learn how to cook and dress ourselves."

Those with younger siblings often assumed caretaking and household responsibilities, as was the case for Enrique, a high school senior, who recalls taking on these responsibilities at a fairly young age: "Since I was thirteen, I've had to pick up my little brother from school, and it's been hard because I have sports and everything. I got to pick him up right away, so they won't take him to the police station or something. I take him home, I check his homework, make dinner for him, make dinner for my parents because they don't get home until about eight or eight-thirty, and then do the homework for all my classes. So it was hard."

Although most students are happy to help their parents by looking after younger siblings and doing household chores, their responsibilities often make it difficult to complete homework. Many students said that their obligations at home often interfered or competed with their school demands.

In some instances, extended family members experience difficulties that have a direct impact on a students' ability to focus on school. One student explained, "We recently got my little cousins from foster care because they got taken away from my uncle, so now both me and my sister have to help my mom with that. Sometimes I feel like me and my sister have to raise them. I have to pick them up from school, take them home, feed them, take care of them, help them with their homework, shower them, and get them in bed by seven o'clock. I have to help them, and that gets in the way of my homework."

In addition to significant family responsibilities, students described severe financial hardships they endured. Many students said their families lived check-to-check during their childhood and recalled constant worries about having the money to pay bills and rent on time. Brianna, a high school senior, explained, "When I was in elementary school, it was a little bit tough just because my dad didn't have a steady job. We had to move around from house to house, and I remember my mom would often say, 'Well, we don't have money,' even though she always tried to keep those things from me . . . She doesn't want that to affect us, but it's kind of hard because I could see that my parents were going through a tough situation and I would get concerned about it."

Like Brianna, most students do not ask their parents for materials they might need for school because they know it is a financial hardship. Some students try to minimize their needs, and other students begin working at a young age to assist the family financially. Enrique, for example, started working when he was seven years old. He would accompany his dad to the factory, where he worked cutting fabric and assembling garments. Interestingly, I found that female students are more likely to reduce their needs for money or educational items, whereas male students are more likely to take on a part-time job. Despite these trends, economic concerns have an impact on low-income students' ability to concentrate and consistently do well in school.

Another challenge faced by low-income students is that their home environments are not conducive to studying. One student told me that she would lock herself in the bathroom to study for important exams, because it was the only room in her house that she could occupy alone and concentrate. Many students, like Enrique, live in apartments with multiple families due to financial constraints. He remembered growing up in a cramped living situation: "We lived in a small house with two rooms for about ten people. We lived with my uncle and they had a lot of kids. My uncle eventually got a house and we went to live in his house. We had one room with a little restroom for me, my brother, and my two parents. We had bunk beds and everything was crowded." Students also mentioned living in poor housing conditions that included dilapidated buildings and apartments. One student, Terry, reported that her home was "dirty with roaches."

In addition to cramped and substandard housing, students worry about their safety. Marissa, a high school student, reported witnessing a lot of violence when she was growing up: "It was a bad neighborhood. Down the street, in the apartments and the trailers, everybody was always fighting. Cops were always there—helicopters looking for people." The violence in her neighborhood also spread to her school campus. She recounted, "When I was in middle school, there was a shooting at the basketball courts." She said it was very scary living in a neighborhood and attending a school where she constantly worried about her safety.

Andrea also described her neighborhood as "dangerous" as she recounted an incident she had recently witnessed:

We went to get food and stopped by the library to pick up my friend's sister. I waited for her in the car, and all of a sudden these kids from my high school started fighting across the street, and the next thing you know, one pulled out a gun and then he shoots two guys. They were in tenth grade. Nobody was helping, people were just walking by! I was scared because it was shocking. It was probably five feet away from my car, so I got out of the car really fast and was screaming for help. Later on, I found out that they both died.

Violence was also a regular occurrence in Rachel's neighborhood. "My next door neighbors were involved in gangs," she said. "There would always be fights and cops there." As decades of research have demonstrated, these living environments have a consistent and long-term negative impact on a students' academic success unless they receive appropriate support.

Students who live in low-income neighborhoods also attend schools with limited resources, unsupportive school personnel, and negative peer influences. Most students are well aware that their schools have bad academic reputations. For example, Rachel noted that her school was "the lowest-performing in the district." Students are also well aware that most of their classmates face uncertain futures after high school, as Veronica explained: "There were tons of people at my high school that would only graduate from high school, if even that, and they didn't really do much with their life." Students from low-income immigrant backgrounds struggle with learning English and gaining access to coursework that would make them eligible to apply to four-year universities.

Additionally, students attending low-income schools seldom get the support they need from school personnel. Instead, they must contend with teachers and counselors who further demoralize them. Andrea, for example, remembered an educator she had who was never willing to assist students when they asked for her help: "If we needed help, and we raised our hand, she would say, 'Have you asked the person next to you?' Or, 'Have you asked your friend before you asked me? Have you looked in the book?' She wouldn't help, so people just stopped asking her questions. More than half of the class had to retake the class the next year." Another student, Kim, recalled one of her teachers belittling her and other students in class: "She used to tell us we had the brains of a gnat. Have you seen a gnat? It's so tiny! She's like, 'If you don't get this, oh my goodness! You guys have the brains of a gnat.'"

Being surrounded by negative peer influences, beginning early in their schooling experiences, is also a fact of life for low-income students.

Rachel recalled, "Some students are already involved with gangs. My brother was telling me that when you walk down the hall, you see all these pregnant girls and this is a junior high school." Another student, Shelly, described how peers who have no college aspirations can derail others from their higher education goals: "Some people that you surround yourself with don't always have the same goal to go to college, and they can bring you down. Then you lose focus and you get unmotivated." In all these ways, growing up in poverty presents students with financial, social, and educational obstacles.

Lack of College-Going Knowledge

Another major barrier for low-income students is a lack of college-going knowledge in their home and community social networks. Students who do not grow up in environments with college-educated adults are less likely to have acquired the information needed to pursue higher education. Without the proper guidance, students are less likely to take the necessary steps to prepare for college, including taking rigorous courses, participating in extracurricular activities where they take on leadership roles, and studying for college entrance exams. Students who are the first in their family to attend college have parents who are unfamiliar with the school system and unable to provide concrete guidance. Shelly, for example, commented, "My parents don't really know about college since I'm first generation. When I go to them and ask them what classes should I take they say, 'Oh, I really can't help you with that because I don't know anything about it.' So basically, my mom and dad aren't that involved."

Another student said, "They [his parents] don't really have high school experience. They didn't go to college either, so they rather get me supplies for school because they can't really help me with my homework." It is not uncommon for students like Kim to make educational decisions without advice from parents: "I have been choosing my schools since elementary school. Right after I finished elementary school, they sent me this paper that said, 'What school do you want to go to?' My mom left it up to me." Although most students said their parents are very supportive of education and promote the idea of going to college, the parents could not provide guidance.

As students progress through the increasingly complicated educational system, students do not always make decisions that provide them with the best higher education opportunities. Although she got herself into a magnet school with a college-going culture, Kim opted out of a critical academic enrichment program that would have better prepared her for college. "You had to do writing, college essays, stuff like that,". And I was like, 'I'm not going to college right now. I'm only in ninth grade. I have an idea of what's ahead, and that's good enough for me.'" Similarly, Valerie did not apply to more selective universities, even though she was eligible, because she did not want to write the extra essays that were required:

> I did not want to write a personal statement because in my English classes, they weren't preparing us for that. In the AP classes, they were making the students write a personal statement to apply to the UCs [University of California schools] and since I didn't have to write one for my classes, I wasn't going to apply to a UC. I did start, but I did it on my own. I didn't really have someone to tell me. The counselor only told me to apply to college and sent me reminders, so I took it upon myself to go through the application process.

With no one guiding her decisions, Valerie did not maximize her options when applying to college. Also, because she had opted out of the honors track early in high school, her school options were further limited.

Lack of information about how to prepare for and apply to college is a constant and significant barrier for low-income students. Joanna, for example, did not feel that she had anyone to call on for assistance as she navigated the college application process. "I wasn't curious enough to ask. I really don't remember people going out of their way to talk about the whole process." She also did not have the resources to visit college campuses before making a decision. "I really didn't get to see schools. I had no way to go see them—just online research." When I asked her whether she asked her counselor for help, she stated, "They don't talk to us. He would always be busy all the time. If he had time, he would help."

Without her counselor's assistance, Marissa, too, had very few alternative sources of information about college in high school. She recalled,

"Even teachers don't know how to apply for FAFSA [Free Application for Federal Student Aid]. They know about it, they know we should do it, and they do tell us, but that's all they know. So, I would have to figure it out on my own." Not having critical information to make an informed decision about college, she only had a vague notion. "I didn't know much at all. I just knew categories, like UCs are supposed to be above Cal State, and private colleges are above everything—Stanford."

Another student, Andrea, also felt that she knew virtually nothing about college: "I didn't know anything about the paperwork that you have fill out for college. I was clueless." Rachel noted, "Since I'm the first to go to college, I didn't have anyone to tell me, 'OK, this is the process, this is how you do it,' or the school never offered those programs where you can go after school to get help with the application process. What do you write about in your essay? How do you write it? I didn't even know there was a fee to apply to universities or how many you could apply to." Valerie also ended up figuring things out on her own. "My dad tried to help but he didn't really know. During my senior year, sometimes I would go to my counselor, but a lot of it was figuring it out on my own through trial and error."

These few examples provide a glimpse into a broad array of obstacles and challenges low-income students must overcome to be successful in school and gain access to higher education. Overall, students from low socioeconomic backgrounds disproportionately attend high schools that do not focus on preparing students for college and have fewer counseling resources.[20] They are also more likely than high-income students to lack access to rigorous course work and be tracked away from honors and advanced placement courses.[21] Instead, schools direct low-income students toward vocational programs and away from college preparatory courses, resulting in lower academic attainment for these students.[22] Low-income and minority students also have fewer resources and know less about the admissions process and the differences among college types.[23] Moreover, they are less likely to view college as a realistic option.[24] Without any significant forms of support and guidance, most students do not live up to their full academic potential and their educational achievement takes a downward turn over time.

Even for high-achieving students, the process is often fraught with uncertainty as their lack of academic knowledge hampers their success. Unlike middle-class students, who enter the school system with various educational resources embedded in their familial social networks, low-income students start school with numerous disadvantages that they must overcome to be successful.

THE MIDDLE-CLASS ADVANTAGE

It is well documented that low-income students do not enter the school system with the same knowledge, skills, and dispositions as their middle-class peers. According to sociologist Pierre Bourdieu, children of upper-class origin inherit substantially different cultural capital (knowledge and skills) than children from low-income backgrounds. Specifically, the set of dispositions, attitudes, and beliefs—which he calls the *habitus*—that is transmitted from one generation to the next in households that include college-educated adults is qualitatively different from that of households where adults have low levels of education.[25]

Moreover, through parental socialization and daily interactions with various college-educated adults, children from these homes develop a skill set that is virtually identical to that of the highly educated personnel who run educational institutions. These students develop the linguistic and cultural competencies that not only guide their actions and behaviors but are critical for school success. Whereas the attitudes and beliefs of children reared by college-educated parents are rewarded and valued in school, those of low-income students are ignored and devalued, and that, along with the economic and social constraints they face, places them at high risk of educational failure.

Not only are the linguistic and cultural competencies of low-income, and often minority, students not recognized in school, placing them at relative disadvantage, but also the accumulation of negative experiences in educational contexts over time and across generations shapes their attitudes and beliefs about the purpose and value of formal education.[26] For these students, persistent negative educational experiences affect their attitudes toward schooling, often resulting in the perception that their future possibilities are limited. For most students, deciding to invest time and energy in their education by studying hard and taking steps to prepare for college depends on their expectations of whether other students like them are successful at those same academic pursuits.[27] Growing up in an environment where educational success and college-going are rare makes students much less likely to develop strong ambitions for high academic achievement compared with those growing up in a social world surrounded by college-educated parents and family members who have "made it" and where the connection between effort and reward is visible. For example, a young woman may aspire to become a nursing assistant because her mother is a nursing assistant and all the adult female figures she knows have similar jobs. When she asks them for advice, they are more likely to suggest a similar path because that is what they are most familiar with. In addition, these older role models may have faced various barriers in previous unsuccessful attempts to pursue a profession that required a higher level of education, and they may transmit that disillusionment to the young woman pondering her future. Because of her perception of insurmountable barriers, this information could discourage her from developing ambitious educational aspirations similar to those of young adults with college-educated parents.

Sadly, the advice received by the young woman in this example is more likely to reinforce social and educational inequality rather than be transformative. If this young woman does not have positive experiences in school and positive relationships with educational agents who provide a sense of broader future possibilities, she may ultimately follow the well-intentioned advice she receives from those close to her and may begin to believe that career options that require a college or higher levels of education are not viable. Unlike their middle-class counterparts, low-income students undergo educational experiences that are fraught with dilemmas and contradictions, making their education choices both difficult and uncertain.[28]

Under optimal circumstances, however, low-income and minority students may experience the types of changes in internal disposition that support high educational aspirations and achievement, as noted in a growing body of educational research. The American achievement ideology's capacity to mystify structural constraints and encourage high aspirations may further drive adaptive change in these students. In describing the experiences of low-income girls who were in the same college-going courses as their middle-class peers, Julie Bettie notes that the girls not only consciously tried to pass as middle-class but also were acquiring the dispositions, as well as the linguistic and cultural competencies, of their middle-class schoolmates.[29] Although the upwardly mobile low-income girls in Bettie's study were occasionally passing as middle class as their internal dispositions were being reshaped by their experiences in the college-prep curriculum, the academic skills they developed did not completely enable their mobility. Some researchers have argued that low-income students who succeed in the educational system must abandon, or at a minimum drastically change, certain features and dispositions of their social class origins.[30] Although it is not exactly clear what kind of changes or alterations need to take place, it is becoming more evident that the accumulation of key academic skills and knowledge is important in helping low-income students overcome the obstacles they typically encounter in the education system.[31]

If a student's attitudes and beliefs are continuously changing as previous research suggests, then it's important to consider the potential influence of the adults with whom low-income minority students come in contact in school who can nurture new dispositions that facilitate educational success. To date, the dynamic and adaptive character of students' attitudes, beliefs, and dispositions have not been fully explored to explain how low-income students persist in school and successfully complete a four-year college degree. Is their story one of complete transformation? Can educators reshape students' dispositions in a way that nurtures educational success? Can these students affirm their low-income or ethnic identities with pride and use them as a source of strength to gain access to higher education? The educational Pivotal Moment framework proposed in this book seeks to identify the actual contingencies and structural opportunities that facilitate achievement and educational success for low-income minority students. It is my hope that these insights can help guide educators in re-creating the necessary conditions across various educational settings.

2

THE PIVOTAL MOMENT FRAMEWORK

Blanca and Terry

An *educational Pivotal Moment* is a significant academic intervention initiated by a college-educated adult who intentionally reaches out to a student to provide the student with the guidance and support to reach an educational goal. In this exchange, students learn from educators how to efficiently and effectively navigate school processes, knowledge that ultimately enhances their academic skill set. The transmission of important academic information from educator to student allows the relationship and intervention to be transformative for students who have not been exposed to this type of academic knowledge before by anyone in their families or communities.

An example of an educational Pivotal Moment is as follows: a middle school teacher initiates and helps her student apply for a scholarship to attend a private preparatory high school. Over the course of several months, the teacher helps the student through every part of the application process, including helping him write a personal statement, study for the entrance exam, and prepare for the interview, and even driving him there. The student is accepted to the school, and with his teacher's assistance in making a decision, he attends the school, an action that permanently alters his educational trajectory. From this experience, the student learns how to develop a meaningful relationship with a school agent as well as the steps it takes to reach an educational goal.

Transformative academic interventions like this become significant and life changing, because through them, low-income minority students gain hands-on experience to learn how to effectively navigate the school system. And, for the very first time, these students begin to develop the academic skills and behaviors that launch them on a path to educational success and advancement.

The main components of educational Pivotal Moments include establishing a trusting educator–student relationship, providing advocacy, transmitting academic knowledge, and lastly, developing positive educational outcomes from these interventions (see figure 2.1). Pivotal Moment interventions must include all these important elements to be effective.

Building trust and rapport is the foundation of a Pivotal Moment intervention. Students need to know that an educator cares about them and their futures. They need to know that an interested adult (e.g., a Pivotal Moment educator) is available to them and understands their concerns, continually helps them explore their educational options, and wants to help them pursue their career objectives.

Students form relationships with educators through regular classroom instruction, participation in extracurricular activities, and other oppor-

FIGURE 2.1

Educational Pivotal Moment process and outcomes

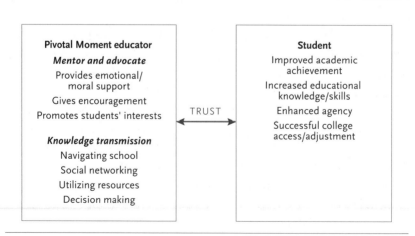

tunities that connect students and school personnel. These relationships often play a significant role in helping students make the transition from high school to college.[1] Educational expectations and postsecondary participation are higher among students who talk with their teachers and have positive feelings toward them. These interactions and positive feelings contribute to enhanced educational outcomes when student relationships with educators are based on trust, mutual respect, and a sense of obligation.[2] Through such positive relationships, students can learn more effectively and can more fully experience the numerous resources available from their schools. When students perceive that educators have high expectations for them, then their own expectations increase, as does the likelihood they will pursue postsecondary education.

Initially, Pivotal Moment educators build a trusting relationship with the student in order to serve as advocates and facilitate the transmission of school knowledge. Educators often build trust with students by showing respect, being honest and trustworthy, demonstrating caring, and sharing personal experiences to lower rigid educator-student boundaries. Trust is usually achieved when students consider educators both as professionals— whom they respect and go to for advice on navigating school processes— and as friends whom they can turn to for emotional and moral support and encouragement. The transmission of knowledge about navigating the school system, social networking, utilizing academic resources, and making decisions helps students develop the academic skills and orientation toward school that allows for educational advancement.

Mentoring and advocacy, without the transmission of educational knowledge and academic skills, is not sufficient for educational success and advancement, and it does not have the impact of Pivotal Moments. This type of educator–student connection has been characterized as "fool's gold" by researcher Ricardo Stanton-Salazar, because even though both student and educator might perceive the relationship as supportive, it is not authentic or transformative because the educator is not passing on critical academic information to assist the student in her educational pursuits.[3] Many students I interviewed described meaningful relationships with educators that had the potential to be Pivotal Moments, but because educational knowledge was never transmitted, it did not positively alter their educational trajectory.

Pivotal Moment educators play significant roles in the lives of low-income minority students and employ various actions during academic interventions (see figure 2.2).[4] They are *mentors* for students by showing them behaviors associated with effective participation in educational institutions, strategic navigation of school processes, and resilient coping with stratification forces that hinder school success.

They are *advisers* in helping students make decisions or plans about academic-related matters such as course selection or college choice. They also advise students on building and managing relationships with other educators, coaching them on communication strategies and approaches. At times, they also advise students on personal or family matters.

They are students' *advocates* in all school-related matters to ensure that students' academic progress and advancement are always considered and prioritized. They even develop relationships with important and influential school personnel to further advocate for students.

Finally, they are unrelenting *supporters* of students in providing emotional and moral support as well as constant encouragement of all students' academic pursuits. According to my educational Pivotal Moment framework, school personnel can provide low-income students with all the necessary information and support to help them successfully navigate the school system and, in the process, develop important characteristics and an orientation toward schooling that allows them to circumvent the stratification forces they encounter.

The one-on-one mentoring relationship students develop with educators becomes exceptionally important for those interested in pursuing a four-year degree.[5] Mentors can serve a variety of roles during college preparation. Early on, mentors can monitor students' academic progress by reviewing report cards and discussing students' high school course work.[6] Mentors can advocate for students who are struggling academically to receive tutoring or additional support. During the college application and selection process, mentors can help students research college options, fill out college applications, proofread essays, and assist with financial aid applications. To fulfill these roles, mentors usually need to communicate regularly with students—meet at least monthly with freshman or sophomore students, and weekly with juniors and seniors who are more intensely engaged in college application and selection.[7]

FIGURE 2.2

Characteristics and impact of educational Pivotal Moments

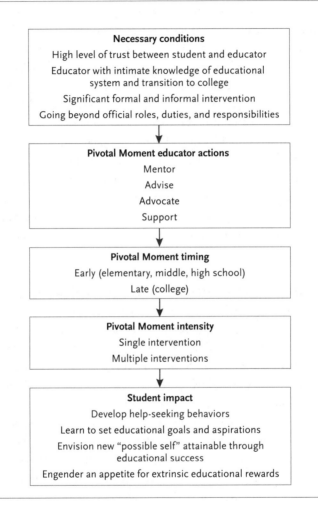

A key outcome of an educational Pivotal Moment is the gradual transformation of a student's psychological disposition toward schooling. There are four characteristics students develop as a result of Pivotal Moment interventions: adopting help-seeking behaviors, envisioning a new possible self, becoming effective in setting educational goals and aspirations, and developing an appetite for extrinsic academic rewards (see figure 2.2). Through the development of help-seeking behaviors, students learn to seek support by mobilizing relationships with individuals around them in educational settings. Students often activate these behaviors when they need to get information about academic opportunities or to figure out how to navigate a specific school process. Pivotal Moments also shape the development of a broader set of future possible selves, or students' aspirations of what they could or would like to become. As a result of the intervention, low-income students begin to develop a self-image and identity of being "college material." A Pivotal Moment crystallizes an image of themselves in the future that can be reached through educational achievement and advancement.

Another dimension of a student's disposition that is reshaped during Pivotal Moments is learning very concretely how to set educational goals and learning the necessary steps to accomplish those goals. Additionally, it is not until after a Pivotal Moment that many low-income minority students set educational aspirations such as planning to go to college. Finally, Pivotal Moments change students' desire for academic rewards because of the affirmation they increasingly receive through their educational success. Students become driven to be rewarded by the educational system and work toward those extrinsic rewards such as winning a writing contest or getting accepted to a selective college.

There are numerous positive long-term educational outcomes associated with comprehensive educational Pivotal Moments. The next section illustrates the flow and major characteristics of transformative academic interventions by examining two case studies of low-income, first-generation minority women—Blanca (Latina) and Terry (African American)—who are now at the top of the educational ladder in graduate school. Both stories highlight how educational Pivotal Moments occur in practice and documents the specific actions educators took to initiate them.

BLANCA'S PIVOTAL MOMENT

Blanca is a Latina in her sixth year of doctoral study at a highly selective public university in California. She is from a low-income background; her mother is a sales clerk, and her father works as a painter. Neither of her parents graduated from high school. She grew up in a household with her mother, father, and three younger siblings. Blanca had numerous family and household responsibilities growing up, which included cooking, cleaning, and caring for her younger siblings. In addition to her household responsibilities, Blanca was expected to be a good student in school.

Blanca experienced educational Pivotal Moments in high school through the intervention of three high school teachers. During tenth grade, her English teacher, Ms. Ryan, took her aside one day and insisted she be in Honors-level English and "wouldn't leave her alone" until she took the entrance exam for the class. Ms. Ryan not only encouraged her to take the exam but also counseled her through the testing process, building her academic confidence along the way. As Blanca recalled, this was the first time an educator reached out to her and made her feel like an exceptional student:

> My sophomore year English teacher insisted that I take the entrance exam for the Honors English class junior year. Up until that point, none of my teachers had indicated that they felt I was exceptional. I certainly did well in my courses, but no one had said that they felt I wasn't being challenged enough. So her insistence that I could do Honors-level course work really had an impact on me. Until that point, I hadn't even considered trying to place into Honors-level courses, and so her comments and support began to change the way that I saw myself as a student and the way that I perceived my intellectual abilities. Thanks to her, I took that placement exam and got into Honors English.

In addition to receiving a boost of confidence about her academic abilities, Blanca explained the impact the Honors English course ultimately had on her college aspirations and planning, because, as she noted, "A significant component of the course entailed preparing us for college applications."

The academic intervention Blanca's teacher initiated had profound long-term consequences on her educational trajectory. For the first time, she began to develop a process to set and work to attain educational goals. As a result, Blanca learned to advocate for herself in school and to get into more-rigorous courses to prepare for college. "Once I figured out how things worked, I also asked my counselor to sign me up for Honors Chemistry and AP Government," she said. "Once on that track, I didn't think twice about taking Honors and AP course work my senior year." The advanced courses also made Blanca more academically prepared and competitive for college admissions. The effort her English teacher made to connect her with academic information at this critical time in her education placed Blanca on the path to seeing higher education as a possibility after high school.

Blanca's biology teacher, Ms. Sullivan, also initiated an academic intervention with her during high school. She recounted how their relationship started: "I met her when I took her biology course as a sophomore, but then she requested that I be her AP Biology teaching assistant my junior and senior years in high school." In addition to counseling Blanca academically when she was her teaching assistant, Ms. Sullivan connected with her on a personal level by making an effort to understand her family situation. Blanca explained many of the roles Ms. Sullivan played in her life as her Pivotal Moment educator:

> I developed a very close relationship with my biology teacher. Not only did she support and advise me academically in high school, and encourage me to consider a number of colleges, but she was there for me when things with my father were rocky, when we didn't have money to do things that she felt were a crucial experience for high school kids (e.g., go to prom, buy a yearbook), and generally provided me with emotional and moral support . . . She bought my prom dress so I could go, talked to my parents when they adamantly refused to let me go on the senior class trip to Yosemite, and generally tried to mediate between the very rigid and strict method of child rearing that my parents were accustomed to, and the kind of freedom and experiences that seem "normal."

At a critical time during Blanca's senior year, Ms. Sullivan also enlisted the support of Blanca's humanities teacher to intervene and alter her path to college. Blanca had planned to apply only to community colleges and two-year vocational schools until Ms. Sullivan stepped in: "They [her biology and humanities teachers] really pushed me to aspire to more rather than feel limited by my parents' financial situation . . . my biology teacher played an instrumental role in advising me on my decision and helping me break the news to my parents. Her support was very, very important to me. I'm not sure that I would've had the courage to go against my parents' wishes if she hadn't reassured me that it was okay to want to go a hundred miles away for college."

As a result of Ms. Sullivan's academic intervention, Blanca attended a selective public four-year university. Blanca did not think that would have been possible without the constant support and guidance of her teacher throughout the college application and decision-making process. Blanca's academic achievement indicates that the transformative intervention that took place over three years had an enduring impact on her ability to succeed and advance in the educational system, putting her on the path to higher education.

Several years later, Blanca entered graduate school with a large amount of academic knowledge and skills that she has accumulated since her educational Pivotal Moment in high school. She employs her new skill set to effectively navigate graduate school in similar ways to middle-class students who grow up with college-educated parents. Blanca is good at finding people in her department who are invested in her success and professional socialization. "I've found really supportive people in my department who are invested in not just me doing well in the program, but eventually getting a job." She has become an expert at seeking out academic resources to successfully navigate the various hurdles of graduate school, highlighting her well-developed help-seeking behaviors.

Blanca's seamless adjustment to graduate school is a reflection of the educational knowledge, skills, and dispositions she has developed since she experienced her transformative academic intervention in high school. Her early educational Pivotal Moment has resulted in various positive academic outcomes and has given her an orientation toward schooling so that she actively seeks out resources and develops connections with key school agents. Blanca's story shows how a Pivotal Moment occurs in practice and provides insight into the specific actions educators take to establish trust, advocacy, and the transmission of academic knowledge to their students.

Blanca's experience underscores the fact that working-class parents' ability to help their children plan for college is very limited even though they highly value the pursuit of a college education.[8] Their educational experiences and social and economic realities make it very difficult for them to assist their children in the college choice process. They do provide other types of support that are instrumental in students' ability to plan for college. Some of these efforts include driving them to the post office to mail their college applications, providing monetary support to cover some of the costs associated with the college choice process, and, most important, giving them emotional and moral support for their college aspirations.[9] These forms of support are important enough to encourage and motivate students to persevere through the college application process. Some students discuss their college planning process with their parents to inform them about college but still seek out college information from other individuals.[10] In many cases, siblings replace parents as sources of information when parents are not able to assist.[11] Older siblings, especially those who have some higher education experience, play an invaluable role by transmitting important college-related information and knowledge.[12]

TERRY'S MULTIPLE PIVOTAL MOMENTS

Terry is an African American woman in her third year of a doctoral program at a highly selective private university in California. She has overcome many of the hardships that low-income minority students encounter. Terry was raised in a city she describes as "predominantly black and poor" by her godmother (a woman not biologically related to her) until she was seven years old. Terry's godmother was a single parent raising both Terry and her own two biological children. Terry described growing up in poverty: "I just remember it [the apartment] being dirty and with roaches . . . I also remember being hungry. I remember that because we would get food stamps at the beginning of the month, and then the food would only last for so long and so the last week and a half or so we were really hungry!"

At age seven, Terry went to go live with her father and new stepmother. When she found out about her new living situation, she was

42

distraught because her father's new family treated her very badly by making jokes and always pointing out how poor she was. She recounted, "They would take my clothes out of my bag and be like, 'Look at these clothes—they are so raggedy!' So they would talk about them in front of me, like I should be embarrassed about these things . . . I just remember feeling really ashamed." Terry moved from a very loving home with her godmother to a very abusive environment with her stepmother, who was "very physically abusive, verbally abusive, emotionally abusive to all of us—but mostly to me!"

Terry had a lot of household responsibilities growing up. She was the oldest child, and her parents, who worked full-time, counted on her to care for the house and her younger siblings. She was responsible for making sure all the chores were done in the evenings before her parents got home. In addition to family responsibilities, Terry was expected to do well in school: "They [her parents] expected us to do well, even though they didn't help us with homework. They were just like, 'You better not come home with less than B pluses.'" Doing well in school, however, was never a problem because Terry saw it as an "outlet to get away from my crazy, abusive stepmother." In fact, she said she was an avid reader growing up because it helped her momentarily escape the reality of her harsh home life.

Terry's academic successes in school are not solely the result of her individual hard work and determination. Rather, she has experienced numerous academic interventions that have allowed her to get on the path to graduate school. She experienced her first educational Pivotal Moment at the end of junior high school. Terry developed a good relationship with her Spanish teacher, Ms. Barrera, who took an active role in trying to get Terry into a private high school in the city where she grew up. In this intervention, Ms. Barrera went beyond her role as a teacher to nurture Terry's academic talents and shape her future educational path. Terry recounted how her teacher served as her educational advocate:

Señora Barrera said, "You're so good at this [Spanish language]." She realized that I was a really smart student and felt that I needed to go to a better high school. So she thought she should try to get me into either a Catholic school or a private school, something that would be more challenging.

She took it upon herself and drove me around to all these private schools. She would just walk up to the admissions office and be like, "I have this student and she's very smart, and you need to have her as a student at your school!"

Terry's teacher also set up times for her to visit the schools she wanted her to attend. "Sidwell Friends is the school that she [Ms. Barrera] thought I should go to . . . so she took me there, and I visited classes and met the teachers." This was the first time Terry had an educator reach out to her and advocate to provide her with an opportunity to advance her education. Even though Terry's parents expressed concern about the idea of her applying to private high schools due to the high cost, Ms. Barrera continued to encourage and guide Terry through the application process, knowing that she would be competitive for full financial aid. Over the course of a few months, Ms. Barrera advised Terry on every part of the application, from writing her personal statement to preparing for the entrance exam and, in the process, exposed her to new academic knowledge and skills.

Although Terry was accepted to her first-choice private high school, her stepmother prevented her from attending by refusing to fill out the financial aid paperwork. Both Terry and her teacher tried to get her stepmother to complete the forms, but she would not comply, and eventually, the opportunity was lost. Ms. Barrera's last resort in this intervention was to make sure Terry at least attended a public high school that had an accelerated program to challenge her academically, a school Terry did attend. Terry's initial Pivotal Moment taught her important information about navigating school processes to reach an educational goal, and this intervention set the stage for additional Pivotal Moments as she made her way through the educational system.

Terry's second Pivotal Moment took place in high school when her politics teacher, Ms. Marks, encouraged her to apply for a scholarship to study abroad in Mexico. The scholarship was a very prestigious award that only a few students received each year. Terry recalled hearing about the study abroad opportunity from her teacher, who insisted she apply. "Ms. Marks said, 'I think you should apply for this fellowship to go to Mexico. I mean, you're really good at languages, at Spanish, and that does seem to be your favorite language—you have a knack for it. I really think that this would be a great opportunity for you to study abroad.'" Ms. Marks even assisted Terry with properly filling out the application, and she wrote her a letter of support. Ms. Marks was so adamant Terry go to Mexico that, after she officially received the award, Ms. Marks met with Terry's parents. "My teacher had to come to my house and sort of convince my parents that this was a phenomenal opportunity, that I couldn't pass it up—it was a scholarship, and the school was paying for it." As a result, Terry's father realized the immense opportunity for his daughter and stopped her stepmother from trying to block it. With her dad's support, Terry was able to take full advantage of the scholarship and study abroad in Mexico, an event she describes as "one of the best experiences of my life."

Terry had another distinct Pivotal Moment in high school with her academic counselor, Ms. Latham, who assisted her with researching and applying to college. During the process, her counselor insisted she apply to Middlebury College, a highly selective liberal arts school that specializes in foreign languages. Terry recalled the conversation with Ms. Latham when she introduced her to the idea: "'I'm going to Middlebury?' I didn't make that choice on my own. My school counselor insisted, 'You're going to Middlebury!' I said, 'All right.' Because I knew I wanted to go to college, but I didn't know anything about the process." In fact, Ms. Latham guided Terry through applying to Middlebury for early admission. As a result of her counselor walking her through every step of the application process, Terry was successfully admitted, a forecast of her future educational opportunities.

Now in graduate school, Terry has adjusted to her doctoral program very well. As a result of multiple educational Pivotal Moments, she has accumulated a large stock of academic knowledge and skills that she employs in educational contexts to succeed. Terry has well-developed help-seeking behaviors and is an expert at finding academic resources to successfully navigate her doctoral program. She is very strategic about identifying key faculty, staff, and peers who can support and guide her academic pursuits. She has developed a close relationship with three female faculty members at her university who advise her research and progress in the program.

Terry's early and multiple Pivotal Moments have helped her develop the educational knowledge, skills, and dispositions needed to successfully navigate the educational system. Her story illuminates the actions numerous educators took to initiate a comprehensive academic intervention that changed the course of her educational trajectory. By nurturing a trusting relationship, these educators were able to transmit the necessary academic knowledge that allowed Terry to overcome the social class and racial and ethnic disadvantages she faced in school.

PIVOTAL MOMENT EDUCATORS AND ETHNIC MINORITY STUDENTS

The trusting relationships ethnic minority students develop with Pivotal Moment educators can significantly strengthen their educational values and goals. These relationships help them take advantage of the knowledge and experiential resources schools have to offer.[13] Most ethnic minority students care about what school personnel want for them and find comfort in knowing that their teachers, counselors, and other school staff are interested in their futures.[14] Given what we know about the tendency for ethnic minority students to rely on their schools—their only viable source—for college information and support, Pivotal Moment educators can play this role early in a student's academic career by encouraging postsecondary exploration and helping students develop the necessary academic skills for college plans.

Talking with teachers outside the classroom about academic issues has a positive effect on students' educational expectations and postsecondary participation. Because teachers provide information and opportunities that enhance students' academic experiences, direct interaction may compensate for a school's potentially lower academic emphasis and may propel students to higher education. Unfortunately, ethnic minority students are less likely than white students with similar educational goals to talk with their teachers outside class. Thus, they do not develop (to the same extent as white students) the types of school relationships that can support educational goals, channel academic information, help them take advantage of educational opportunities, enhance their school expectations, and ultimately increase their postsecondary participation.

This is a concern especially for Latino and African American students in low-income urban communities, because school personnel may be the only potential source of college and career planning information.[15] These students' families and communities often lack the information and resources to help them succeed in school and make the transition to college. Thus, it is up to educators to encourage these students, monitor their academic progress, assess and nurture their social development, and maintain a general interest in students' futures so that they can turn educational expectations into realistic goals.[16] Teachers, counselors, and other school staff who take on the Pivotal Moment educator role can help close the gap between ethnic minority students' educational expectations and their postsecondary attendance.

To be successful, Pivotal Moment interventions must include three main components: build trust, mentor or advocate, and transmit academic knowledge and skills. If trust, mentoring, and advocacy happen without the transmission of educational information, the effort will not reach the full transformative power needed to disrupt school inequality. As a result, low-income minority students will not experience the positive educational outcomes associated with Pivotal Moment interventions, including higher academic achievement, increased educational skills, enhanced agency, and, most important, college access. Additionally, students' psychological dispositions toward schooling will not be altered.

The findings raise important questions about exactly how low-income students from minority racial or ethnic backgrounds circumvent the sorting process of schools via intense academic interventions: How common are the Pivotal Moment experiences among low-income minority students? How frequently do educators make academic interventions? What prompts Pivotal Moments from both the educators' and students' perspectives? For low-income minority students who experience a Pivotal Moment intervention, how are their educational trajectories different from those of the same background who do not experience one? Do Pivotal Moments have an enduring effect on students' adjustment and success in higher education? And lastly, does the timing of a Pivotal Moment intervention in a students' school career matter? This last question will be addressed in the next chapter.

3

WHY PIVOTAL MOMENT
TIMING MATTERS

Carmen and Valerie

D ora is a fourth-year Latina doctoral student in a social science discipline at a selective public university in California. She is from a low-income background; her father is a cook, and her mother is a nanny. As a first-generation student, Dora's path to higher education and graduate school has been fairly linear. After high school, she attended a highly selective private liberal arts college. Three years after her undergraduate studies, she entered her doctoral program, and she has been having a very successful graduate school experience. She began her program as the recipient of a prestigious multiyear fellowship and, since starting graduate school, has received funding every year. As you will see in the next chapter, Dora is well adjusted to graduate school based on her exceptional performance, and she has actively participated in her academic department as a graduate student representative on various committees. Her approach to graduate school shows she has developed excellent help-seeking behaviors:

I've gotten really good about seeing them [colleagues] as my best resources. I was very good from the beginning in finding those people who wanted to be helpful and just asking them, "So what is this process like? What should I expect from this professor? This class?" Just trying to get recommendations from them about what to avoid, what to look for, what their experiences had been like. Finding those people was probably the hardest thing. But they're definitely there.

As the quotation illustrates, Dora is very strategic and intentional about seeking out colleagues and asking them questions to obtain information to effectively navigate her graduate studies. Her approach demonstrates she has a large accumulation of the educational knowledge and skills imperative for academic success.

In contrast, Carmen, a third-year Latina doctoral student in a social science discipline at a highly selective private university in California, also from a low-income background, is having a very different experience in her doctoral program. Carmen is a first-generation student who has taken an indirect path to higher education and graduate school. She graduated from public high school with a 2.0 GPA and, as a result, started higher education at her local two-year community college. After two years in community college, Carmen transferred to a selective public four-year university for her bachelor's degree. She then earned a master's degree at a different state university and, shortly thereafter, applied to doctoral programs.

Unlike Dora, Carmen has not adjusted well to her graduate school program. Although Carmen has not had any problems finding research assistantships to fund her graduate education, she finds doctoral studies difficult and lonely. She seems to feel very isolated in her program and has become distrustful of her new environment: "At the very beginning, I was rejecting everybody. I was really defensive, and I thought, 'I'm not telling anybody anything, and everybody's out to get me.' I just felt that, and now I know I don't have to develop meaningful relationships with anybody [at school]." Carmen's approach to graduate school demonstrates she has not developed all the academic skills and behaviors needed to excel in her new educational environment. Sadly, she does not see any value in developing relationships with colleagues and faculty in her department, and a lack of such relationships ultimately can have negative long-term consequences.

Dora and Carmen share many of the same social characteristics, including race and ethnicity, social class origin, and gender. So why are they having such different experiences in their doctoral graduate programs? In brief, Dora is doing better in graduate school because she experienced an "early" educational Pivotal Moment (in junior high school), whereas Carmen experienced a "late" educational Pivotal Moment (in community college). The timing of each woman's academic intervention has had consequences for their routes to higher education as well as their academic outcomes.

This chapter highlights the fact that even though educational Pivotal Moments have a permanent effect on students' educational trajectories, those that occur earlier—particularly before or at the beginning of high school—have a significantly stronger impact than those that occur at the end of high school or during college. I explore these variations through the experiences of low-income minority students at different points along the educational pipeline—high school, college, and graduate school—to provide a detailed analysis of the procedural knowledge and significant relationships students develop as a result of these transformative academic interventions. As stated earlier, educational attainment trends show that despite evidence of high academic potential, a significant proportion of low-income students does not complete high school or continue to college. Without a comprehensive academic intervention, countless promising students face virtually insurmountable obstacles both inside and outside school—obstacles that ultimately result in educational failure.

CARMEN'S PIVOTAL MOMENT

> *Before I met her, I didn't think I was academically, financially, or socially capable of going to college.*

Carmen, the Latina doctoral student introduced at the beginning of this chapter, underwent a change in her educational trajectory when she experienced an educational Pivotal Moment in community college. Carmen is the second oldest of four siblings and the daughter of immigrant parents from Latin America. She grew up with her mother, father, and four brothers until her parents divorced when she was nine years old. Afterward, she was raised by her mother and stepfather. Carmen described her childhood as "financially difficult" because her mother was always working to "put food on the table and pay the family bills."

As a result of growing up in a single-parent household and because she was the only girl, Carmen had a lot of household responsibilities.

She recounted her mother's insistence that she take care of most household chores, such as cleaning and cooking, because "I was the girl." At a very early age, Carmen resisted the gendered role imposed on her. She felt that if her brothers did not have to help out around the house, she should not be required to either. A role she willingly took on was caring for her youngest brother when her mother was working. She recounted, "I would say the role that I did play the most would be with my youngest brother. He's nineteen right now, and I'm six years older than he is, so he was like my baby because he was about two or three years old when my parents got divorced. Then my mom had to work to support us, and so when he was a little baby, he would sleep in bed with me and I did everything for him."

Unlike other students I interviewed, Carmen did not mention that doing well in school was a priority in her family. She had a poor academic record and discipline problems in high school. She described her high school experience as "crazy and unstable" and said she does not recall any educators with whom she connected. Carmen's primary goal in high school was "just to graduate and get my diploma." After graduation, she remembered, "I was so happy and proud, and I thought, 'I'm never going to go to school again!'" During her turbulent high school years, no one had ever thought Carmen would go to college, including Carmen. Up to that point in school, no educators had ever reached out to Carmen, and she felt that most of them generally had very low expectations of her. She graduated from high school with a low 2.0 GPA and enrolled at a community college. The main reason she initially enrolled was to "get my mom off my back and show her I was doing something productive with my life after high school." As it turned out, her decision to go to community college became a turning point in her life.

It was at the community college that Carmen experienced her first educational Pivotal Moment. For the first time in her education, she had an educator reach out to her and assist her with her academic development and educational planning. Until that time, Carmen had never felt connected to an educator in such a deep and significant way. Her professor, Ms. Romero, took an interest in her and, during their interactions, started talking to her about the "next steps" in her education. Carmen developed a strong relationship with Ms. Romero, who eventually became both her academic counselor and her mentor. In fact, Ms. Romero played a significant role in helping Carmen transfer from the community college to a highly selective public university to finish her bachelor's degree. She recounted the story:

> While I was in community college she was my instructor for two courses, my academic counselor, and the director of the Transfer Incentive Program [a program for underrepresented students] that I was a part of. In these three roles she became my primary provider of academic information. I really had no idea how college or community colleges worked. She spent two and a half years explaining it to me. Some of the things that she helped me with were picking my classes, helping me choose a major, and making sure I was on track to transfer. She taught me the differences between higher education institutions (community college, University of California school, California State University school, and private colleges), explained what different degrees such as the AA, BA, MA, PhD were, and helped me learn about many of the resources available at the community college and at four-year institutions.

Carmen's professor took an extended amount of time to explain to Carmen all of her school options and the different educational paths she could take. Before meeting Ms. Romero, Carmen did not have anyone in her social networks who could explain the schooling system to assist her with making informed decisions about her education. In a very intentional and hands-on way, her professor introduced Carmen to the academic knowledge and skills she lacked.

In addition to providing her with concrete academic information, Ms. Romero also constantly encouraged her along the way. According to Carmen, the emotional and moral support was critical in helping her realize that she was capable of getting accepted and succeeding in higher education:

> She was also the person who made me really believe that I should and could pursue a college degree. Before I met her, I didn't think I was academically, financially, or socially capable of going to college. I also did not see the importance of a college education and the impact that it could have on my life. She really encouraged me to pursue an education

and shared a lot of her personal experiences to show how she had done it. She believed in me so much and was willing to invest so much time on me that I started thinking that maybe I was "college material."

Carmen found it particularly useful that her professor shared a lot of her own personal experiences in school as a first-generation college student. Ms. Romero was a Latina who grew up in a similar socioeconomic background, and that made Carmen trust and feel that her professor truly understood her struggles. For Carmen, an important factor in the mentoring relationship with Ms. Romero has been the fact that she can identify with her on a personal level, and Carmen has learned that everyone faces challenges and setbacks in school. Importantly, whenever her professor shared stories about her challenges, she would always follow it up with a discussion of how she overcame them, a practice that transmitted knowledge to Carmen about navigating school. Through Ms. Romero, Carmen had access to a source of academic information that helped her transfer to a four-year university and eventually get on the path to graduate school. Because her professor helped her through every part of the college application process and explained in detail why she had to do certain things along the way, Carmen has now developed important skills for achieving her educational goals.

Carmen's late educational Pivotal Moment, however, affected the amount of academic knowledge and skills she could accumulate and develop before entering doctoral studies, a limit that has substantially impacted her adjustment. As noted at the beginning of this chapter, Carmen has been struggling to adjust to her new educational environment. She feels overwhelmed and isolated. In our interview she said that graduate school caught her completely off-guard and made her question her academic capabilities. She has not been able to make important connections with faculty and graduate students since she began. As a result, she often seeks support outside the university from individuals not affiliated with school and who do not have the knowledge to help her successfully navigate the numerous hurdles of graduate school.

Typical of most first-generation college students, Carmen initially did not feel a sense of belonging when she arrived on her graduate school campus. She felt that the culture was very different from the predominantly Latino environment she was accustomed to, as she explained: "I felt, 'This place is not for somebody like me, and nobody gets me,' you know, I just felt like, 'Everybody else is exactly the same,' and that was really, really hard for me to deal with. I guess I was just naïve." In addition to not being able to find a supportive community in graduate school, Carmen has had negative experiences with her colleagues, and these experiences have compounded her isolation.

She described a class discussion during her first semester with another student about the merits of affirmative action in university admissions. She explained the exchange they had, which really disturbed her. "He patted me on the shoulder and said, 'Well, I'm sure you would've gotten in without affirmative action anyways.' And I thought to myself, 'Yeah, motherfucker, I had a 4.0 when I transferred, you don't have to be telling me shit.' It was really patronizing." Carmen was deeply offended by her classmate's condescending remarks, which made assumptions about her academic abilities. These types of exchanges with her colleagues made her become even more guarded about sharing her personal experiences and discussing her research ideas with others. She said, "It's been hard because I feel like . . . I can't get any real feedback from people, because all they're doing is questioning why I want to do what I want to do."

Carmen dreads attending school-related informal social events. After attending a few, she felt so uncomfortable that she stopped going altogether. She explained, "I would try to go to those social events, but everyone just kisses ass, and I can't stand it. I couldn't stand going to those social events to stand around looking for a normal person to talk to. I would end up leaving fifteen minutes later. That was during the first year. Now I don't go to those events any more."

Carmen's withdrawal from these social events prevents her from connecting with professors and fellow graduate students and benefiting from those social relations to successfully complete her doctoral studies. Her negative experiences have led her to seriously consider dropping out, an action she came close to during her first year. Although she has reached the highest level of education, completion is not guaranteed. Carmen's late educational Pivotal Moment provided her with a lower stock of academic knowledge and skills to draw from as she tries to adjust to her graduate school program.

VALERIE'S PIVOTAL MOMENT

Seeking help from professors is not something I would actually do.

Another student who, like Carmen, experienced a late educational Pivotal Moment was Valerie, a fifth-year college student at a four-year public university. Valerie is the daughter of immigrant parents from Latin America, and the eldest of four siblings. She is from a low-income background; her father is a mechanic, and her mother is a housewife. Even though her parents are not highly educated themselves—neither of them has a high school diploma—they strongly encourage their children to excel in school.

Growing up, Valerie realized that she would be the first in her family to accomplish the educational milestones that her parents were never able to, and she knew that her younger siblings would be measured by what she accomplished. "Even today, I'm the role model of the family," she said. "I'm the one who went through school, did the honors society, all the clubs, the involvement, going to a four-year university. They push my sister by telling her, 'Why can't you be more like your sister?'" Although one of her sisters resents being compared to Valerie, her younger siblings look up to her: "My younger sister is like, 'I want to go to your school. I want to be a teacher,' and she's eight. And then my brother, he's like, 'I want to go to your college.' Both are really smart. They're in Honors and GATE [Gifted and Talented Education]. My other sister and I weren't. I think because my sister and I went through school, they're thinking, 'I can do that too.'"

Like most children raised in immigrant homes, Valerie went through a transition learning English when she first started school. "Growing up, I didn't really speak English. My kindergarten was all in Spanish. By second grade it was a lot more English. By third grade, I was already in a full English class." Unlike the parents of most students I interviewed, Valerie's mother took an active role in her schooling: "My mom was actually really involved when I was in kindergarten. The teachers loved her. It was really nice because my mom got to know the teacher and her aide."

Her mother's involvement was facilitated by the teachers' ability to speak Spanish. By the time Valerie reached second grade, as she transitioned into English-only classes, her teachers did not speak Spanish, and it became more difficult for her mother to communicate with them. "She'd volunteer to go on field trips, but by the time I got to second or third grade, she kind of backed off . . . The teacher didn't speak much Spanish. I don't think she felt a connection with the teacher." Valerie's father was also involved in her schooling. Because he spoke English a little better than her mother, he usually attended parent–teacher conferences. "As far as grades and going to the conferences, it was mostly my dad because his English was better than my mom's, because he uses it a lot in his shop, so he practices it more."

From a very young age, Valerie recalls being liked by many of her teachers. She said, "I always tried to be the teacher's pet. All the teachers liked me." She exhibited great interpersonal skills when interacting with them, and that frequently provided her with unique opportunities to establish strong connections. For this reason, she enjoyed being at school even during the summers when only a few instructors were around campus: "Every summer, during the last few weeks of August before school started, my sister and I would go to the school to play, and we'd run into the teacher, so we'd end up helping them set up for the class. We'd end up cleaning bookshelves and throwing out old books and stuff."

In middle school, Valerie developed a strong relationship with her physical education teacher, Ms. Hart, whom she described as one of her mentors: "It started when I went to talk to her about afterschool sports. After that, I would always go talk to her. Just kind of like, 'How are you doing?' Just kind of seeing if she needed help with the sports equipment or anything. She was kind of like a mentor for me during eighth grade. I was having some problems with my friends, and I wanted to talk to somebody so I think I was talking to her about it."

When I asked her to describe in more detail how Ms. Hart mentored her, Valerie stated, "We would just talk. I remember my mom was pregnant with my little sister, so she would always ask, 'How's your sister?' and that was our connection. I just used to go talk to her about my family." Although Valerie referred to Ms. Hart as a mentor, her teacher did not seem to provide more than occasional emotional and moral support. Unlike a Pivotal Moment educator, Ms. Hart did not use the trust that Valerie placed in her to transmit educational knowledge and skills.

Valerie was also involved in a semester-long college awareness program in middle school that had the potential to be a Pivotal Moment, as she explained: "We would stay after school a few times a week, and somebody from the local university would come to talk to us about college, kind of like a mentor. They would tell us, 'You're going to go to college!'" Interestingly, Valerie initially volunteered to participate in the program because it was an excuse for her to stay after school. "I enjoyed staying after school. I wanted to be in school, because I really liked school and the school environment." Her involvement was not because she or her family necessarily understood the benefits of participating in an academic outreach program that promotes college.

Even though Valerie always did well in school, participated in short-term academic outreach programs, and developed a close connection with her teachers, she still lacked important knowledge about navigating the educational system. This was evident when she was initially placed in Honors courses based on her test scores and made the unwise decision to opt out of them. She explains:

> I think I might have tested high enough to place in those classes, but I was not happy that I was in the Honors classes. I talked to my dad, and he's like, "You know, just try them out," but I still went and talked to the counselor and told her, "Hey, I just want to be out of the Honors class." She asked me why, and I told her, "I don't want to be in them. I want to be in the regular classes like everybody else." And she said, "No, you qualify for them, you should stay in those classes. I'm not going to change you."

Even though Valerie had a close relationship with at least one teacher and participated in programs that emphasized the importance of college, no one stepped in to keep her from going through with it when she was making this decision on her own. Even the academic counselor who initially refused to change her schedule eventually gave in to her demand and let her out of the Honors track. Sadly, none of the educators that Valerie trusted, or even her counselor, took the time to explain the importance of taking more-rigorous classes to prepare for college. Valerie had acquired some information about this school process but still lacked important insights about how to successfully navigate it.

In high school, Valerie was very involved. She played in the school band, ran track, was on the soccer team, was elected class officer her freshman year, and was a member of the Honor Society. She also took on various leadership roles, including captain of her soccer team, secretary for the honor society, and vice-president of the band. She again developed a close relationship with an educator, her chemistry teacher, that in many ways was similar to her relationship with Ms. Hart, her eighth-grade teacher:

> I had a love-hate relationship with him [her chemistry teacher]. I was the rowdy, smart-ass kid in the class, but we still got along. He would tell us stories about how he almost flunked out of college. Through all of that, I didn't do very well in his chemistry class. I think I got a C. But he was okay with it. I ended up taking his physics class, too. I got a D in that class, but he was still very encouraging and supportive. He would tell me, "I know you want to go to college. I had a hard time, but I had to buckle down, and I know you can do it."

As with her eighth-grade teacher, Valerie's relationship with her chemistry instructor, Mr. Sholtz, could have been an educational Pivotal Moment, but he did not intervene, advocate for her, or attempt to transmit academic knowledge and skills. Mr. Sholtz also did not provide extra tutoring assistance when she repeatedly received low grades in his classes, even though he had gained her trust and seemed to recognize her academic potential.

Despite Valerie's high level of involvement, multiple leadership roles, and close connection with her chemistry teacher, one of the most striking details about Valerie's high school years is that she finally got her way and did not enroll in the Honors track. Her chemistry teacher could have advised her to enroll in the Honors courses, but he did not. In the short term, being in the regular classes helped boost Valerie's self-esteem, because she was the smartest student in the class. "A lot of my classmates were in gangs. They were the slackers. Because I was not in the Honors class with the students that would challenge me, honestly, I felt superior to the rest of them because I would get straight A's." Her decision not to enroll in Honors courses, however, greatly impacted her educational trajectory, and despite her promising academic potential, eventually led her to attend a lower-tier, less-selective university, where more often than not, first-generation college students enroll but do not complete their degree.

After I interviewed Valerie, I was puzzled why a student with such exceptional academic potential did not attend a more-selective institution of higher education—especially because she was ambitious from an early age. "I always knew I was going to go to college . . . My parents always said, 'You're going to go to college. You should work your best so you can go to college.'" Valerie was even adamant about not wanting to go to a community college after high school, because most students in her neighborhood take that route and get stuck there, never getting to a four-year university. Even though Valerie aspired to more than a two-year junior college, she did not have anyone advising or guiding her to apply to more-selective schools. Also, because she was not in the Honors classes, she was not getting the type of encouragement and support that those students receive. Most students who take Honors courses are prompted to think about college applications and writing personal statements during their senior year. Valerie explained, "I did not want to write a personal statement because in my English classes, they weren't preparing us for that. In the AP classes, they were making the students write a personal statement to apply to the UCs, and since I didn't have to write one for my class, I wasn't going to apply to a UC. I just did it on my own. I didn't really have someone to tell me how to do it. The counselor just told me to apply to college. We also had reminders over the school P.A. system every morning."

Valerie's experience demonstrates that it is not enough for schools and educators to tell students to apply to college or remind them about application deadlines. Low-income minority students need much more guidance and support. Valerie explained that she followed the reminders but still struggled doing it on her own: "When I had questions I went to my counselor a few times during senior year, but a lot of it was on my own, through trial and error." Lacking the proper guidance, Valerie did not make informed decisions when she applied to college and just followed what her peers were doing. "My best friend, who's two years older, went to one of the local universities, so I decided to go to that university because that's where my friend was." Despite the lack of college-going knowledge and support from educators, Valerie was driven to figure out the process as best she could on her own. Her motivation to go to college has always been her family. "The reason I'm in college now is because of the push from my parents, especially my dad. In my head I thought, 'I'm going to go to college because I want to please my parents. I want them to be proud of me, but I also want my siblings to see me going to college, and I want them to go to college too.'"

When I interviewed Valerie as a college senior, she seemed like a very different person from the high school student she described. Not surprisingly, it was because during her first year as a college student she finally experienced an educational Pivotal Moment when she got involved on her college campus as an orientation leader in the student affairs office. "Second semester I decided I wanted to be involved, so I applied to be an orientation leader here on campus and I got the position. And that pretty much changed my experience here." Before she got involved in the orientation program, she had spent very little time on campus; she would go to class and then go straight home.

Valerie gained valuable leadership skills through her participation in the orientation program but, more importantly, also developed a relationship with two academic affairs staff who helped guide her through college. "I had a mentoring relationship with our supervisor. Over the past three years, I've been able to open up to her about academic and personal struggles. Not only her, but also with my other supervisor." When she was having difficulties balancing school obligations with her parents' rule to be home early, she turned to one of her mentors for assistance: "I talked to one of my supervisors and asked him for advice. After that, I talked to my dad and he was understanding. Over the past few years, I've talked to them about why I needed to be out late, or why I needed more freedom. I think it was more trying to explain everything to him, because they don't really understand a lot of the things that I do here on campus. After that, he got it." Valerie's involvement in the orientation program was pivotal, because she gained access to school agents who significantly changed her orientation toward school and helped her succeed.

Another source of support for Valerie has been an academic outreach program that helps low-income, first-generation college students adjust to college. Similar to other academic outreach programs she has participated in, Valerie serendipitously, and without knowing much about it, applied to the program through her admissions application:

In the application, there was a little box that asked if you want to apply for it. I wasn't sure what it was, but it said that you have a counselor assigned to you and I was like, "Okay, that's cool." I think I just applied for it because my friend was applying for it. So I applied for it in high school, and then I just started meeting with a counselor since my freshman year . . . The first semester, it was required to meet with your counselor three times just to make sure your transition was okay. During registration they went over what classes I could take.

Although Valerie relies more on her supervisors and mentors for help with both personal and academic matters, the outreach program provides an important second source of guidance and support. When she was struggling to decide on a major and career path to take after college, she turned to her academic outreach program counselor for assistance. "I've seen her every semester since I started, even though I don't have to go anymore. I just want to make sure I'm still on the right track . . . I came in as a psychology major, and I wasn't very happy with that after I took my first psych class. I knew I wanted to go into some type of counseling field, but I didn't know exactly what. She told me to explore different things. She encouraged me to consider graduate school."

Among all her sources of support in college, Valerie considers her two supervisors in the academic affairs office her most influential mentors. Her male mentor, Mr. Williams, provides support with school, work, and personal matters. She said they frequently have coffee together to talk about her academic progress. He also gives her valuable career advice and takes her to professional conferences to increase her networking skills. Additionally, Mr. Williams connects Valerie with other educators he knows who can assist her with reaching her professional goals. He put her in touch with one of his close friends, Dr. Taylor, who is now helping her prepare for graduate school. Dr. Taylor is the assistant to the Vice President of Student Affairs. Dr. Taylor and Mr. Williams, Valerie said, have been "my guides for the past few months." Dr. Taylor has become a Pivotal Moment educator for Valerie as she guides and mentors her through graduate school applications.

In seeking out the assistance of Dr. Taylor, Valerie demonstrates that she has started to develop initiative and help-seeking behaviors, a characteristic typical of students who have received extended support through Pivotal Moment interventions:

I got to know her better, so I approached her and I told her that I had heard from my supervisor that she may have an internship position available. She didn't have one, but she wanted to know what I planned to do after graduation. So I set up a meeting with her, and when we met she asked me what I wanted to do. She asked me lots of questions about my background and my interests, and then she asked me if I wanted to go to grad school. When I told her I did, she offered to guide me through the whole process.

Unlike when Valerie was in high school applying to college, now her new mentor is providing Valerie with concrete and specific educational information and is walking her through the process of applying to graduate school step-by-step:

At our first meeting she told me, "I have a map for you if you want to go out of state. We'll choose schools from there. But first, we'll have to get you an internship." So that's what I worked on last semester. She and my other supervisor took me to the conference to explore the field of student affairs to see if I still like it. At the conference, she helped me pick out different workshops that she thought would benefit me. There is a purpose for everything she does. She had me practice informational interviews with some people on campus that I might be interested in interning with. After that, I secured my internship site. Then we worked on me joining the professional association, NASPA [Student Affairs Administrators in Higher Education]. I'm now a member. This year, we are applying to a fellowship program called the NASPA Undergraduate Fellowship Program. It's a formal mentoring relationship, and she'll be my mentor and we'll go through exploring the field together and preparing me for grad school. This summer, I'm prepping for the GREs and just getting everything done so in the fall we'll be working on applications.

With the kind of support and preparation she's receiving, it's very likely that Valerie will be successful in graduate school and continue to increase her educational knowledge and academic skills. As she reflected on her undergraduate experience, she credited the orientation program and her two mentors as the source of her knowledge and insights on being a successful college student. "I didn't know much at first, but the orientation program changed my whole college experience."

Despite the new academic skills Valerie has acquired in college since her Pivotal Moment, she is still too intimidated to talk to professors. "Seeking help from professors is not something I would actually do. I think I'm okay relating to staff and asking them for help. But as far as professors, I haven't really done that." As she looks toward her transition into graduate school, she hopes she will be able to find supportive individuals like her undergraduate mentors to assist her with being successful. Like many first-generation college students, Valerie fears the next step in her education because she has not developed the stock of academic knowledge that would help her adjust to her new school environment seamlessly as a result of her late Pivotal Moment.

Carmen's and Valerie's experiences demonstrate that for struggling as well as academically promising students, late Pivotal Moments can have a dramatic impact on students' educational trajectories. Valerie's story highlights that it is not enough for educators to offer a sympathetic ear or just give students encouragement and expect that they will know how to figure out the rest. Rather, low-income minority students need more support and guidance as early as possible in school. The earlier that students experience Pivotal Moment interventions from teachers, counselors, or academic outreach coordinators, the better they do in the long term. Regardless of the type of educator, however, the intervention must occur over a substantial amount of time to allow students and educators to develop a trusting relationship and open up a space to transmit the academic knowledge and skills necessary for school success. In the following chapter, Dora's and Brianna's educational Pivotal Moments highlight the importance and advantages of an early academic intervention.

4

EARLY PIVOTAL MOMENTS ARE BETTER

Dora and Brianna

The timing of Pivotal Moments—whether they occur early or late in a student's educational career—has significant implications for the long-term academic achievement of students from low-income and minority backgrounds. As you will learn in this chapter, early Pivotal Moments have a deeper educational impact than later ones. Early interventions allow students to acquire and accumulate the academic knowledge and skills needed to effectively navigate the educational system. As a result, students who experience early Pivotal Moments get a head start in developing the behaviors and orientation toward schooling that will enhance their academic success. The stories of Dora and Brianna illustrate the numerous benefits of early Pivotal Moments.

DORA'S PIVOTAL MOMENT

I didn't want to go, but eventually my teachers really pushed me to do it.

Dora, the Latina doctoral student introduced at the beginning of the previous chapter, experienced an early educational Pivotal Moment. She was five years old when her family immigrated to the United States from Latin America. She is the oldest of four siblings and grew up in a household with both her mother and father. Dora described her biggest family responsibility growing up as "going to school and being a good student." As a young girl, she did not have many of the responsibilities typical of low-income children and she recalls that her parents "were good at taking care of the adult stuff in my family." Generally, Dora's parents assigned her only a few household chores. Her parents even protected her from chores, at times, so that she could focus on school. She explained, "Their perspective was that my job at that age was to go to school and to be a good student. So I had very few chores at home. They really just wanted me to focus on school." Even though Dora's parents were not able to help her with schoolwork, they always expressed the importance of getting an advanced education and encouraged her to strive for more than the low-paying service sector jobs they had.

Focusing on school was sometimes a difficult task for Dora, however, because her home environment was not always conducive to studying. Because her mom took care of children all day to earn money, the house was typically very noisy, making it difficult for Dora to focus on her homework. Dora had to develop a strategy to get her homework done, as she recounts: "At some point it would get so crazy that I'd have to go home [after school], wash dishes, eat, then nap until everybody left, and then I could do homework after everyone was gone. That kind of thing was pretty common."

Unlike Carmen and Valerie, Dora had her Pivotal Moment in middle school when she joined the Cosmopolitan Club, which she described as "a casual group that got together every other week to basically go out to eat different kinds of food." Near the end of middle school, her English and math teachers, with whom she had developed a trusting relationship through the Cosmopolitan Club, encouraged her to apply to a highly prestigious private preparatory high school. They explained the application process to her and insisted that she seriously consider applying.

At first, Dora was extremely skeptical and was not interested in going to a private high school. She knew that private schools cost a lot of money, and her parents were barely making ends meet financially. Dora was torn about telling her teacher she was not interested in applying because of her family's financial situation. However, her teachers were so insistent she apply that they set up an appointment to meet with her parents to explain to them that it would be an important educational opportunity for her. She explained, "I wasn't interested. I really didn't want to do it, but I just didn't know how to say no. They talked to my parents, and so my parents said, 'Okay, you should apply.' So I applied."

Unless Dora received a scholarship, however, her family would not be able to afford the cost of her attending a private high school. Although Dora's parents fully supported this great educational opportunity, they reminded her about their limited financial circumstances. She recounted a conversation she had with her father: "We were driving back home and my dad told me, 'Look, you deserve this. It would be great. But I don't think you should get your hopes up,' because in his notion of what a scholarship is, even if you get up to 90 percent from them, we can't pay for this. At the time, it cost like $10,000 a year to attend that school, and my dad was making like $14,000 a year or something like that, so there was no way."

Once Dora informed her teachers of her decision to apply, they immediately started helping her with every step of the application process. Over the course of several months, her two teachers—going beyond their official duties—counseled her through the logistics of applying, such as filling out the application and writing her personal statement; they even drove her to the admissions interviews. She explained how her teachers reached out to her during this process: "She [Dora's English teacher] took an interest in me and was really the main person who looked up programs and things for me after junior high. Mr. B, who taught me algebra and geometry, was also involved . . . They helped me with all the parts of my application. Once they sent out the application, the school contacted me for interviews and that's when the teachers got involved again and drove me to the interviews because my parents couldn't."

Without this intense transformative intervention, Dora would never have applied nor attended one of the most prestigious private high schools in the country. Her parents supported her throughout the process and were happy when she was accepted. She recalled, "They were excited for me . . . about going to private school. It was their first time going through something like this, so they thought it was cool that my teachers were looking out for me. They were supportive about the whole thing."

Even after being admitted with a full scholarship, Dora needed to be persuaded that going to an elite school was a decision that would give her better options in the future. Unlike Valerie (see chapter 3), who did not have anyone advising her against leaving the Honors track, Dora's teachers intervened and insisted she take advantage of the opportunity:

> I didn't want to go, and I was kind of set on not going and then we got the letter that I was admitted and that the school was paying for all of it. So they [her English and math teachers] were really excited and I wasn't. I didn't want to go, but eventually my teachers really pushed me to do it. I had also applied to magnet schools, and I had gotten into this one teaching program and I was set on going there and my teachers said, "No, you can't!" They just wouldn't let me make that decision not to go.

As with Valerie's decision to transfer out of the Honors program, Dora's first instinct was to decline the private school offer and instead attend the local magnet school. The magnet school was close to home, whereas the private school required her to take public transportation every day for thirty minutes each way to get to school, which was located in an "intimidating, wealthy, and predominantly white neighborhood"— a very different social environment from the working-class Latino immigrant neighborhood where she grew up. Eventually, Dora attended the private prep school and did very well academically, and upon graduation, she gained admission to a similarly prestigious liberal arts college. Shortly thereafter, continuing on the impressive academic success of her undergraduate career, Dora decided to pursue a PhD.

Ten years after her educational Pivotal Moment in middle school, Dora entered graduate school, bringing with her a decade's worth of educational knowledge and skills. The years of accumulated academic knowledge allowed her to effectively navigate graduate school in similar ways to students who grow up in college-educated, middle-class homes. In contrast to Carmen, who had a late Pivotal Moment and only five years of accumulated academic knowledge and skills, Dora became an expert in seeking help and nurturing her social connections to expand her professional knowledge in graduate school. As a result of her early Pivotal Moment, she is proficient in locating the academic resources she needs to successfully navigate her program. She has developed keen help-seeking behaviors and actively looks for people who can provide strategic information about getting through the hurdles of graduate school. Dora has also become an expert at finding key allies among her graduate student colleagues who can provide her with academic information and advice:

> So the first thing was to look for students of color and figure out what their experiences were like. Who did they like to work with? Who wasn't supportive? To me, that's a basic thing. My department doesn't have that many students of color, so I wasn't going to limit myself, either. My peer mentor when I started was a white woman who comes from a very privileged background and is very aware of it. She is very involved and very politically active. I felt comfortable talking to her, so she made me realize that if you act entitled about the responsibilities that professors have with their students, I could expect them to help me.

Although Dora is effective at extracting the information she needs to plan her graduate school career, like Valerie, she is apprehensive about approaching her professors; she struggles with "acting entitled" to ask for her professor's time and help when she needs them. In fact, this was the case for most students of working-class origins. Many of these students were baffled by middle-class white students who went into professors' offices without a clear agenda but "just to talk," whereas they felt that unless they had something specific to discuss with the professor, they should not be "wasting" the professor's time.

According to sociologist of education Annette Lareau, the "entitled" approach taken by white middle-class students toward faculty is a characteristic developed by a middle-class parenting style she called "concerted cultivation."[1] Lareau asserts that because middle-class children are encouraged to speak up and ask questions when interacting with institutional agents such as teachers, they develop an entitlement to assert their individual preferences and manage those exchanges to their benefit. In contrast, the parenting style of the working class—"accomplishment of natural growth"—does not nurture the same sense of entitlement, and, as a result, children are less assertive and more deferential to authority figures. This could possibly explain why a student like Carmen, for example, does not seem comfortable networking with colleagues and faculty in her department.

Although Dora observes this networking behavior among her white middle-class colleagues, she said that she remains ambivalent about emulating it, even though it seems to be a part of "playing the game" in graduate school. Her ambivalence, however, does not keep her from forging the necessary connections that will guarantee her success in graduate school. In almost every instance when she feels conflicted about her academic environment, she still manages to extract the necessary information, support, and guidance she needs to be successful. Dora's strategy for finding supportive advisers highlights this process. Since starting graduate school, she has sought out two faculty members with whom she feels connected and who can relate to her own social and economic experiences. These faculty members help her navigate different aspects of graduate school. She explained that she looks for people who can provide emotional and moral support and can mentor her by "breaking down the processes of graduate school." Dora has become an expert at finding strong supporters and has developed such a keen fluency in this process that she often does not recognize she is doing it.

Dora has been very active in her academic program since starting graduate school. She has held graduate student positions on department committees, positions that have consequently expanded and strengthened her social network. Although she became active in her department to give students of color a voice, she was also positioning herself to be noticed by faculty. Interestingly, Dora said that she did not feel that participating as a graduate student representative has had any direct benefits to her academic experiences. Nevertheless, through her involvement she continues to develop social connections and has established a good reputation with her professors. "I'm on the admissions committee, and I've found it really useful in understanding how they think about students, how they talk about students, who they value, what kinds of ideas they value. I feel like I've learned a lot."

Dora's involvement has given her a perspective on the administrative processes of her department that Carmen has not been able to develop. This new knowledge adds to Dora's ability to access all the resources she needs to navigate graduate school and greatly contributes to her positive adjustment. Her graduate school experience is characteristic of most low-income students I interviewed who experienced early educational

Pivotal Moments. Students who received early academic interventions were well adjusted and exhibited better academically successful behaviors and outcomes than students who received a later intervention.

BRIANNA'S PIVOTAL MOMENT

I knew I had someone who I could count on that cared about my education.

Brianna, a first-year Latina college student at a highly selective private college, also had an early educational Pivotal Moment. Brianna was born in Mexico and came to the United States when she was only two years old. She grew up with her mom, dad, and two younger sisters. Her family moved around frequently when she was a child. She remembers living in so many different places that she eventually lost track of the number. As she grew up, her father worked various jobs, ranging from loading oranges to washing high-rise windows. When I interviewed Brianna, her father had recently lost his job and was unemployed; her mother continued working part-time in multiple restaurants.

Although Brianna's family struggled financially during her childhood, her parents always stressed the importance of education. She recounted her mother's advice when she was young: "She always told me I had to get an education. She would say, 'You don't want to end up in a restaurant or in a job where they're going to treat you bad or you don't have your job guaranteed. Sometimes I wish I had an opportunity like the one you have.'" For this reason, Brianna tried to be a diligent student in elementary school. She performed well academically and, as a result, always gained the positive attention of her teachers. When I asked her whether any teachers stood out during the early part of her education, she told me about her third-grade teacher, Mr. Ricks, who encouraged and actively nurtured her academic skills:

> I had the same teacher up until third grade, and he helped me a lot. I remember there were times I wouldn't go to recess but would stay and help other girls learn their multiplications. He would tell me, "Why don't you go around and help anybody that needs help?" or, "If you don't mind, stay after school to see if anybody needs help." I would stay because I just liked helping out. Even in fifth grade, I still had a really close connection

with him. He would always ask, "Are you okay in school? Do you need any help?"

Her teacher's efforts led Brianna to trust him, and that gave him the opportunity to nurture her academic self-confidence. According to Brianna, even seemingly mundane activities helped forge a connection between them. "I would help around and just like staple or stamp papers. To me it was really fun, and it helped to build a really close connection." Mr. Ricks encouraged her to do well in school and also provided the support and mentoring for her to be successful.

It was in ninth grade that Brianna experienced a second, more intense educational intervention—which became her educational Pivotal Moment—when she joined an academic outreach program. In fact, she said what she remembered most about high school was "all the activities I have done in the academic outreach program. It was the biggest part of my life." Two of the most important academic skills that Brianna learned were effective class note-taking and organizing her time to develop good study habits. She recalled, "During freshman year, they started teaching us note taking, and we all hated it. We didn't see the point. I would still do them because it was part of my grade." Before the program, she remembers that she did not have the slightest idea about taking good notes. "I would just get a piece of paper and write a couple of questions and a few sentences in really big letters so that it looked like I was taking lots of notes, but it wasn't helping me." The program was very focused on helping students develop key academic skills and required students to review effective note taking at the beginning of the academic year. "They would always have two days to review how you're supposed to take notes, things like how to develop questions, write a summary." After three years of being forced to take class notes, she began to notice a significant and permanent change in her note-taking and study habits:

Junior year of high school, I started noticing that I was getting used to it. I didn't even have to think about taking notes. I would just take a piece of paper and started taking notes. I think that's what helped me get good grades in high school—I learned how to take good notes and to be organized. Even now a lot of my college friends go, "Oh, my gosh, you're totally a college student. How do you do it?" That's just how I see things now. I can't have a messy folder. My brain doesn't work like that anymore. I think it helped me a lot. Otherwise I wouldn't be here [in college].

In addition to developing academic skills through the academic outreach program, Brianna had access to various supportive teachers whom she formed connections with: "Ms. Smith was a very influential person throughout my high school years. I had her as an algebra teacher too, and she was always there helping me with everything. Having her as a teacher, I always wanted to do things right. I didn't want to let her down. I thought to myself, 'OK, I'm going to be organized so she knows that I'm an organized person.'" One of the reasons Brianna wanted to impress Ms. Smith was that they had developed a strong relationship. Over the course of two years, spending time with her informally during lunch helped to forge a strong bond:

> I would always stay during lunch in her classroom just because it was always quiet and sometimes I needed help with math . . . We had a really close relationship. She would tell me, "Why don't you major in math?" She always asked, "How are you doing, Brianna? Do you need any help? Do you know what classes you're going to take next year? I recommend you to take this." Spending time with her during lunch and having her as a teacher for two classes helped us develop a really close relationship.

Not only was Brianna driven to develop her academic skills to impress her teachers, but also she was motivated by other students in the program who helped raise her expectations: "Once you realize that everybody in your class is doing the same thing and everybody is organized, you push yourself to show others that you can be organized too." Even after Brianna no longer had Ms. Smith as a teacher, she remained connected to her through various informal interactions. In this way, her teacher found ways to transmit important knowledge about higher education such as picking a college and a major.

Brianna developed a similar relationship with her math teacher, Mr. Allen:

I had him for three years, so he knew me since I was a freshman. Last year he told me, "I remember as a freshman you were the quiet girl that would sit in the corner and would hardly ever talk, and throughout the years, you talked more and you think so differently now. I can't believe now you're going out of state to go to college. You've matured so much and accomplished so many things." I had respect for all of my teachers, but with him a lot more, just because I've seen him stay every day after school till late at night to help out students. So we became really close.

Another Pivotal Moment educator who played a critical role in Brianna's transition to higher education was her academic counselor, Mr. Chang. She explains how Mr. Chang assisted her with college advice and guidance:

If it wasn't for Mr. Chang, I don't think I'd be here. He was one of the people that let me know about deadlines for colleges and how to apply for scholarships. He's the one that let me know about this college. That's the only reason why I applied. He got in touch with some of the counselors here so that they were able to pay for me to visit the campus. He always asked, "How are you doing in classes?" or he would tell me, "You have to get these SAT scores" or, "Here's information on another scholarship, and this is what you need."

Not only was Mr. Chang a valuable source of college information, but also he motivated Brianna and eased many of her concerns along the way: "I knew I had someone who I could count on that cared about my education. He did a lot, not just for me, but a lot of students. He's always helping out. He seems really dedicated, and I really liked that . . . He always made sure I was doing the right things, and that made me feel confident about what I was doing. Whenever he talks, he makes people get so encouraged."

Mr. Chang began to connect with Brianna when she went to see him at the end of her junior year. She expressed to him that she was unsure about her plans after high school and did not know what she wanted to major in. He quickly gave her several information resources to look over during the summer and told her to come back and see him at the beginning of the year. When she returned to school her senior year, she had narrowed her list of schools based on Mr. Chang's advice and resources. Interestingly, she compared his support to that of a college-educated parent:

> He was like a parent . . . although my mom always pushed me, if they knew more, they would help me more, but they couldn't, so I was really relying on whatever information I could get on my own until Mr. Chang stepped in and was able to do all that for me . . . I feel like he's part of my family because he played that parent role by encouraging me, always guiding me through the right path and letting me know what's out there and making me feel like there's someone here that cares.

Mr. Chang has been influential in the lives of many students at his school, so much so that when the school experienced budget cuts and decided to eliminate his position, the students began a campaign that resulted in the school hiring him back. "He got a pink slip when they were trying to cut down counselors and teachers," Brianna said. "So another student and I got signatures and letters, and we went to the school board to talk to them."

As a result of Brianna's early and multiple educational Pivotal Moments, she has adjusted very well to higher education as a first-year, first-generation college student: "When I came to visit the school, I really felt the connection here. As a freshman, everybody goes through being homesick, and my first term was a little bit tough because I was getting all these classes and I didn't know what was going on, and I was stressed. The second term started, and I began meeting more people and making friends. I love my school even more, and I don't really miss home. I really like being here." Brianna has joined a multicultural sorority that volunteers to tutor middle school students, and, similar to Valerie, she also joined the freshman orientation team. These activities helped Brianna become integrated in to her college community: "That's how I made friends, and that's how I became more comfortable when I started college."

Brianna is doing well academically considering that the courses she enrolled in during her first year included calculus and chemistry. "I've done really well, but I have to work for it . . . There were little things that I still had to learn, but other than that, I feel like I was really prepared for it." As a result of her early educational Pivotal Moment, Brianna has developed effective help-seeking behaviors. When she struggles in her courses she goes to see the professors and the tutoring center for help. Unlike Valerie, who remained apprehensive about approaching professors even as a college senior, Brianna has already developed relationships with a couple of her college professors: "I'm really close with my Spanish professor. He gives me articles to read, and he's told me, 'I could give you a couple of books if you want to read over stuff,' and that made me feel really good . . . I made another really good connection with my calculus professor, because I went to get help from him a lot and I always went to his study sessions. He wrote a letter of recommendation for me for an RA [Resident Assistant] position that I applied for."

Reflecting on her educational success, Brianna credited her high school academic outreach program for the educational knowledge and skills she has accumulated. "The program helped me a lot in being responsible and being able to communicate and have confidence in myself." As a testament to the dedication of her former academic outreach program teachers, she still stays in touch with them, and they continue to provide emotional and moral support: "The program has been a really huge part of my life, and still is because I still have connections with my teachers . . . Some of them text me, 'How are you doing in classes? Is everything OK? When are you coming back? Are you coming to visit?' I have a really close family connection with everyone . . . They're always calling to make sure I'm okay, if I need any help with anything, or just to check in to see how I'm doing."

Brianna's case illuminates the long-term academic benefits of early Pivotal Moment interventions. It shows how students who learn academic knowledge, skills, and behaviors early are better able to navigate and succeed in new educational contexts. Whereas Valerie, who had a late academic intervention, expressed fears about transitioning to her new graduate school environment, Brianna, who experienced an early intervention, did not have the same worries and immediately adjusted to her new college environment.

THE IMPORTANCE OF PIVOTAL MOMENT TIMING

Table 4.1 illustrates that the timing of a student's Pivotal Moment can significantly impact their higher education experiences and outcomes.

TABLE 4.1

Educational Pivotal Moment timing and long-term academic adjustment and success

	Pivotal Moment timing	
	Early	**Late**
Higher education adjustment	Good adjustment to higher education; reports more positive experiences; feels well supported.	Difficult adjustment to higher education; reports more negative experiences; does not always feel well supported.
Navigating the educational system	Exhibits various help-seeking behaviors such as reaching out; feels confident asking school staff for help.	Exhibits few help-seeking behaviors; feels bothersome asking school staff for help.
School involvement	Participates in various types of school activities; feels more integrated.	Uncomfortable participating in most school activities; may feel marginalized.
Social support networks	Support networks are broad and diverse, including one or more educators.	Support networks are small and include mostly individuals who are not educators, such as family and friends.
Academic accomplishments	High academic success; various academic awards and much recognition.	Limited academic success; few academic awards and little recognition.

Students who experienced early interventions, like Dora and Brianna, had a more positive adjustment to higher education. These students felt more integrated and supported and had broader and diverse support networks. Early Pivotal Moment students also exhibited better help-seeking behaviors that enable them to access institutional resources to accomplish educational goals. In contrast, students who experienced late interventions, like Carmen and Valerie, did not transition to higher education as smoothly. As a result, late Pivotal Moment students felt less integrated and supported and had dense and homogenous support networks. These students also exhibited negative help-seeking behaviors, and that hampered their ability to attain their educational goals.

With so few low-income minority youth successfully navigating the educational system to gain access to higher education, it is critical to understand the important factors that place them enroute to college enrollment and completion. Academic interventions, or educational Pivotal Moments, initiated by supportive educators are one of those notable factors. When I mapped out the various types of academic interventions students experienced, it became clear that the timing of a students' Pivotal Moment was significant in determining her long-term educational success. Those who had an earlier Pivotal Moment (before or during early high school) tended to have a smoother path to higher education and were better adjusted than those who had a later Pivotal Moment (late high school or after).

The educational Pivotal Moment framework argues that the knowledge and skills gained from an academic intervention—developing a new orientation toward schooling and accompanying stocks of academic capital—have a cumulative effect that allows students to exponentially develop more over time.[2] Because instrumental educational knowledge and skills are important for success in higher education, students who have a higher stock are more likely to be successful than those with less. If early Pivotal Moments provide significant educational benefits to low-income minority students, we need to make sure that they happen as frequently as possible in educational practice. Thus, educators need to know about the impact of Pivotal Moments so that, as practitioners, they can be intentional during their interactions with students to increase the number of early academic interventions with low-income and minority youth, to ultimately enhance their overall academic achievement and college completion rates.

PART II

Creating Pivotal Moments in School

5

"THEY DON'T FEEL LIKE THEY ARE JUST A NUMBER"

Building Trust

When I arrived for our interview, Mr. Chang had a group of three senior boys in his office whom he was counseling on college and scholarship matters. As the students exited his office, he politely introduced each one to me while mentioning where each had applied to college. I was very impressed that all three students had applied to top-ranked colleges and universities. The attention Mr. Chang paid to introducing me to his students while naming the schools they applied for is indicative of his counseling style, which he describes as "being a student's greatest advocate and support system—not only motivating them, but treating them with respect and caring for them, letting them know you have high expectations for them to go to college."

Mr. Chang takes his role as a high school academic counselor very seriously and exemplifies the key characteristics of an effective Pivotal Moment educator: he has a personalized approach to working with students that helps him earn their trust. He mentors them through the college preparation and application process, and, during the process, he passes on important academic knowledge and skills. As a result, he gets many of the low-income minority students he works with accepted into highly selective colleges and universities.

Few students are as fortunate as Mr. Chang's students. First-generation students generally spend less time in high school talking to teachers or counselors about their educational aspirations than their peers with college-educated parents.[1] In fact, high school staff sometimes discourage low-income and minority students' college aspirations and limit their access to college prep classes.[2] These students have less access to information about college and the application process, and they attend less-selective institutions.[3] They also face obstacles in their preparation, access, persistence, and graduation from college, as well as in their subsequent graduate school enrollment.[4]

Educational disadvantages begin to emerge in middle school, accumulate throughout high school and college, and have a negative impact on students' career paths.[5] In college, low-income students have less time to study and participate in student clubs and organizations, because they hold jobs to pay for school. They are less likely to visit faculty during office hours and in their homes than high-income peers, gaining fewer incentives to raise aspirations or attainment.[6] They are also less likely to expect to finish college.[7] First-generation and low-income students' aspirations and plans for educational attainment are lower than those of non-first-generation and higher-income students.[8] Additionally, they are less likely to aspire to a law or medical degree, and they attend graduate school less frequently.[9]

Efforts by educators like Mr. Chang have the potential to dramatically change current educational trends for low-income and minority students. Through his intentional guidance and support, his students develop resilience, show positive adaptation despite adversity, and are able to beat the odds and circumvent the sorting process of school to gain access to higher education.[10] In the presence of stressful events and conditions that place them at risk of doing poorly in schools, and ultimately dropping out, resilient students become academically invulnerable and sustain high levels of achievement motivation and performance.[11] Under proper conditions, resilience can develop to buffer a student from social forces that can potentially interfere with normal development and effective participation in school.[12] Resilient children learn to manipulate and shape their environment to deal with its pressures successfully.[13]

Contemporary resilience theories explain the role of protective factors that mitigate the risks of adverse conditions and circumstances for children and young adults, allowing for healthy development where hazardous conditions would predict otherwise.[14] Resilience research has helped us understand the conditions that enhance young people's potential by optimizing their coping and adaptation, minimizing detrimental impacts of external conditions, and subsequently facilitating resilience building. Social ties, such as the ones Mr. Chang develops with his students, are thought to buffer the adverse effects of social and economic disadvantage because they serve as resources for effective problem solving.[15] In this chapter and the two that follow, I discuss how low-income minority students' social ties to Pivotal Moment educators in public schools positively impact their long-term educational success.

THE MULTIPLE ROLES OF ACADEMIC COUNSELORS

Secondary school academic counselors perform various functions in their schools. They are trained to provide all students with educational and career planning and college counseling services. They work with teachers to conduct guidance lessons in classrooms on topics such as college planning, conflict mediation, and violence prevention. In small group formats, individually, or in consultation with parents, teachers, and administrators, counselors also provide responsive services to students experiencing problems that interfere with their school success.[16]

A major role for counselors is assisting students as they decide, plan, and pursue post–high school education.[17] Unfortunately, most high school students do not consider their counselors to be very helpful and rarely utilize them for guidance about college.[18] Students who are the first in their families to attend college are less satisfied with the assistance they receive from their high school counselors.[19] One of the reasons may be that in the schools they attend—which are characterized by low test scores, low Advanced Placement course enrollment, and fewer seniors applying to multiple colleges—counselors are inundated with clerical and administrative duties such as photocopying, mailing deficiency notices, serving as testing coordinators, substitute teaching, and administering discipline. In recent decades, counselors' responsibilities have multiplied and changed, with their primary energies being devoted to scheduling, discipline, and monitoring dropouts.[20] As a result, they are less likely to provide low-income and minority students with educational and career planning and college counseling services.[21]

These trends are worrisome because for low-income minority students, schools are one of the few potential sites where their college plans can be nurtured.[22] Sadly, the schools they attend have too few teachers and counselors who are trained in helping them think about and prepare for college.[23] In many schools, counselors may be the only available source for advising students and their families on appropriate classes, providing basic information on the reasons college is important, and being sounding boards for college choices, but the structure of counseling departments in public schools does not always allow them to be effective in this role.[24] Counselors in large high schools can carry caseloads of up to one thousand students.[25] Moreover, they may be grossly underinformed about college types, college entrance requirements, and other important information about higher education.[26]

All these trends highlight the obvious: Pivotal Moment educators such as Mr. Chang are rare, but their potential impact can be profound. Although most educators who work closely with low-income minority students are caring and encouraging, not all of them intentionally intervene in students' schooling to transmit knowledge about navigating the educational system. As noted in chapter 2, cheering students on or simply encouraging them to do their best is not enough to be transformative. Pivotal Moment educators serve as mentors, connect students to resources, guide and expose them to critical information, and provide specific academic knowledge such as communicating strategically, dealing with school bureaucracies, networking, problem-solving, and developing help-seeking behaviors. They engage in these practices in schools with high levels of poverty, high minority student populations, low achievement levels, and low college-going rates. They foster academic success and college enrollment in places where most educators are not able to do so. The practices of Pivotal Moment educators, therefore, can help others learn and adopt their strategies to increase low-income minority student achievement and enrollment in higher education.

PRACTICES THAT BUILD TRUST

For Pivotal Moment educators, the foundation of all their practices lies in the establishment of a trusting relationship with their students. Mr. Chang, an Asian American, has been a public school educator for fourteen years, the past three as a high school counselor. Before that, he spent eleven years as a middle school teacher and counselor. He took his current position because he wanted the opportunity to help high school students prepare for college. The high school where he works serves low-income students, with 76 percent of them eligible for free or reduced-cost lunch, 66 percent Latino, and 24 percent white.

Mr. Chang has a large student caseload. In 2009 he advised 425 students, a number that grew to 560 in 2010, including 110 seniors. He works with students beginning in ninth grade through twelfth grade. Over the years, he gets to know his students well. Despite his large caseload, he prides himself in knowing all his students by name: "I feel like when students know that their counselors know them by name, they feel special. They don't feel like they are just a number, that the counselor really wants to support them, and they can trust what I will offer to help them. Some of them, I may have only met them once or twice and they go, 'How do you still remember my name?'" His students are always amazed by how quickly he learns their names at the beginning of each school year. I was not surprised that Mr. Chang was good with names and uses it as a strategy to build rapport with his students. Throughout our interview, he would respond to my questions with, "That's a great question, Roberta!" I was impressed that he found a way to personalize our interview and build a friendly relationship with me during our brief interaction.

A key to Mr. Chang's success in supporting students is earning their trust. One of his strategies is to share his personal story of being a first-generation college graduate from a low-income family. Like most Pivotal Moment educators, he finds that sharing his own educational experiences with students helps him earn the trust he needs to effectively reach out to his students: "I share with them that high school was never easy for me. Being a first-generation college-bound student myself makes me want to make sure they don't have to go through what

85

I went through in high school. Whatever services they need, I do my best to offer that to them."

Mr. Chang said that part of supporting students is to let them know that they are important. His efforts create a level of rapport that allows him to be an influential counselor. He has learned that his ability to reach students depends on their perception of his availability: "In counseling, sometimes you feel that with a vast caseload of students, you might not be able to focus much on an individual student, but sometimes students need that and I wouldn't want to close the door on a student and say, 'Sorry, I don't have time to see you,' because word gets around and that is not good when there's a perception that counselors are not available to see you. So I try to make myself available."

Because of his great reputation, students who are assigned to other counselors often seek out Mr. Chang for guidance. Typical of most Pivotal Moment educators I interviewed, he does not turn any students away who come to him seeking his assistance. "I have students that see me often because their friends tell them, 'Go see him. He'll tell you about the private schools, the information you need,' and that's great. Whether the student belongs to me or not, I'm willing to help. I wouldn't say, 'Sorry I can't help you because I'm not your counselor.'" He said that as an academic counselor, he should be available to serve all students on his campus, and he makes every effort to do so.

Pivotal Moment educators go out of their way to build relationships with their students, but other educators, such as Mr. Carlson, take a different approach. Mr. Carlson, who works with low-income minority students in a large public high school, explained that he had been advised by more-experienced counselors not to make himself available. He remarked, "I'm not supposed to be available. Top-notch people in my profession have told me not to be available because then it looks like I'm not doing anything. I've been told not to do random acts of guidance." He further stated, "I'm very unavailable as a freshman counselor. I always tell kids, 'Hey, don't walk in and expect me to be here for you because I'm not.'" He even told me about recently having to "run a student off" who kept coming to his office after school to talk with him.

Mr. Carlson's comments are typical of most counselors I observed. Unfortunately, their views indicate a significant disconnect between, on the one hand, what counselors learn in graduate programs that train and license them, and, on the other hand, guidelines developed by national professional counseling organizations. Contrary to the view of many counselors, the American School Counselor Association calls for school counselors to utilize advocacy to ensure educational equity and access within their schools.[27] Advocacy has been formalized in the counseling profession through the "advocacy competencies" developed by the American Counseling Association.[28] These competencies describe the dispositions, knowledge, and skills essential to the effective practice of counselor advocacy.[29] They are based on a social justice philosophy and emphasize the impact of social, cultural, economic, and political systems on students' development. Unfortunately, most counselors do not learn about the national counseling organization's guidelines and suggested competencies during their graduate education.[30] Although they did not specifically mention or refer to counseling guidelines or competencies, the Pivotal Moment educators I interviewed exhibited practices consistent with those guidelines, particularly in their efforts to build relationships with students.

Ms. Reyes, a Latina academic counselor at a magnet high school, builds trust with her students by asking them questions about their daily lives. Even with an advising caseload of 365 students, she tries to find time to ask all her students about their families to get to know them and build a caring relationship. "I want the kids to know I'm a safe person to talk to," she said. "I ask them a lot of questions, and sometimes they don't answer because they're not ready to trust me yet, and that's okay because trust takes a while to build with the kids." Ms. Reyes recognizes that it can take time for students to warm up to her, but she knows that with her efforts, over time they will eventually learn to trust her. Like Mr. Chang, she shares with them her own struggles as a student. "My first year in college, I was on academic probation. I tell them I'm not perfect. I made a lot of mistakes." She feels that it is important for students to know that she struggled academically in college but sought out resources that helped her overcome the challenges she faced. In asking students questions about their lives and by sharing her story, Ms. Reyes builds trusting relationships with her students that facilitate her ability to better counsel them.

According to Ms. Pineda, a Latina academic counselor at a large public high school, making students feel comfortable around her is what eventually builds trust. In her school 85 percent of students are low income, and 98 percent are Latino. Despite her caseload of 340 students, she works to create a sense of comfort with her students: "We're first generation, and we can relate to the challenges of the school system—and the intimidation factor. A lot of what we try to do from Day One is to set a very informal tone. We want to send the message that we're here to assist and guide them and that we're not here just to reprimand, discipline, or judge them. Whether it's with the low-achieving kids or the high-achieving kids, it's about creating that sense of comfort." Her ability to create a comfortable space for her students stems from being a first-generation college graduate who can personally relate to the educational experiences of most of her students. She knows that being sympathetic to students' struggles inside and outside school is important in showing them she cares about their personal lives.

Unlike Ms. Pineda, however, most educators I studied were not as sympathetic to low-income students. One example was Mr. Ortega, a high school counselor. He stated, "If a student is on the free or reduced-price lunch list, they don't want you to know that they're on that list because you're supposed to handle 'those people' with care because they're embarrassed, which is ridiculous because you're trying to give them free services. You're trying to get their SAT for free, planning college for free, go to college for free." Mr. Ortega does not seem at all sensitive to the stigma low-income students may feel being on the free and reduced-price lunch list at a school where only one-fifth of the student population is low income.

Ms. Johnson, an African American woman who is the head counselor at a large public high school, believes that if she does not build trust with her students they are not going to be receptive to her academic advice. She works at a school where 86 percent of the students are low income, 80 percent are Latino, and 13 percent are African American. Currently, she has a student caseload of 540 that includes 225 seniors. Unlike Mr. Chang, who works with his students all four years of high school, Ms. Johnson works exclusively with seniors during their final year of high school. As a former teacher, she learned early in her career that to effectively help students, she first must earn their trust: "For me, it started in my classroom when I used to teach, and I noticed that a lot of my kids had no rapport with adults, had no one they could trust to give them information that was beneficial to them. You can talk to them all day, but the trust factor is big. Every student that I have that connection with, I feel the opportunity is there to provide them with information that they can use at that time, and it works because they trust what I have to say and they come back for more." Ms. Johnson believes that students must first trust educators before they can provide information to assist them with academic and personal issues. For that reason, she makes a concerted effort to connect with her students on a personal level whenever opportunities present themselves.

Similarly, Mr. Montes, a Latino high school science teacher, said that connecting with students in the classroom was important to get them engaged with learning and to build rapport. Mr. Montes works at a high school that is 89 percent low income, 92 percent Latino, and, based on state achievement tests, low performing. He estimates that only 15–20 percent of the graduating seniors at his school go on to four-year colleges. Like all Pivotal Moment educators, before fully beginning his intervention with students, Mr. Montes works to establish a strong connection with students: "If you don't connect with them, forget it. They'll be here just to pass the class and to get a D or a C and they won't care about your class. They won't care about you because you don't care about them, and so it won't work, and instead you will have students who give you trouble, rather than students who will try to do something for you." He feels that connecting with students builds trust, engages them in the course, and creates a platform to talk about college.

In contrast to Pivotal Moment educators, most educators I interviewed shared the perspective expressed by Mr. Lewis, a counselor at a large public high school. When asked about connecting with students, he replied, "To be candid, five hundred is too big of a caseload. Sometimes you start to get to know the frequent fliers, the bottom and top ends, very well. It's that kid who does everything right and has a 2.7 to 3.3 grade point average that might get lost in the shuffle, because they don't seem to need it as much. They don't want or need my services. They're low maintenance." Unlike Mr. Montes, Mr. Lewis does not feel that he needs to make an effort to build rapport with all of his students.

With this approach, however, the likelihood of those kids in the middle experiencing an academic intervention is extremely low regardless of how much they actually need it. Like that of many educators, Mr. Lewis's approach ignores the fact that school relationships can help integrate students into the school environment and help them take advantage of the educational and social resources it has to offer. To ensure optimal use of educational resources and learning experiences, educators must develop cohesive relationships with students to facilitate the transmission of information that can help students succeed academically and socially and make a successful transition to college.[31]

Educators can foster academic norms and values through their general interactions with students. Students who have cohesive relationships with school personnel value the educational process and are often more committed to the school. They come to see the importance of education as they learn the value of attending school regularly, completing assignments, and performing satisfactorily in the classroom.[32] These values are emphasized by educators who take a special interest in students and make them feel that someone in the school really does care about them and their academic progress.

In college settings, student–faculty interactions are positively associated with a broad range of student educational outcomes.[33] In general, more contact between students and faculty, both inside and outside the classroom, enhances college students' development and learning outcomes. Informal (out-of-class) student–faculty interaction has significantly positive associations with career plans and educational aspirations, satisfaction with college, intellectual and personal development, academic achievement, and college persistence.[34] Formal (in-class) student–faculty interaction, as well as the informal interaction, positively affects students' success in their courses, their cognitive skills and intellectual growth, their attitudes and values, their educational attainment, and their career choice and development.[35]

Race, ethnicity, and social class also shape the nature of relationships between students and faculty as well as affect students' educational outcomes.[36] Student–faculty interactions have a significantly positive effect on white students' educational aspirations, but not on those of minority students.[37] Although undergraduate research experience is positively associated with college GPA for all students, the relationship is notably stronger for minority students. This experience also predicts higher degree aspirations for all racial groups, but the effect is more pronounced for white students than for Latino, Asian American, and African American students. Asian American students are more likely than other racial or ethnic groups to be involved in undergraduate research experience, but they are least likely to interact with faculty regarding course-related issues. African American students tend to interact more frequently with their faculty for course-related matters than other racial or ethnic groups, but they are least likely to assist faculty with research. As a student's social class rises, so does frequency of communicating or interacting with faculty. First-generation college students tend to assist faculty with research, communicate with faculty outside class, and interact with faculty during lecture class sessions less frequently than high-SES and white students.[38]

Because of these trends, there is an urgent need for faculty at the college level to develop trust with low-income and minority students to become their Pivotal Moment educators. The college faculty I studied employ similar strategies to those of high school teachers and counselors to establish trust with their students. Professor Ruiz, a faculty member at a highly selective private college, says she helps first-generation students in a variety of ways. Her first priority is to provide students with a safe space to earn their trust: "I think I'm helpful in being a listener. I also try to provide a space for students to share with me how they are doing." Professor Garcia, a faculty member at a large public research university, is sympathetic to the challenges first-generation college students face. "They are not very comfortable approaching their professors. I always wonder, 'Why don't they come talk to me? I'm so accessible!' They say, 'Oh, it's kind of awkward. I feel uncomfortable going to see professors.'" For this reason, Professor Garcia continually looks for ways to connect with students so that they feel more comfortable approaching her or asking for advice. Over time, she has come to develop caring relationships with many of her students: "I invited one of my students to my wedding, so I felt pretty close to her. It depends on the student, but I do develop a close relationship with certain students. It was funny because one of my students was presenting her research at some campus symposium, and I was there watching her presentation and she was so good! I just felt so proud of her, like a parent!"

The most effective college mentors build trusting friendships with students and share with them knowledge about the academic culture of the university.[39] Establishing trust, developing friendships, and sharing personal life stories are key components for building strong mentoring relationships.[40] Mentors and mentees enter into these relationships because they believe they can either provide or receive important academic knowledge and resources.[41] Talking to professors and teaching assistants, sharing knowledge by studying and socializing with classmates, and developing positive beliefs and expectations about their own competence are important means for students to come to know and feel comfortable navigating college.[42]

The powerful influence of educators on low-income and minority students is unmistakable. Close connections with the adults in a school helps students achieve higher levels of academic success.[43] Relationships with high school teachers, counselors, and administrators help students prepare for higher education, because they are trusted adults students can readily go to for information and advice. In fact, college students often mention by name secondary school educators who make a significant impact on them by encouraging them to attend college and making them believe they can succeed.[44] Clearly, educators at all levels have tremendous potential to positively impact the academic success of their students by developing trusting relationships.

6

"JUST STAY FOCUSED
AND I CAN GUIDE YOU"

Mentoring and Advocating for Students

After gaining students' trust, one of the most common ways Pivotal Moment educators support students is by exposing them to knowledge about college and encouraging their academic potential. Mr. Chang, introduced earlier, recognizes that his students lack critical college-going information, so he works to ensure they receive it from him: "The vast majority of our students' parents don't have a college education, and that's where I come in to guide them and let them know that there are a lot of great opportunities out there with financial aid and scholarships." Mr. Chang said that it is one of his primary jobs as an educator to provide first-generation students with information and support that they cannot get from home.

Ms. Pineda also described the lack of college-going knowledge in the students' families she works with: "Sometimes their family is trying to be supportive, but because they don't know the process, they can't. They don't know what they should be doing. They just don't even know what they need. For the academic support, they need to find somebody that understands—whether it's other students their age, a teacher, or a counselor."

Because parents and other individuals in students' social networks cannot provide important information and guidance, Pivotal Moment educators must assume that urgent role. Educators play a critical mentoring role for students by helping them see the importance of education, identifying and helping them develop their talents, and guiding students as they make educational and career decisions. Through classroom instruction, tutoring, and extracurricular activities, school personnel can encourage students and help turn their educational aspirations into realistic and attainable goals.[1] According to the National Association of Secondary School Principals (NASSP), all students need to know that there is at least one adult in the school who continually cares about them and their future after high school. NASSP recommends that all high school students have a "personal adult advocate" to help personalize their educational experience.[2] These advocates can be teachers, counselors, principals, or other school staff members who are committed to mentoring and guiding students. NASSP recommends that they work with about twenty students and follow their progress throughout high school, and that schools structure their time so that students and advocates can meet at least once a week.[3]

Pivotal Moment educators can be particularly important for African American and Latino students.[4] These educators can develop relationships with students to ensure that they are well integrated into the school and engaged in the learning experience. Educators who can relate to individual students and understand the challenges each student faces help foster a school climate in which students can easily access school resources.[5] They can also facilitate students' relationships with other adults and students in the school—including identifying problems that should be taken up with counselors, mediating conflicts with teachers and students, and visiting students' homes. A Pivotal Moment educator can serve as a buffer to help students navigate through high school and prepare for postsecondary education.

However, most educators believe that providing the necessary information is enough for students and their parents to understand and use it. For example, rather than try to convince parents and students to pursue a four-year degree, Mr. Lewis, a typical high school counselor, feels that by providing information, warning parents and students about the consequences of not taking all the necessary courses for college, and documenting his efforts, he has done his job properly:

They ask the questions. I give them the answers. I point them to the resources. [I tell them,] 'If you get stuck, give me a call, or come back and
check with me.' I try to set up all my kids on schedules so that they're
going to be in a four-year college. When they start to deviate from that,
I'm on the phone with the parents, letting them know that if the student
is not going to do a second year of a foreign language, he might not be
able to go to a four-year college, but instead a community college. And
that's fine. I've told the kid, I've told the parent, and I've documented
everything . . . You encourage everybody, and when they drop off, it's
of their own choosing.

Unlike Mr. Lewis, Pivotal Moment educators recognize that it is not
always as simple as just giving students information, especially for those
from families having low levels of education. Pivotal Moment educators understand you cannot just give students and parents academic-
related information and expect them to know what to do with it. As
Pierre Bourdieu explains, you can give people a machine, but in order
for them to know how to use it, they must have access, either in person
or by proxy, to that specific knowledge.[6] So putting a machine in front
of people and assuming they know how to use it, when in fact they do
not, could set them up for failure.

Mrs. Johnson understands that even the most high-achieving students, who you might assume know what they are doing, struggle with
college applications, and therefore she intentionally intervenes early.
She explained how she assesses what students know (or do not know)
and then works with them according to her assessment of their needs:
"I've had meetings where they have no clue, and they may be sit-
ting there with a 3.8 GPA and haven't done anything, haven't applied,
haven't thought about applying, don't know the steps to take because
they're first-generation students. Those are the students that I actually
sit down and have a longer discussion with. It could be an hour, it could
be two hours."

When she identifies students who need guidance, she takes the time
to counsel them so that they leave her office with the necessary information about college. In those exchanges, she realizes that students
need not only information but also a lot of encouragement and constant

reminders about their potential to gain acceptance to and succeed in college. Essentially, Mrs. Johnson has to build students' academic self-confidence while counseling them.

HOW PIVOTAL MOMENT EDUCATORS CAN HELP

Teacher advocates play an essential role in the academic success of their students, including increased grade point averages and college-going rates.[7] School counselors, through their professional roles and responsibilities, are in a unique position to advocate for increased college access for underrepresented students. Counselor advocates can teach students how to help themselves by educating students and parents on how to navigate educational bureaucracies and how to access support systems to promote academic success.[8]

In contrast to Pivotal Moment educators, the one-size fits all approach practiced by Mr. Lewis of helping students, despite their varying needs, is typical of most educators I studied. Mr. Lewis characterizes his approach as "honesty." He stated, "As far as the relationship, it's being honest with the kids, and being consistent with the communication and the message. I don't deviate from that message. 'Prepare to be ready for a four-year college.'" If students decide to attend a two-year community college instead of a four-year university, he reasoned, "it's because they *want* to, not because they *have* to." Instead of insisting that students go to a four-year university and putting them on that path as do Pivotal Moment educators, Mr. Lewis lets students make that decision on their own. When he says that it is their choice not to actively choose the four-year path on their own, he is not acknowledging that they may just be intimidated or overwhelmed by the process. As you saw earlier with Valerie, however, her decision to get out of the Honors track—a decision she made completely on her own—worked against her when she applied to college, by limiting her school options.

Despite the great potential to positively impact students' lives, counselors sometimes have difficulty turning a critical eye on themselves and their schools. They also have difficulty with the concept of advocating only for a particular group of students, such as low-income or minority students.[9] Even though they collaborate with teachers, administrators, and families, counselors rarely intervene at their schools to promote equity. They often blame the families and the communities for low student performance and apathy. Counselors highlight the value of family involvement, but at the same time they may not be sympathetic to family situations or may not value the importance of taking on a parental role for students who do not have strong parental involvement.[10]

As noted earlier, one of the major tasks of Pivotal Moment educators is to build students' confidence about succeeding in college. Mr. Chang observes that sometimes students just need a sense of belief and hope because they don't even think that they can get into four-year colleges. That's when he tells them, "Yes, you can do it [go to college]. Just stay focused and I can guide you." Often, he has to motivate students to even consider applying to college: "This year, several of my seniors that I thought for sure would not want to go to college, I was actually able to convince them to go. All they need is assurance and confidence in themselves. So I tell them, 'Apply. Take your SATs. You have what it takes. College is going to open up all kinds of doors for you.'"

Over the years, Mr. Chang has developed a reputation on campus as the counselor who goes out of his way to guide students and provide personalized time and attention. Students who come to him know they can trust his advice, because they have heard from other students that he is a student advocate and, as such, always has students' best interests in mind. Because students trust him, he can motivate them when they have doubts: "Some of them doubt themselves because of their SAT scores. Others feel like they can't go to college because nobody believes that they can. Sometimes it's because they don't know whether they can get there or how to get there. That's when I have to show them the steps and guide them."

In addition to motivating students, Ms. Reyes stated that she needs to insist in guiding them to pursue college by "pushing if necessary": "It's more than just talking to the kids about college. You're reinforcing their self-esteem and their motivation, telling them, 'You can do this. There's a reason why you worked so hard all this time. There's a reason why you got all these grades, and this is the payoff.' A lot of it is just getting them to feel sure about themselves."

Ms. Pineda, too, spends a lot of time convincing students and addressing their fears before they are ready to absorb information about college. Sadly, the extensive time she spends with her students is often perceived negatively by her colleagues as doing too much hand-holding: "Some people believe that it's the student's responsibility. If they really want it, they're going to do it. I don't believe it's a matter of they don't want to do it, I believe it's a matter of how to do it. They don't understand how the process works. So I really believe that hand-holding is not necessarily taking away their responsibility, it's helping them trust the system and the process that's in place."

Whereas Ms. Pineda hand-holds students through the college application process, Ms. Johnson lets them figure out some things on their own so that they begin to develop help-seeking behaviors. "I definitely walk them through the process," she said, "but I leave some work to them, because it shows me if they're truly, truly serious about it." She gave an example of a student she had recently counseled through the process of preparing for the SAT. She first gave him all the information about the exam, such as what is on it, the different sections it includes, how to study for it, and when he needed to take it. Then she sent him to the school library to check out an SAT study guide so that he could begin preparing for the exam. She told him to study for a week or two and then come see her again for additional guidance.

In sharp contrast, Mr. Carlson and Mr. Ortega, two high school counselors who did not exemplify Pivotal Moment educator behaviors, expressed the view that the push to get more students into four-year universities is misguided. Mr. Carlson explained:

> A recent interest of mine has been to get kids to redefine college. Our district is all about creating a college-going culture, and I hate that we've for so long made that to mean a four-year college. To me, if you go to the community college and you get a certificate in welding, you went to college, and you completed something and you just empowered yourself to do better in life. You may have done better than the kid who went with no clue what they wanted to do, and got a four-year degree, and racked up lots of student loans and came out with no skills that are marketable. So getting technical career information to kids and just validating that as a great pathway is an important thing.

Similarly, Mr. Preciado, a high school teacher who, like several other educators I studied, felt that college was not for everybody, said, "I don't know if we would really want everybody to be college material. Would that really work? Would that be a better society? The students make you think, and the answer is no. College is not necessarily the best thing for all students."

Although they were not in the majority, several other educators expressed the view that college is not for everyone. Their perspective echoes what I consider a settled debate among educational researchers, practitioners, and policy makers. In the past two decades, high schools have moved away from preparing students for work that does not require a college education. Most of the largest school districts have declared a commitment to getting all graduates into college and have systematically reduced vocational programs.[11] Occasionally, the college for all debate reemerges. Most recently, in early 2011 a group of researchers from the Harvard Graduate School of Education released a report that suggested that not all students should be pushed to pursue a college degree. The report asserts that by concentrating too much on classroom-based academics with four-year college enrollment as a goal, the nation's education system fails vast numbers of students, who instead need solid preparation for careers requiring less than a bachelor's degree. They propose that schools articulate students' career options as early as middle school and define the course work and training required so that young people can chart an informed educational path.

Most education advocates are alarmed by such proposals, given the virtual absence of career counseling in the K–12 or community college system to help level the playing field between disadvantaged students and more-fortunate ones. Previous tracking efforts have always sent disproportionate numbers of low-income and minority students to the lower tracks. Until we can find a way not to do that, despite the protests of some, I, along with most educators, will object. The work of Pivotal Moment educators provides concrete practices that are resulting in educational excellence among low-income and minority students despite the characterization of such efforts as an "impossible task."

Pivotal Moment educators recognize that once students feel comfortable with the resources that will help them get to college, they still need to be convinced that they have the necessary knowledge and skills to succeed academically. For example, Ms. Pineda explained, "One student that I'm working with said to me that he didn't want to apply to Stanford University because only 'smart kids' go to Stanford. This kid had a 4.3 and was taking six AP classes as a senior!" She expressed surprise that a student with such a strong academic record did not believe that he was smart enough to go to Stanford. When she heard him say that, she knew she needed to step in and convince him he should apply to Stanford as well as guide him in that effort.

In contrast, Mr. Carlson often discourages his students from aspiring to professions, such as medicine, that require numerous years of schooling: "There's an amazing amount of kids that say they want to be pediatricians, and then when you tell them, okay, so four years of high school and then like eleven years of college and graduate school after that, then they're like, 'Uh!' So I tell them that if they want to work with kids, nursing can be done in two years. And they're like, 'Okay, I wanna do that.'" Instead of encouraging his students to pursue high-status occupations, Mr. Carlson lowers their career and educational aspirations.

Ms. Reyes, a Pivotal Moment educator, works to raise students' expectations: "One challenge is just having them see beyond what they're familiar with. That's a real big one." She said that students need help seeing the possibilities available to them through encouragement and providing resources. She said that students can feel overwhelmed by the college application paperwork, which can sometimes discourage them, but that's when she knows it is her time to give them an encouraging push: "When they start the process of applications, it can be overwhelming sometimes and then they start to step back and fall back on, 'Oh, maybe this isn't something that I really need to do . . . maybe I shouldn't be doing all these schools.' [And then I say,] 'No, no, you need to be doing all of it.' That's when sometimes I push them." Ms. Reyes doesn't push only the academically stellar students but all her students, even those whom other teachers might not consider college material. She stated, "I see the potential . . . If I see kids that have C's and maybe two D's, I still tell them that they're going to go to college, that they should apply. I say, 'No, you're going to go. You're still going to apply.'"

Unlike Pivotal Moment educators, other educators had lower expectations of students, particularly those who struggled academically or
faced particularly difficult emotional hardships. Mr. Lewis said, "Some
kids got so much going on at home that school is their last priority, and
if you see them perpetually failing, sometimes you counsel them to attend a continuation or alternative learning setting that might be a little
bit more conducive to their emotional needs."

Similarly, another counselor, Mr. Soto, said that he actively helps
students transfer to alternative or adult schools if they are having academic difficulties rather than offer them additional help or support or
insist that they stay at the traditional high school so that they can take
the necessary course work to go to college. Some educators feel that
students have inherent abilities to perform well in school that cannot be
changed and thus believe that certain students are just not capable of performing in rigorous courses and going to college. Mr. Lewis expressed
this belief when he described his frustration with the expanded Honors program at his school, which was intended to increase access to the
more-rigorous curriculum for all students:

> Part of our WASC [Western Association of Schools and Colleges] goals
> were to make it more inclusive, not to make it so hard to be in an Honors
> course, and we've had mixed results with that. When you have a third
> section of AP U.S. History, your talent pool isn't as good as if you have
> one or two sections. In a true Honors program, you got about thirty-five
> kids that are truly gifted, maybe a few more, so two sections should be
> enough, but we have three to make it open to more people. The reality
> is some kids are there, they work hard, and they get their B. They're hard
> workers, but in order to be a true Honors student, you have to have the
> intellect *and* industry. You have to have both. If we have too many kids
> that signed up for AP Physics you call those kids in your office, and you
> say, how about regular physics? It still counts."

Sadly, educators like Mr. Lewis let their opinion that some students
are just born gifted and more intelligent determine which students they
let stay in the Honors courses versus those they counsel not to enroll.
He does not work under the assumption that all students are capable of

being in academically rigorous courses—even if they demonstrate the diligence and motivation to succeed.

In contrast, Pivotal Moment educators like Ms. Pineda do not like to label students based on perceived ability. She said that labeling students can hinder them from developing the sense of possibility that they can and should go to college. She insists that all students should have the opportunity to go to college and that academic counselors like her should send that message to all students they work with, regardless of their current achievement level. She explained her philosophy of working with students: "It's not our job to decide who's ready and who's not. For me, you send the message that it's for everybody. Try not to label kids. Open access to whoever is willing, because we're already stereotyping that student. So really have an open mind, have a philosophy that all students have the opportunity, and don't wait for them to come to you. You reach out to them." Ms. Pineda also said it is imperative for educators to proactively reach out to students and communicate the message that college is for everyone. She believes that if students hear this continually, they will start to internalize the possibility of going to college and work toward it in high school.

Most Pivotal Moment educators share a similar philosophy, and it motivates them to go beyond the call of duty for their students to ensure that they are mentored and guided properly. Mr. Chang is exemplary in this area. He is so dedicated to helping students that he often works long hours after the school day ends to assist them. "I'm always here," he said, "sometimes late in the evening to five or six answering questions, providing them with the guidance they need." Although he, like Ms. Pineda, often gets criticized by his colleagues for doing too much for his students, he explained that it is necessary to get them successfully through complicated academic hurdles such as the college application process: "There's nothing worse than when you disappoint a kid that really wanted your help and support, and feel like you've let them down. Sometimes people say, 'Why are you spending so much time with them? Let them do it on their own. Have them research it on their own,' and I say, 'You don't understand—they need help. They want your support. You can't just turn a kid away or say after ten or fifteen minutes, I don't have time anymore. You have to do it on your own.'"

Even when it creates resentment from his colleagues for seeing their students, Mr. Chang's rationale is that "at least I can go home feeling like I did what's best for the student." Student advocacy is central to Mr. Chang's philosophy as an academic counselor. He knows that without his advocacy, students would be lost in the college planning process from the very beginning: "I advocate for them because some students don't know where to begin." He said he feels an obligation to guide and support them.

Most educators, however, do not share Mr. Chang's student-centered ideology. Mr. Lewis, for example, has a very different philosophy of working with students. He stated that he thinks he should direct students to resources but does not feel obligated to mentor them or be an advocate. In fact, he was quite critical of educators who go above and beyond: "I keep making that effort, but when he doesn't graduate, I'll have a clear conscience. A lot of people in education still have the Jesus complex of, 'I'm going to save everybody.' You can't!"

As a high school teacher, Mr. Montes spends a lot of time talking about college in his science classes. In fact, he builds it into his course curriculum. He sets aside specific days in his class to talk about college so that all students know early in high school it is a possibility and they should be planning for it: "In my mind, I need to make sure that at least once a month I do something about college. Sometimes I do it more [often]. I identify students, and in my mind, I keep a list of the students I am working with. So when they come the following year, I have goals for them, I try to get the best out of them. What I try to do is reach out to a few tenth-graders every year in my classes, and those are my targets. And within those targets, hopefully they'll move on to AP class . . . and eventually go to college."

Mr. Montes is very intentional in making sure all his students have information about college. Additionally, he continues to work closely with a select group whom he connects with and that take multiple courses with him. In fact, he actively encourages students to take numerous courses with him so that he can continue to guide them in preparing to apply to college when they are seniors: "If students are lucky enough to take my class in tenth grade, and I see that they have the interest, I usually tell them to enroll in any one of my classes in eleventh grade so that

I can continue working with them. If I'm lucky, I'll have them for three years. I constantly tell them that they need to get high grades, they need to take the SAT, have they done this, have they done that."

Mr. Montes began to do this several years ago when he noticed that most of his students, including the top students, lacked college information. He said that the academic counselors at his school focus more on a generic four-year course plan without linking it to information about college, a practice he finds problematic. "The way counseling takes place is more like, 'These are the classes that you're gonna take, and there you go,' rather than counseling where you sit down with them and say, "Okay, this is what you should do, this is the path, and this is how you get to college,' and provide more guidance. I think that piece is missing."

As a result, low-income minority students at his school remain uninformed about college, because they do not have teachers or counselors providing them with that information. So, as a Pivotal Moment educator, he takes on that task: "Year after year, I talk to students and they don't know the difference between a community college, a state university, or a private university. They don't know the costs. They don't know what it takes to get there. There's a lot of confusion, so they're worried about getting their classes. I hear from students that there are only a few teachers at this school that actually spend some time in class to explain how college works." He lamented that even students ranked in the top 30 of their graduating class were going only to community colleges, even though they were eligible to attend prestigious four-year universities.

Additionally, students at his school worried about college admissions because they were never given enough information: "Even the top three [ranked] students worry, because they don't know if they're gonna get accepted. I keep telling them they just need to decide where to go, because they will get accepted." When students begin to worry, he tries to dispel their concerns and reaffirms their possibilities.

Mr. Montes is starting to see the results of his efforts to help students see college as a reality. "What I think I've accomplished over the years is that the more I talk to them, I see less and less students that are in the top thirty going to community colleges. Now, they're more committed to go to a four-year university." There is no doubt that Mr. Montes's students are more committed to going to four-year colleges because he is instilling in them the confidence and guidance to pursue that path. As a teacher, Mr. Montes intentionally tries to reach out to students early in high school so that he can work with them consistently for several years, providing the mentorship they need to get into college. He also builds college into the curriculum in all his science classes. From these two efforts, he opens up the option of college to his students and provides the needed guidance and information to help them apply. As a result, an increased number of students at his high school are now going to four-year colleges and universities.

His efforts are critical, because the majority of teachers and counselors do not identify issues of equity in their schools.[12] The small proportion of educators who, like Mr. Montes, believe advocacy should be added to their traditional role tend to be more comfortable as educational leaders and in collaborating with other educators.[13] Educators who feel advocacy is a part of their professional responsibilities stress the importance of relationships and getting to know students well so that they can advocate for students when needed.[14]

College-level professors, especially those at two-year institutions, also expose students to information about how to transfer to a four-year university or to continue to graduate school. Professor Lopez, a part-time faculty member who teaches at three different community colleges, quickly realized that at the campuses where most of the students are first generation and minority, many lacked information about the transfer process. Her students do not know what it takes to transfer to a four-year institution, and she knows what that feels like: "For a lot of students, no one's ever talked to them about transferring to a four-year. And I understand that because I came from a community college too." As someone who understands the struggle, Professor Lopez includes extensive information in her courses about the transfer process. Like Mr. Montes, she began to include transfer information in her politics courses when she first started teaching five years ago: "I talk about the transfer process. I tend to teach evenings and weekends, and so my students are not typically on campus when all the counseling services are provided. The transfer center is not open on Saturday, and counselors aren't readily available on evenings or weekends. In the past, I've invited universities to come talk about their transfer processes."

Professor Contreras, a faculty member at a large public university, also provides information about graduate school. "I talk about grad school throughout my courses," he said. "I don't sit down and say, 'You should go to grad school.' I do it through the curriculum itself. At the end of the semester, I let them know that I can help them with whatever they need if they want to talk about graduate school. I also tell them about past students that have gone to graduate school at Yale, Harvard, USC, Cal State Fullerton, and here." Professor Contreras said that his university—which has a high percentage of first-generation students—is not exposing them to the possibility or the information to go to graduate school. Thus, he believes it is important for students who take his courses to know it is the next step in the educational pipeline that they should be thinking about.

Pivotal Moment educators are important at the college level for providing information on the next steps in transferring from either a two-year to a four-year university or being exposed to graduate school information. The types of advice educators provide reflect both the level and the type of school at which they teach. Faculty at two-year schools expose students to transferring while faculty at four-year schools introduce students to graduate school.

ADVOCACY WITH PARENTS AND EDUCATORS

Pivotal Moment educators also advocate for students with their parents, who worry because they do not understand, for example, why their children stay up late at night studying or are considering going away for college. Mr. Montes often advocates for students with their parents: "I've talked with parents who tell me they're worried because she's staying up until eleven or midnight and she's doing homework, and they don't think that's good for her. Some students tell me, 'I've got to do this homework, and my mom does not let me stay up after ten o'clock.' Parents have absolutely no idea what it takes to go to school because most of them are not educated." When he can, Mr. Montes tries to help students resolve such situations with their parents. Additionally, when students feel that their parents don't understand all the hard work they put in to get ahead in school, Mr. Montes counsels students on understanding their parents' point of view. "They cry when they get their "A" or their "B" in AP classes, and they work so hard and they get home and they feel their parents don't appreciate it or they don't care. So I tell them, 'You know what? You can't blame them because they don't understand what you're doing. They don't know anything about it.'"

Mr. Chang is also very sympathetic to the many challenges his students face outside school: "Sometimes students are telling me, 'Life is just tough. I can't keep up with my AP courses. My parents don't understand why I want to go to certain colleges.' So sometimes you have to counsel them and just reassure them. 'Yes, everything will be okay. Do you want me to meet with your parents? No problem.'"

Unlike Mr. Montes, who understands that parents express concern because they are not familiar with school processes, Mr. Soto faults parents for not being more involved in their children's education. He expressed the opinion that students are making their own decisions about how to proceed with school because parents are just too unmotivated to get involved: "The students are the ones making the decisions on what they're gonna do regarding the alternative schools. I send letters home to come see me anytime, but I think that such unmotivated parents just go along with it." In Mr. Soto's view, immigrant parents in particular are responsible for some of the poor decisions students make about their education, because they lack proper parenting skills: "Recent immigrants are very uneducated to the high school process, and to the parental process. When I talk to them, there doesn't seem to be many rules at home. I can just see it without getting into it. I think parents are having a very tough time just providing basic needs for their students and having to work quite a bit and having to deal with their own life processes, which doesn't really let them invest the time to be better parents."

Mr. Lewis also characterized low student achievement as a lack of individual student effort: "I spend most of my time with the lowest kids, just trying to get them a diploma and holding their parents' hand who don't know what to do or why their kid doesn't want to get good grades." Pivotal Moment educators, in contrast, understand the challenges associated with poverty and the lack of information due to low levels of education. Educators who acknowledge these two important factors do not hold negative views about parents or blame them when students have poor academic performance.

In addition to working with parents, Pivotal Moment educators mentioned advocating for students with other teachers on campus. Ms. Johnson's work as an advocate is particularly valuable for her students, because according to her, the teachers at her school hold low expectations of them:

> My biggest challenge is getting the staff to understand that all kids can learn. I have teachers that write kids off before they even set foot in their class. They automatically say, "These kids aren't performing because they're from here, and that's just the way it is. They don't ever go anywhere." We have about 175 teachers. I would say about 30 percent have a great impact. They tend to be teachers that have been in the profession longer. The rest are close minded. They don't believe in doing things differently.

Ms. Johnson regularly advocates for students to get the necessary support from teachers to help students accomplish educational goals. She explained the situation of Keith, one of her students: "Keith is a first-generation student to go to college. Mom didn't graduate high school, and she's not really able to support him. He wants to study performing arts in college, so last year I told his dance teacher, 'You need to help him create a portfolio.' So I make the connection with the teachers as well. I tell the teacher, 'He's college bound—could you help him?' As head counselor, I have that ability to talk to teachers on that level, and they respect the fact that I'm emailing them saying, 'Do this!'"

Ms. Johnson knows that because teachers have low expectations for students, it is her job to enlist their support in helping students move forward with their college plans. But unlike Ms. Johnson and other Pivotal Moment educators, most counselors do not advocate for students.[15] They are often very hesitant to critique their own schools and challenge the status quo. The lack of student advocacy by counselors—who often strive to be likable and promote harmony and are reluctant to appear confrontational by challenging policies, practices, and inequities in their schools—has been described as Nice Counselor Syndrome.[16]

College Pivotal Moment educators also frequently advocate for students and support them in various ways. Because she relates to her students' experiences, Professor Lopez feels an obligation to provide encouragement, information, and guidance about transferring. She has been successful in helping students get accepted into academic support programs and private universities by encouraging them and advocating on their behalf: "I had two students who got into the USC scholar programs, and I wrote their recommendations. These two students were just exemplary. They were stellar. And I was like, 'You guys need to be on a path to go to USC,' and they were like, 'I can't do that—I work, I have kids,' and I was like, 'Apply for this program. I will endorse you and recommend you,' and both of them ended up getting in. And one of them has since transferred and was accepted to USC."

Professor Garcia also described a vivid example of a young woman, who, even though she was a top student, lacked the confidence and information to continue to graduate school. She would have applied to a less challenging and prestigious program had Professor Garcia not insisted that she apply to a top graduate program:

I had this one student—she was so smart! She is the kind of student who already has straight A's but is doing the extra credit. She's just so intense and engaged and just like on top of everything. I knew she wanted to go to a private school, and so she came to me in her senior year with some applications from a couple of California State University schools, and I asked her why she wasn't applying to USC and UCLA, and she said she missed the deadlines. I told her if she went to one of these other schools she would have more resources and connections available to her. I told her to think about the prestige that USC or UCLA was going to put on her resume. And she was like, "I just don't know if I'd get in." I told her, "Don't think, just apply please!" I'm begging her, "Please, please apply! You are such an excellent student. You are exceptional! If anybody is going to get in, it's going to be you." So she applied, and I wrote her this great letter and in two weeks, she told me, "I got in!" Not just that, but she got a scholarship. She was top notch, but she had such a hard time believing that she could or that she even deserved to apply to a school like that. I have to push them to trust themselves, that they can do it. I feel that part of my job is to be a counselor/cheerleader. Si se puede! [Yes you can!]

Similarly, Professor Martinez, a faculty member at a highly selective private college, actively advocates for students in the graduate school application process:

I call professors on their behalf. I'll say, "You know, I have this student that will be applying," and generally they're very receptive. I had a student who totally bombed the GRE, so I got a call from this professor at the graduate school asking, "What happened? The GREs are low, the letters of recommendation are good, the personal statement is good, the GPA is good, the classes are good." I told him that I knew he would make it there. He's a PhD now . . . So I try to connect them to schools and to people that are going to be supportive so they can thrive.

The mentoring and advocacy work that Pivotal Moment educators do is extremely effective in getting low-income and minority students on the path to college and graduate school. They expose students to information about higher education as well as provide the encouragement and support to help them envision future possibilities. It is the trusting relationships educators develop with students that facilitates their ability to shepherd their academic success and educational advancement.

7

"TANGIBLE WAYS OF MAKING IT REAL"

Transmitting Academic Knowledge and Skills

Most low-income minority students have the desire to attend college but do not always have the informational resources and personal support networks to attain their postsecondary education goals.[1] Students often lack adequate advice, particularly if no one in their immediate family has completed a four-year college degree. As a result, a large part of the obligation to enable students to gain the academic, social, and cultural skills to gain entrance to college falls upon teachers, counselors, and school administrators.[2] Educators can increase college access by providing emotional support, educational information, and assistance in navigating the college admission process.[3]

Students face a daunting task in applying for college admission and financial aid, and yet few educators realize that lack of information about these two processes is a considerable barrier for low-income minority students.[4] One of the most significant components of Pivotal Moments is the transmission of critical educational information and academic skills. Pivotal Moment educators use their trusting relationships with students to pass on knowledge in a variety of ways. They teach their students skills about navigating school, social networking, utilizing educational resources, and making effective decisions. These educators are intentional in transmitting this information to students in both formal and informal ways. The transmission of knowledge about navigating school processes is a critical part of a transformative student–educator relationship.

THE IMPORTANCE OF COURSE PLANNING

In working with students, Pivotal Moment educators often walk them through course planning in high school, school selection in the college application process, and decision making about college choice. Mr. Chang constantly reminds his students about the importance of course planning if they want to attend highly selective schools: "I want to challenge them to take rigorous courses, because academic rigor is so important nowadays for students that want to go to competitive colleges and universities." Unlike course selection, which is just picking courses to take in high school, course *planning* helps students choose specific courses with a clear explanation about why the levels and types of courses matter.

In contrast, Mr. Lewis said he does not think educators should insist that students take college prep courses if they choose not to: "My recommendation is to take as much math as they can, but I cannot and will not force them. They're big boys and girls now." When Mr. Chang meets with his students about course planning, he is very deliberate in telling them the educational outcomes they will achieve if they choose a regular course compared to an Honors course. He always ties his academic advising to being competitive for college so that students start hearing about college early in high school when they start meeting with him. He also advises students to get involved in internships and other extracurricular activities where they can develop their leadership skills, something that will look good on college applications.

Mr. Chang's advising creates a college-going culture that gets students thinking about and preparing for college. During students' senior year, Mr. Chang assists them with all aspects of their college applications. He encourages students to apply to highly selective colleges as well as try for prestigious scholarships. He believes that private schools will provide better support and funding for his students who are the first generation in their families to go to college: "The last couple of years, I've been steering students mostly towards the private schools." When students apply, he makes sure that everything is properly filled out. "Sometimes I have to spend a good one or two hours with a particular student, because you really want to make sure nothing is missing," he said. "Several of them come to me to proofread their scholarship or college applications." In these exchanges, he is passing on information about how to be successful in achieving educational goals.

When I asked Mr. Chang about his student success stories, he described three students. One is a Latino, now at Harvard University, whom Mr. Chang helped with applications and coached through the interview process. Another student is a Latina who is now at Worcester Polytechnic Institute, whom he worked closely with since her junior year and walked through every step of college preparation and application. The third student, a Latino who is now at a public four-year university, had said that he planned to go to a community college after high school. Mr. Chang makes an effort to work with students individually based on his assessment of their needs. He works with all students, regardless of their academic records, holding each student to high expectations.

Although it was clear Mr. Chang has helped all three students in numerous ways, as an exemplary Pivotal Moment educator he provided some of the details that demonstrate how he transmits information. He explained the interview coaching he did for the Latino student who is now at Harvard University:

> We have not had a student go to Harvard in over thirty or forty years. Even though I was not technically his counselor, he came in to see me about how to prepare for a college interview. I tell them to be themselves, that the schools only want to get to know them and not grill them. I tell them not to think of the interview as a make-or-break situation but to use it to learn more about the college. I tell them that they are going to be interviewed by one person, and it's very casual. I remind them to offer a firm handshake, make good eye contact, and just answer to the best of their ability. I tell them some of the questions they're going to ask. When I tell them all that, they start feeling better.

He said that first-generation college students should be coached through the entire application process to be successful. Even though he played an important part in this student's going to Harvard, he humbly stated, "It was not because of me, but because of his accomplishments." For Mr. Chang, no detail is too small for students to make the best impression possible. When another student had a college interview, he also helped her prepare. "I gave her special bonded paper to print her resume. I tell the students to impress the interviewers with some good bonded paper. It makes a difference. Presentation is important."

For the Latino student whom he encouraged to look beyond community colleges and apply to four-year universities, Mr. Chang explained how he walked him through every aspect of his application. The student told him he wanted to go to the local community college, but Mr. Chang kept telling him that he should aim higher and apply to four-year universities instead. The student was initially very skeptical but finally gave in after Mr. Chang kept bugging him about it, but he needed assistance and encouragement along the way that Mr. Chang happily provided. He recounted, "There were times that he'd come in to ask me about the FAFSA, about scholarships, or to review applications. He had trouble filling out applications because he didn't know certain things." Mr. Chang held this student's hand through the application and financial aid process, and the student now attends a public four-year university and is earning his bachelor's degree.

These types of efforts make all the difference. For example, students who are eligible to attend college after high school but do not enroll express uncertainty about their academic preparation. A majority of these students see themselves as not very well prepared for college-level material, as did the Latino whom Mr. Chang advised.[5]

Similar to Mr. Chang, Ms. Pineda puts all her students on a course plan to attend college when they enter high school in ninth grade and first meet with her. Her philosophy is that all students, especially low-income minority students, should be told they are expected to go to college, and not have it presented as an option. She explained by saying, "Don't give them too many options, because they're always going to opt for the easiest and the less scary one." She said that first-generation students need assistance getting on the path to higher education. She also acknowledged, however, that she needs to actively "reach out to students" and "not wait for them to come to you for guidance." She stated that students need guidance throughout high school, and educators like her need to take on that responsibility: "Plan A is prepare yourself for postsecondary education. So let's not talk about the application, but let's fill out the application, even if it's a sample, even if you're doing it in tenth grade. Let's not talk about the SAT, let's give sample questions of the SAT. Let's not look at the college online, let's go visit a college. Tangible ways of making it a real experience for them—that's not always easy."

Ms. Pineda argued that if students are properly supported and guided, they would all choose to go to college to have better lives and futures. As an academic counselor, she works under that assumption and steers students to college accordingly. In contrast, other educators, such as Mr. Ortega, steer students in different directions after high school based on their parents' educational backgrounds: "A lot of the parents I work with got their bachelor's degrees back in the seventies and eighties. That's all you needed to get a good job. Now it's not. Now you really do have to get your master's. So I'm pushing those [middle-class] kids to do that. And then my [working-class] kids, whose parents haven't been to college, step one is to get them to the career college."

When I asked Ms. Pineda about her student success stories, she told me about a few students she worked with the past few years whom she recently had guided through the college application process. One student in particular was a Latina who has been accepted to several highly selective colleges. Ms. Pineda said, "She's already been accepted to University of California schools—we've done all her paperwork." She also elaborated on the details of how she provides information to students. When she first started working with this student, Ms. Pineda encouraged her to take academically rigorous Honors and AP courses, which she knew the student was capable of. She explained her course load her senior year as an example: "She's done AP English, AP American literature, AP government, AP psychology, pre-calculus—she's that kind of kid." Ms. Pineda told the student to take these types of courses because it would make her a competitive applicant for college when she was ready to apply senior year.

As a result, the student had numerous college options. During the student's senior year, Ms. Pineda counseled her through the entire application process during a very difficult time when the student became homeless after the death of one of her parents. Despite the severe obstacle, the student stayed focused and followed Ms. Pineda's instructions: "I have been walking her through every step of the way, and the same with scholarship applications—rereading her essays, editing, making sure she submits whatever forms she needs, faxing things, and whatever else was needed. I actually sat with her and filled out the FAFSA. I also drove her to colleges . . . Right now we're working on how we are going to get her financial aid for summer school because she needs a place to live."

Not only did Ms. Pineda help her student navigate the college application process but she is also assisting her with making a decision about which college to attend. Ms. Pineda also explains to students exactly why they need to do certain things—the rationale behind it—so that they can take those skills with them to the next level of their education.

When I asked her about her student success stories, Ms. Johnson proudly told me about a Latino student named Raymond who she counseled the past few years and helped get into college. Raymond was a promising young man who became homeless when his family was deported back to Mexico. Ms. Johnson's educational intervention during his junior and senior years in high school completely changed the course of his life. In recounting the story, Ms. Johnson elaborated on the details of her relationship with Raymond and explained how she was able to pass on information to him. She first described how they met: "One day during his junior year he ends up in my office, and he says, 'I want to graduate early.' And I said, 'Okay kid, whatever. Everybody wants to graduate early.' He was really not giving me a lot of information, so I told him I needed to know why. He told me he was having problems at home. He was in honors classes, had all A's. I spent the whole morning trying to get to know this bright, well-mannered kid that wanted to leave school early."

She described in great detail how she made an effort to get to know Raymond better to learn about his family situation and circumstances:

It was a Thursday and I had to buy the counselors lunch, so he says, "I can get you a discount." And I thought, "Whatever." But he insisted, "No, I'm the nighttime manager there." So I said, "You're the manager of the Pizza Hut down the street?" So I called, put the order in, the driver showed up and gave me 25 percent off the pizzas. The pizza delivery guy, an older man in his sixties, goes, "Hey, Mr. Tito, is this your school?" and he shook his hand. He had so much respect for [Raymond], and I was like, "This kid is a nighttime manager, good grades, straight A's, all Honors classes—what is going on?" So we had pizza and talked, and he told me that his mother was deported and his stepfather had kicked him out and he was living on the streets and actually sleeping on campus under the bleacher area. Most recently, he had been riding his skateboard from a nearby city, where he found a friend that would let him stay with him. He would ride his skateboard fifteen miles when he couldn't get bus money.

After getting to know Raymond, Ms. Johnson knew that she needed to intervene and help this young man get to college, an option that he had not even considered. He was initially asking to graduate early so that he could join the workforce full-time to earn enough money to pay for his own living expenses. Ms. Johnson knew he had college potential, so she acted on it. For more than a year and a half, she advised him academically on finishing high school on schedule rather than early to increase his chances of getting into college. During his senior year, she guided him through the college application process, helping him every step of the way. She also taught him the value of social networking, which helped him get strong letters of recommendation for his college applications:

> I walked him through the college process, and showed him how to get in. I introduced him to Ms. Harrison, the principal. She fell in love with him. Ms. Harrison and I wrote letters of support, and we advocated for him with the president of the local public university and he ended up giving him a full scholarship. He ended up graduating number six in his class, with a 4.6 GPA. He's now a sophomore in college, straight A's, and a math major. He's a calculus tutor now on campus. He wants to come back here and teach math.

In the process of helping Raymond navigate both the rest of high school and the college application process, Ms. Johnson also showed him how to utilize all the school's resources to get the support he needed to succeed academically and get accepted to college.

Typical of other educators I interviewed, Mr. Lewis also had experience working with homeless and foster care kids. But unlike Ms. Johnson and Ms. Pineda, Mr. Lewis had a more hands-off approach to working with these students: "There are those that you take under your wing and you do the best you can, but sometimes they still fall. I got one this year. His dad threw him out of his house. I bought him a tank of gas, took him down to family services, got him set up with an apartment for a couple weeks, and said, 'Okay, you got a tank of gas, there's no reason you can't be coming to school for a while. If you need anything, come see me.' That was the last time I saw him." Without the extra support, mentorship, and advocacy of educators, the most vulnerable students fall through the cracks of the educational system. Thus, academic interventions for these students are imperative.

Mr. Montes adopts creative ways to engage his struggling students. He vividly described one of his student success stories. Gabby was a Latina student who was flunking his class. He decided he was not going to let that happen and explored other ways to help her learn the material. He eventually tapped in to her artistic talents:

> She wasn't doing well at all. I told her that I didn't know what I was gonna do, but that we would work something out and to just stay with it. And then one day I was passing by and I noticed a drawing of a flower on her notebook. So I said, "Who drew this?" And she said, "Oh, I like drawing." So I told her I wanted to see her draw. She was absolutely phenomenal. And I said, "Okay, let's try something. Instead of taking notes, read the book and create images, create stories with pictures and colors. If you don't learn, then we'll try something else. She showed me her notebook, and there were all these pictures and drawings and colors that meant nothing to me. One day I told her I was going to teach class like I always do, but I wanted her to take notes like she does every day but on the board so everyone could see. So I went ahead and gave the lecture, and she started drawing. We were doing something with ecology, and she drew all these images—I mean I still have the picture in my mind. So then I asked her, "What did I just say?" She just started looking at her

pictures and explained everything I said. It was amazing! Since then, I try to give all students opportunities to learn in different ways.

Gabby is only one of the students Mr. Montes connected with early in their high school careers and, at his suggestion, kept taking his classes to continue receiving his mentorship. "I believe that all students can learn," he stated. "They just have different challenges, different circumstances, different backgrounds. I want to see everyone succeed." Mr. Montes's relationship with Gabby stayed strong, and, during her senior year, he helped her apply to college. Similar to the other Pivotal Moment educators, he assisted Gabby with every step of the college application process, and she now attends a selective private liberal arts college.

Mr. Montes acknowledges that being able to work with a student for an extended period is most beneficial to keeping students on track for college. It also helps with building a strong teacher–student connection. Once he gains a student's trust, he identifies the information students are missing and begins to fill in the relevant academic knowledge: "They don't know the steps, they don't understand FAFSA. They worry about how they are gonna pay for it, they worry about so many different things. College is there, but it's blurry, it's full of questions, and they don't know how other students got there. And the thing is that they probably don't have many places where they can ask." Mr. Montes said that there are only a handful of teachers who are willing to help students with college questions, so he tries to be one of those teachers whom students know they can come to with questions.

College professors provide academic knowledge and skills to students in similar ways, particularly on how to navigate higher education once they have entered college. Professor Lopez often hears from former students who come back to thank her for helping them figure out how to transfer from a two-year college to a four-year university. "Students have come back to tell me I really helped them, that they learned where to go, how to navigate the process, or who to get help from. It's a good feeling 'cause I want them to do well." Professor Lopez said that her community college students need support not only with learning how to transfer but also with developing their academic skills: "We have to have those conversations sometimes about taking notes.

I started using PowerPoints and providing the PowerPoints ahead of time so students can print them out and then take notes, because I realized when I was just lecturing, they weren't able to keep up because all the concepts were so new."

Similarly, Professor Garcia encourages students to connect with their professors and instructors. "I try to tell them to talk to the professors, to make relationships with the professors—it does matter. So I try to talk to them about navigating graduate school." She provides students with academic skills to help minimize their fears and insecurities about college. "I try to prep them about seminars and things like that, because they can be very intimidating. I tell them that some people are just better at performing, that they probably don't understand the material any better but that they just have a lot of confidence in their performance."

Professor Solano, a faculty member at a public university with a large low-income, first-generation population, also provides her students with concrete advice on specific educational processes such as strategies for communicating with instructors: "[One] student was actually emailing some professors to ask them about their articles, and I told him that a lot of these are available online and that he probably shouldn't email someone to ask for their articles if they're available online. It was just a little thing, but I felt like it was part of the professionalization process. I told him that you don't really want to approach somebody who you want to work with as a mentor until after you've read their work."

For students who come to see him to talk about graduate school, Professor Contreras often provides his first-generation college students very specific academic knowledge that he knows they have not yet acquired. Speaking of one student, he said,

> I asked her if she had thought about grad school, because I thought her writing was very strong and she was very analytical. She said she hadn't even thought about it even though she works at job where she encourages students to go to college. No one had ever talked to her about grad school, so that's why she came to see me. She's a triple major, 3.7 GPA, and a senior. She said she had not brought it up before, because she didn't know how and didn't know how she was supposed to think about what she wanted to study. I told her to start researching the areas she was in-

terested in pursuing as a career. I also encouraged her to identify ten schools she wanted to attend and categorize them into dream schools, really good but not dream schools she would love to attend, and then good enough schools where she was confident she would get into. I told her to start looking them up and to meet again the following week to start working on her statement of purpose by wring the first draft. Then I encouraged her to identify faculty at those schools, send them an email of introduction, and to tell them that she's working with a professor. So we went through the whole process and she ended up getting into her dream school.

Professor Martinez also gives students various tips on how to be strategic when they begin applying to graduate school: "What I tell my students to do when they're writing their personal statements is name drop. I tell them that I have colleagues at a lot of the major universities, so they should mention that they took a class with Professor Martinez, or they did this paper for Professor Martinez. I tell them the do's and don'ts, like never talk about any of the professors even if you hate them, because somehow it'll get around and then you're going be in trouble." Professor Martinez constantly provides students with effective strategies and approaches for getting into top graduate schools, something that he knows will be beneficial to their careers in academia. Faculty mentors are critical in the lives of low-income students who attend college. They show students the possibilities that education provides and guide them in the process.[6] Working on a professor's research project and spending time talking to faculty outside class significantly increase the likelihood that low-income students will attend graduate school.[7]

First-generation college students need additional support and guidance from college or university personnel. They arrive at college with the challenge of not having someone at home to call on for direction when they have questions. They are in uncharted territory that no one in their families has experienced. Only a few feel well prepared; most of them feel their preparation was inadequate. They feel they lack the academic, study, and time management skills needed for college-level work. Low-income students often lament missing opportunities in high school that would have better prepared them because they did not realize how important such participation would be in college. Missed chances include not taking challenging courses, not filling out scholarship applications, not starting the application process early, and not taking high school course work seriously. Additionally, students feel that high school teachers did not encourage them to become independent learners, a critical skill for college-level work.[8]

The three chapters in this part of the book present various examples of how Pivotal Moment educators provide support, guidance, and advocacy and pass on critical academic skills to help their students excel and advance in school. Pivotal Moment educators have a very intentional and personalized approach to working with students that allows them to build trust and rapport with their students. These educators' efforts to establish a caring relationship with students provide an avenue for passing on educational knowledge necessary for long-term academic success of their students. They understand that students need to have explained, in various ways, the full menu of educational and career choices. Pivotal Moment educators purposefully connect students to other educators when needed and coach them on effective communication skills. They also take the time to walk students through important processes in a step-by-step way that might otherwise create significant obstacles in their school success. By doing all these things, Pivotal Moment educators give low-income minority students the tools to circumvent the sorting process of schools and gain access to higher education.

In contrast, non–Pivotal Moment educators have an approach to working with students that tends to be generic and formulaic, with an emphasis placed on getting them through high school without planning for postsecondary education. These educators generally have lower expectations for their students and do not engender the possibility of attending a four-year college after high school. Although some do connect students to key educational agents, they do so minimally and without a thorough understanding of the pivotal role they could play. They also are not intentional during their interactions with students and, as a result, fail to pass on the institutional knowledge and support low-income minority students need to successfully transition to higher education. Unlike Pivotal Moment educators, they have a one-size-fits-all approach to working with students. They hold low expectations, lack empathy, and often blame parents for their children's academic difficulties. In many ways, these educators' interactions with students serve to reinforce educational inequality rather than disrupt it.

The analysis of the Pivotal Moment educators in this chapter highlights the critical role school agents can and must play in the schooling experiences of low-income minority students. All institutions from kindergarten through university need to make sure that educators, particularly those who have direct interactions with students, learn about Pivotal Moments and understand how they can play a significant role in the lives of disadvantaged youth. Just as educators need to be intentional with students, schools need to make a concerted effort to train school personnel by providing formal opportunities, such as professional development workshops, that present information on the importance of setting high expectations for all students and explain how educators can become effective student mentors and advocates. Educators need to learn best practices for connecting with students and also need to be equipped with the appropriate knowledge to transmit about navigating the educational system and planning for college.

PART III

Pivotal Moments in Other Contexts

8

BUILDING TRUST IS NOT ENOUGH

Challenges of Academic Outreach Programs in Creating Pivotal Moments

There has been a substantial increase in precollege academic outreach programs at the federal, state, and private sector levels in the past several decades. More than one thousand programs operate in the United States, each offering a unique mix of educational support and information to a diverse student population.[1] According to the National Survey of Outreach Programs, more than two million students are served in outreach programs each year.[2] Most outreach programs offer services to students beginning in ninth grade or earlier, and the rest focus on the later years of high school. Most programs are hosted by colleges or universities, although they may also be hosted by K–12 schools or community organizations.

Two distinct models of college outreach programs are currently operating in U.S. high schools: a traditional model that focuses services on a relatively small number of targeted students, and a newer, schoolwide outreach model offering services to all students in a given school cohort. The most frequent program goals include promoting college attendance, awareness, and exposure, followed by improving academic skills, building student self-esteem, and providing role models. Academic outreach programs are all based on the same general principle: encourage underrepresented students to set their sights on higher education and improve their chances of enrolling and graduating from college.

Academic outreach programs are designed to facilitate the path to college for students who have traditionally been underrepresented in higher education, including low-income, first-generation, and minority students.[3] Programs have improved college access specifically for minority students as well as doubled the odds of college attendance for moderate- to high-risk students.[4] Unfortunately, only about 5 percent of at-risk students participate in outreach programs each year.[5] For students whose family incomes fall at or below the poverty line, academic outreach programs are a particularly important part of their path to higher education. Because low-income students generally attend large, underresourced high schools having counselors who carry large caseloads, it is difficult for them to obtain important information and guidance about college.

Outreach programs, therefore, serve to compensate for the shortcomings of the public education system by offering a comprehensive approach to college access for disadvantaged students.[6] These programs provide first-generation, low-income minority students with the necessary information, support, and guidance to successfully enroll in college. Given their particular goals to support students, staff who work in academic outreach programs hold great potential to be Pivotal Moment educators for their students.

GOVERNMENT-FUNDED ACADEMIC OUTREACH PROGRAMS

Since the launch of the federal TRIO programs in the late 1960s, most precollege outreach programs have pursued a targeted intervention model in which college outreach services are provided to a relatively small, hand-picked group of students.[7] The Upward Bound and Talent Search programs as well as the Posse Foundation, the Quantum Opportunities Program, Summer Bridge, and dozens of other privately funded programs fit this model.[8] These programs differ from one another in several important ways. Many are built on collaboration between schools and universities, whereas independent nonprofits and community-based organizations operate alone. Some offer instructional services and college counseling to students during the school day, and others provide afterschool and summer activities. Some are targeted exclusively at high-performing students, and others are geared specifically toward students with B and C averages in high school. The services that outreach programs offer vary considerably, including academic services such as tutoring, study skills, college tours and information sessions, and counseling and leadership training, as well as parental services.[9] Despite the variation in their funding sources and designs, all programs grouped under the targeted intervention model are based on the assumption that direct intervention can change the educational trajectory of participating students.

Academic outreach programs like Upward Bound, Gaining Early Awareness and Readiness for Undergraduate Programs (GEAR UP), and other state, local, and privately sponsored programs typically begin working with students within the K–12 system to strengthen their academic experiences and assist in making the transition to college.[10] Studies of Upward Bound and other TRIO programs have generally found that students in these programs have higher academic achievement than similar students who are not involved in such programs, but lower achievement levels than more-advantaged students.[11] However, participating students do have a need for remedial or basic skills courses when they enroll in college, and remediation increases persistence and bachelor degree attainment.[12]

By contrast, schoolwide outreach programs aim to have broader effects. The GE Corporation's College Bound Program, the federally funded GEAR UP program, the AVID program, and several university-based outreach programs founded in the wake of state-level affirmative action bans also operate on the schoolwide outreach model, targeting college information and recruitment opportunities to all students at particular high-poverty high schools.[13] Offering outreach services to all students at targeted high schools, these programs aim to catalyze schoolwide improvements. Rather than attempt to identify students in advance who stand to benefit from outreach, these programs attempt to raise educational outcomes for all students, whether or not they actively participate in outreach activities. These programs typically offer fewer services to students than targeted outreach programs do, but they make these services available to a far larger number of students, attempting to create an academic culture in targeted schools that is more conducive to student success. One well-known example of the schoolwide college outreach model is the I Have a Dream Foundation, launched in 1986 when New York businessman Eugene Lang promised to pay college tuition for any sixth-grader at East Harlem Elementary School who finished high school.[14]

Summer Bridge programs are one solution universities have used to address the gap in preparation and achievement levels and retain underprepared students, most of whom are from low-income families or are the first in their families to attend college. Such programs typically provide academic preparation and transitional support in the summer prior to freshman year.[15] Participating students achieve higher grades, stay in school longer, and have higher completion rates than comparable nonparticipants.[16] Participants also have increased locus of control, increased confidence, and increased self-esteem—important factors related to meeting the social and academic challenges of their first year of college.[17] Furthermore, students who participate in bridge programs have closer contact with other students and faculty during their freshman year and complete more core courses than nonprogram students.[18] Participating students also develop leadership ability, have more-extensive involvement in the university community, and are more likely to take advantage of tutoring and counseling during the academic year than are their nonbridge peers.[19]

The ability of underserved students to persist in the competitive postsecondary academic environment is understandably a high priority at colleges and universities. As demographics continue to change, postsecondary institutions have become critically aware of the need for internal, institutional infrastructure and the availability of support services for underserved students. Many of the federally funded TRIO programs serve as some of the first model programs for the establishment and delivery of academic support services to historically underrepresented, underserved students.

The hallmark of most academic support programs is a quadruple grouping of academic support services that combines ongoing and consistent advising and counseling, tutoring support, and some degree of mentoring. Ongoing and consistent academic advising allows students to meet frequently with student peer advisers as well as faculty advisers in order to refine course schedules, establish academic plans, and stay within a four- to six-year graduation time line. Tutoring in the form of individual, one-on-one support by peers and faculty enables students to maintain high grade point averages, or remediate as necessary on an individual basis. Mentoring also serves as an occasional feature of many programs designed to guide historically underrepresented students through college.

KEY FEATURES OF EFFECTIVE ACADEMIC OUTREACH PROGRAMS

Although thousands of national academic intervention programs exist, designed to pave the way to higher education for low-income minority students, we know very little about how well these programs actually work.[20] Many observers assess a program's impact on college access and persistence, but almost none examine which program features account for or contribute most to the program's success. There is some indication that outreach programs boost participating students' odds of college attendance.[21] Students who participated in a program are more likely to enroll in a four-year college than nonparticipants. These findings are encouraging but far from conclusive. On average, students in outreach programs or enrolled in schoolwide outreach high schools do better across various educational outcomes than their nonparticipating peers; however, the differences are modest.[22] Evaluations of the effectiveness of outreach programs suffer from various limitations. Despite these limitations, academic outreach programs still hold great potential to provide a path to college for many disadvantaged students, so it is important to better understand the features that can make them effective.

The most successful precollege academic outreach programs share several important characteristics, many of which are similar to the required components of a successful educational Pivotal Moment.[23] Effective outreach programs prepare students academically through "untracking" efforts such as tutoring, curriculum reform, or both.[24] In that effort, they provide academic counseling, enrichment, and remediation as well as teach study skills and create personalized learning environments. Like Pivotal Moment educators, these programs address teachers' biases and instill high expectations among all school staff.[25] Effective programs also do a good job of balancing academic support with social support. Social support is a predictor of college attendance and completion.[26] Therefore, successful programs facilitate strong networks that aid in students' academic and emotional development as well as their likelihood of enrolling in higher education.[27] Programs also connect students with one another, because students are more likely to plan to attend college if their friends also plan to enroll.[28] Like Pivotal Moment educators, college-educated mentors play a key role, in addition to peer support, in helping low-income students overcome obstacles to gain access to higher education.[29]

Similar to a Pivotal Moment intervention, effective outreach programs tend to intervene early and provide comprehensive, long-term support.[30] Most programs begin serving students in ninth grade or earlier.[31] It is critical to intervene early in order to facilitate curricular planning.[32] Programs that have the greatest impact offer extensive services and require a high level of involvement over a long period of time.[33] Students benefit more the longer they participate in the outreach program.[34] Highly effective programs also work closely with students during the college admissions process.[35] They also work with parents and families by providing them with college information and teaching them how to support their children's education.[36]

Most outreach programs are peripheral and supplemental to the classroom, a practice that may explain why outreach programs tend to have little effect on students' academic achievement.[37] The most effective programs offer long-term systemic services that are incorporated as part of regular school offerings, rather than short-term supplemental programmatic services.[38] However, very few programs take a systemic approach. Several programs address this issue to some extent by establishing partnerships between secondary schools and postsecondary institutions and by helping ensure that students complete college entrance requirements.

Finally, effective programs provide financial assistance by sending students on college visits, covering the fees for college entrance exams and applications, and awarding scholarships.[39] Although only about half of programs provide scholarships, many provide students with information and assist students in applying for financial aid.[40] Among all effective programs, three stand out as having the strongest evidence of their effectiveness: Indiana's Twenty-first Century Scholars, Upward Bound, and Talent Search.

After interviewing academic outreach professionals and observing their service delivery to students, I discovered that the structures of outreach programs can either help or hinder staff in being effective Pivotal Moment educators. Many outreach staff are exemplary in their efforts to connect with students. I was continuously impressed with the creative strategies they have developed to nurture relationships with students as well as parents. They also do a phenomenal job in mentoring students and providing advocacy to promote students' interests. Where most outreach staff fall short in becoming Pivotal Moment educators is in their inability to transmit academic and college information. Although outreach programs support their staffs' ability to build trust, mentor, and advocate for students, they do not facilitate their capacity to transmit instrumental educational knowledge and skills. As a result, staff's behaviors do not always effectively disrupt educational inequality for the first-generation, low-income minority students they service.

BUILDING TRUST

Preparing for and going to college is a leap of faith for most first-generation students, because no one else in their families have done it before them. Such students need to feel they can trust outreach program staff—who are their guides through this process—in order to take that step forward for themselves and their families. Although few first-generation students are likely to have made the transition from high school to college without the information provided by academic outreach programs, it is the relationships they develop with outreach educators that allow them to be receptive to the services and support these programs offer.[41]

Joanna, who has been an academic outreach professional for several years, explained the importance of building trust with students to maximize the impact she has on their academic success: "I think the kids have to trust you enough to know you care about them. They have to know there's trust and that you care about their futures." She is currently a coordinator for College Prep, a government-funded academic outreach program that serves fifty to seventy students annually and is housed on a university campus.[42]

Like Joanna, many of the academic outreach professionals interviewed for this study highlighted the successful strategies they use to build trust and rapport with students. As noted earlier, trust is the foundational piece to providing advocacy and support, but, more importantly, it opens a pathway to transmit knowledge about the educational system. Building trust with students is often a process that is nurtured over an extended period. Unlike Mr. Montes, the science teacher introduced earlier, who can only hope that he has a student for three years, staffers at many academic outreach programs find that the work of developing trust is logistically easier for them because many of them work with students for three or four years.

Thus, many outreach staff try to recruit students as early as possible in school so that they have extended time to work with them. In general, they try to get students during their freshman year, but no later than sophomore year. Many say that they need to work with students a minimum of three years to develop trust and provide the necessary guidance to successfully transition to college. Sometimes staff turnover can affect a program's effort to develop trust with students. Sonia, for example, who is an academic adviser for College Prep, said that when she started in her position three years ago, there was a high turnover, so students had a new person every year, something that had a negative impact on relationship building with students. More recent cohorts of students have enjoyed more-stable staff connections, and Sonia has now seen several students through the program from beginning to end. This stability has allowed her to get to know her students and their families more intimately.

Similar to teachers and counselors, academic outreach professionals also develop trust with their students by sharing details about their own personal experiences. These stories are often used as a tool for building connections with students because they help them to personally identify with educators. Hector, a director for College Prep, said that sharing his story helps students "buy in to the whole idea of, 'If he did it, then I can do it too.'" He said that sharing his story makes the notion of attending college more palpable, because someone like them has done it. Joanna also said that her students need to hear about her experiences in overcoming obstacles so that they know that with the right tools, it is possible: "I tell the students a lot about growing up. They know a lot about my life story. Anything related to college, how I got there, and the obstacles I had to overcome to get there, I feel it's important to share . . . It's important for them to understand that their shoes aren't that much different than mine."

Karla, a coordinator for College Prep, likes to give students concrete examples about growing up in exactly the same neighborhood they live in so that they know that through her own experiences, she understands the numerous challenges and struggles they face. She firmly stated that connections with students are deeper when you can give them examples that resonate with their daily lives.

In addition to sharing life histories, being accessible and staying in frequent contact with students is an important component of building trust. Students are receptive to educators who make themselves available beyond the normal nine-to-five business hours as well as through various communication outlets such as texting and, in some instances, Facebook. Sonia stated that establishing her availability with students early in the process strengthens her relationships and enhances her reputation with other students as being readily available: "Students tell other students. They'll say, 'She's really going to reply back to you, so if you need to talk to her just text her.'" She said that this type of support lets students know that she's dependable, so that if at any given time they need something in an emergency, they can count on her to assist with getting it resolved right away. She also said that texting gives students the security and comfort of having things in writing from her that they can take time to process. Similarly, David, an academic adviser for College Prep, reported that establishing a connection with students via texting not only makes him accessible to students but also is an excellent way for him to constantly remind them of important upcoming deadlines:

> I get involved with them, find out what's going on, and it becomes a very close relationship. I mean, they have my cell phone number, they text me at random times in the day to remind me of different things, which

I take and use it to my benefit as well because if there's a deadline coming up, I remind them about it through a text. I've had to adapt to that, because they are into cell phones and electronics so I'm using that to my benefit too. So with that, they feel comfortable enough to come to me when there's an issue with their application, financial aid, or whatever, and I can provide them that support pretty much twenty-four hours a day as opposed just eight-to-five.

Like David, most staff who are accessible to students see their jobs not within the confines of a regular nine-to-five workday, but rather as a process beyond those arbitrary constraints. Norma, director for Map to College, stated, "I think my job is one of those jobs that sometimes isn't a set time frame, you know. There's times where the kids need me, and if I'm available, I take the call."

Making students' experiences personal is an important part of academic outreach professionals' connecting with their students. One strategy used by Sonia is to insist that students call her by her first name rather than using a formal title:

The number one thing that I've done is I don't allow them to call me "Ms.," number one, and I started off in the beginning—"My name is Sonia. No Ms., No Ms. Cruz, just plain Sonia"—because I feel that that word in front of my name already begins putting up that wall at the beginning. So as soon as we meet up, even in the interview when I'm interviewing the first-time freshmen, I tell them, "Look, guys, I want you to know my name is Sonia. Just like I call you by your first name, you call me by my first name." . . . I establish what I want them to call me, and I think that kind of makes them feel comfortable.

Sonia said that using first names helps break down the rigid educator–student boundaries and helps her develop a more reciprocal exchange with her students.

Other outreach professionals personalize students' experiences by building a sense of family among students and staff. Some do this through the summer residential programs when they host new students. Many staff, such as Karla, used the term *family* frequently when describing their programs: "I always tell the students to think of program staff as family members that went to college." Similarly, Elva, a coordinator for College Prep, stated, "It's important to build camaraderie and sense of family within the group . . . and showing them that this is the family that you belong to now." They often structure their residential summer programs in groups "as families" so that students can develop a sense of attachment to staff as well as to other students.

For outreach staff, making the experience familiar and "like family" raises the issue of the careful balance between the personal and the professional that many educators face when they develop strong relationships with students. Joanna said that establishing a healthy distance between herself and students is important for developing a respectful and reciprocal relationship with them. She stated, "I tell them, 'Respect my time after work. While I love you guys, this is still my job. I have a family to go home to.' And I've had to show them that my kids see me eighteen hours a week, you guys see me forty." Creating boundaries was cited as the biggest challenge outreach staff face when trying to establish trust and rapport with students, as Sonia stated: "I think that's where our job gets extremely difficult, because we do have to draw that line where we can't be too personable, but then if you're too professional, you put up a wall with students." Karla, a College Prep coordinator, manages these boundaries by thinking of her role as that of an aunt:

> I'm like the cool Tia Karla that they know they can come and talk to, but that they have to respect. So that's the kind of relationship we have— they know they have to respect me but they joke around with me, they laugh with me, I laugh with them, I joke around with them, so it's a respectful friendship. They know they can come to me for anything, and I'm going to help them and tell them the truth if they need to hear the truth, and I'm going to be proud of their accomplishments.

Although creating and maintaining boundaries are important, staff note that it is critical for students to know that they take a special interest in caring for them. Megan, a coordinator for College Prep, stated, "I think it's important because they feel like you have a special interest in them, and that shows you really care about them. I think that they need to understand that somebody's out there to help them and they really have an interest in them doing well." Karla initially builds rapport with her students through her role as an academic counselor: "I meet individually with each student for about an hour, and I talk to them about what their plans are, where they hope to attend, what career they want to pursue, so I kind of advise them on that. I don't just give them their academic plan, because then they won't know how to do it when they get to college."

Sonia is deliberate in her efforts to guide students, because she doesn't want them to disengage if they feel they are being talked down to:

> I think number one is no nagging. If you nag the student, it's not going to work. I think it's more about you making them responsible for what they have to do. Just giving them reminders without it being a nag. They get nagged at home twenty-four seven . . . they get nagged by teachers, they get nagged at school by counselors, by their parents, so they don't need one more person to also be nagging them and telling them, "Why aren't you doing this?" You know, it's more about, here are the deadlines, write it out for them, give it to them. Not being a nag or that voice of annoyance I think has worked very well with my students.

It is the relationships and trust that students develop with the program staff that allow them to be receptive to the numerous support services offered to help them get into college. The process of establishing relationships with low-income minority students, however, can sometimes be difficult, because other adults in their lives have either been unsupportive or untrustworthy. Even adults who encourage students to go to college may let them down by not following through on promises of support to help get them there.[43] Students often feel they are able to develop relationships with program staff because they are "relatable" to them and feel that staff care about them and are consistently available for support. As a result, the relationships outreach staff build with students motivates them to go to and persist in college because they do not want to disappoint them. Additionally, students often leave their programs knowing they can always rely on the staff to continue to give them advice and support even after they graduate.[44]

MENTORING AND ADVOCATING FOR STUDENTS

Establishing trust and rapport with students facilitates an outreach professional's ability to provide them with emotional and moral support as well as encouragement and affirmation. Developing a caring relationship with students makes students more likely to seek out staff for assistance when students are facing a personal or educational problem. As mentioned earlier, low-income students face many challenges living in poverty. Thus, students from lower socioeconomic backgrounds have unique needs that educators must be attuned to and accommodate. Norma, director of Map to College, a university-housed government-funded academic outreach program that serves approximately six hundred students annually, recognizes that poverty affects the families she works with and she understands that they have competing urgencies that often conflict with their students' educational pursuits. She explained, "In my personal experience, sometimes your parents are more concerned with making sure you have your basic needs, which is food, shelter, and somewhat decent clothing. So sometimes I think the parents have to be more concerned with just making ends meet this month."

Once students begin to trust her, Karla, a coordinator for College Prep, often assumes multiple roles as their academic counselor, coparent, confidante, and psychologist. She said she needs to be prepared for everything when students come to see her about issues ranging from friend problems to family issues, such as parents losing their jobs and students worrying about burdening their parents with the cost of college. Most importantly, however, is that students' personal problems are often interwoven with academic issues, so educators who work with them must be aware of both to effectively counsel students.

David, an academic adviser for College Prep, said that he has come to realize over time that students' academic performance is often tied to and greatly impacted by their home lives: "I've had kids cry to me over stuff that sometimes I'm like, 'Wow, something's going on in their home,' and it really makes me understand why the student is getting the grades that they're getting or why their motivation is not there. When they open up about their family, about what's going on, that's when I understand why. Then I know how to try to motivate them."

For David, having insight into students' personal dilemmas helps him develop possible strategies to motivate students to do well in school and work through their difficulties.

Megan, a coordinator for College Prep, also helps students work through family issues. "If they text you at midnight, you're wondering, 'Oh my gosh, what's happening now? What's going on in their life?' A lot of it is family dynamics, so I try to help them get through it . . . I try to be a positive role model. I think that's a key thing when they're going through hard times and bumps in the road. I tell them to stay positive and that they have a lot of potential."

Another way academic outreach professionals support students is by getting parents involved. In fact, many view parent participation as crucial to students' success. Hector, director of College Prep stated, "I think that the difference comes in when we are in sync with parents and students. That's the recipe for success." His program gets parents to help out in a variety of ways. "Our program involves the parents. I work with five schools, and I have set up parent committees to get the parents involved . . . they help me with phone trees. I have five parents that call everybody else about events coming up, help me with fund-raising efforts, and help me put together some of our events." Other programs recruit parents to assist with fund-raising to help pay for additional college visits or student scholarships.

Academic outreach programs use very creative ways to get parents to attend information meetings, something that is sometimes hard to do when parents are busy and work multiple jobs. Norma's Map to College program began hosting evening events she calls "cafecitos" (coffee dates) at her own home so that Latino and Spanish-speaking parents can get information and ask questions: "What I tried to do was create a support group where parents help each other out and we did it in Spanish and English," she said. "My goal was to have it at a house so they don't feel threatened, so it's more of a friendly environment at a home, like a cafecito. And instead of us telling them exactly what they need to know, it's us finding out what parents want to know."

Rather than just talk at parents, something that can sometimes make them feel uncomfortable and intimidated, she treats these meetings more as a parent support group. Not only are these events well attended, but also parents share information with each other at the events. Sometimes parents share academic information, but other times they share basic parenting strategies such as getting students to study. One of the clever ways Norma has gotten parents to attend informational events is by sending parents an elaborate invitation. She explained, "To encourage the parents to come we did the invite more like a wedding invitation . . . a one-page formal invitation. And for whatever reason it worked—we got the most RSVPs." When I was in her office for the interview, she showed me the invitation she sent out, and I could tell why it caught parents' attention.

Karla is also very creative in engaging parents. One of the biggest challenges she faces is getting low-income Latino families to understand the rationale behind allowing their daughters to live in the dormitories for the residential summer program and then go away for college. Many Latino parents are reluctant to let their daughters move away from home for any reason. Because Karla is the first person in her family to graduate from college and is the youngest daughter in her family, she brings her mother to talk to parents: "I brought my mom in because she had to deal with that. The parents could talk to my mom and hear from her that it's okay, that their daughters will be fine, and that it's a good thing for them to go away for college . . . So, I brought my mom because I knew that when she was going through it, it would have been easier for her to hear that it was going to be okay from somebody just like her."

Even at the college level, Connie, an outreach counselor, spoke about the importance of including parents in the effort to educate first-generation minority college students: "You're not only educating a student, but you're educating a community. So if you don't educate the parent on how college is different from high school, that could be detrimental to the student's academic success. You have to provide that orientation not only for the student, but also for the parent, because they are part of the process that allows the student to be successful. I think that's critical."

Academic outreach professionals fully recognize that they are role models for their students as well. They realize that as college-educated individuals, they are in a position to shape students' self-image as future college graduates. As Elva, a coordinator for College Prep stated, "Working with this population, it's important that they see themselves reflected in the staff." To do this effectively, outreach professionals re-alize that they must be able to relate to and motivate students. Karla reminds all her staff, including the tutors—the majority of whom are also first-generation college students—that they must make an effort to be positive role models for the students. "I want the students to see that somebody like them—a first-generation and minority college stu-dent—did it, and they can do it too. We want the staff to motivate the students to do the same things."

Megan also brings in professionals from the community to serve as additional role models and share information with students about their careers: "During the summer, we have guest speakers from our com-munity, and they talk to the students about how they got where they are. We'll invite doctors and dentists. This year we're going to have an optometrist, we're going to have a vet, and we're having an engineer—we always have an engineer. So they get to hear about what they had to do to get there, what type of classes they had to take in college, and how they got their first job."

Although outreach staff recognize that they are role models, I didn't always see them explicitly use that role to transmit knowledge to stu-dents in the way that the Pivotal Moment educators described earlier do. I expand on this point in the following section.

TRANSMITTING ACADEMIC KNOWLEDGE AND SKILLS

Precollege academic outreach programs and the staff who run them are often the most important sources of information about college for first-generation students. Unlike their middle-class peers, most low-income students do not even think about college before high school, let alone start preparing for the application process. Students who are lucky enough to participate in outreach programs in high school are usually ahead of their peers in planning for college early. The program staff plays the most crit-ical role in helping students get to college, because they are the agents who can transmit the academic knowledge and skills to help students ef-ficiently and effectively navigate the educational system.

The transmission of knowledge is one of the most critical compo-nents of a Pivotal Moment intervention. In addition to establishing trust and providing support, Pivotal Moment educators use that connection with students to pass on information that is critical to their educational advancement and success. Unfortunately, even though most academic outreach staff have the potential to create Pivotal Moments, many do not have the knowledge needed. The following comments from Joanna, a coordinator for College Prep, illuminate how outreach educators sometimes miss opportunities to transmit information to students: "I try and teach them autonomy, to try and think outside the box. You just have to remember that each student is a success story if you give them the right tools. And sometimes giving them the right tools is letting them discover that they already have them and you're just the catalyst that helps guide them through it."

Low-income minority students do have numerous strengths, but interviews and observations, in addition to a significant body of research, all suggest that they still need considerable help in acquiring and making sense of educational information. Educators are often the only adults with a college education in a position to play a critical role in passing on to them the same knowledge that upper-class students get from their college-educated parents and relatives to be successful in school. In this case, Joanna is assuming that her students have the "tools" needed to do well in school, and, as a result, she does not make a concerted effort to teach them the skills they need to excel.

One goal of academic outreach programs is to expose students to new experiences and opportunities. This is accomplished by trips to cultural events and college campus visits. Exposure is the foundation of Norma's Map to College program. "I think more than anything is exposing them to opportunities that they don't know they have," she said. According to David of College Prep, it's important to expose students to experiences outside their community. "It makes students leave their comfort zone," he said. "Whether it's emotionally or physically, some students live in such a bubble in their community, and that limits what they know and how they're able to grow as a person. Being exposed to different people, different races, everything that they're not used to really changes their perspective."

When I asked outreach professionals why exposure was important to achievement and college-going, however, many struggled to provide concrete reasons other than noting that it was a component of their programming. I was surprised that many outreach staff could not articulate exactly why it was helpful to students to attend a musical, for example, other than just exposing them to something they would not otherwise experience. For example, Karla, coordinator of College Prep, was quite proud of her cultural activities: "We took them to go see 'Wicked' at the Pantages Theatre. Oh, and we took them indoor skydiving. So, different stuff that they normally wouldn't do with their own families because of cost." Also, Hector, director of College Prep, took his students to see a well-known musical: "These kids had never heard of it, even though everybody's heard of 'Phantom of the Opera' at one point in their lives. They need that exposure. They need to know to be well-rounded individuals. They need to know how to dress, how to react, when to clap."

Even though musicals were a popular choice for cultural activities, I found it problematic that students were not receiving any systematic guidance on how to interpret, engage, and make meaning of the performance or event. They were often just expected to figure it out on their own by mere exposure. Outreach staff were not making an effort to help students make connections with educational processes or to understand the deeper educational value of being acquainted with cultural references in musicals that might come in handy for something like taking the SAT, writing an essay, or contributing to a related class discussion. It seemed as though one of two things was happening: either staff simply did not possess that knowledge themselves, or they did not fully understand it as part of their program's mission.

Another activity academic outreach professionals provide to students is exposure to college campuses. Students go on various campus visits during their time in the program to see and experience different types of colleges. When I inquired about the names of schools students visit, most were less-selective public universities even though many talked about exposing students to all types of colleges. For example, Elva of College Prep explained her program's rationale:

> We try to expose them to different campuses outside Los Angeles. We expose them to University of California schools, California State University schools, and some private colleges. We haven't done a commu-

nity college tour, just because we want to expose them to other campuses that are farther away, but we did have a community college workshop. On the college visits we schedule information sessions, campus tours, and college student panels so the students can actually see students of color on campus. For example, we went to USC in December, and they got some students to talk about where they came from and a lot of them mentioned the high schools that our students attend, so they got really excited because they were able to see themselves as college students on that campus.

Her program works diligently to help students see themselves as college students, but trips to highly selective colleges were rare even though these types of institutions have the highest graduation rates for students from low-income minority backgrounds. I wondered whether the list of schools selected by outreach programs reflected low student expectations or just a lack of awareness about the advantages of attending more-selective private schools that offer better funding to low-income students. I was also surprised to learn that most outreach programs did not make it mandatory for their students to apply to private schools. I frequently heard that it was optional for students to apply to private colleges and universities. As you saw earlier, without fully understanding all the benefits of attending a private university, when given a choice, first-generation college students often decide not to apply because of the additional requirements and essays. Although David's College Prep program does an excellent job of providing students with detailed, hands-on workshops for public university applications—where he walks students through filling out and submitting applications—he does not provide the same level of support for private school applications.

The expectation in David's program is that students apply to four less-selective, and four more-selective, public state universities. The decision to apply to private schools is left entirely up to the student. "For private universities, those are on an individual basis. We don't have a workshop specifically for private universities, but if we know that a student wants to apply, then we work with them on a one-on-one." Although his program supports students who want to apply to private schools, they are not actively encouraged to apply, although this practice would actually give students a greater diversity of college options. Students who apply to private schools must do their own research about the application process and steps for submitting an application. For low-income students, the college application process is already daunting, so knowing they are on their own to apply to private schools often deters them from doing so.

Not all academic outreach programs, however, are the same. Similar to the advice most middle-class students receive from parents and counselors, Megan's College Prep program insists that students apply to top private schools so that they have more options. She explained, "They get four waivers for the public universities, so I make them fill out four applications for each. And then I always have them fill out private school applications too. They get waivers for it, so I tell them to apply because they'll have a lot more options." Megan stated it is important to give students a full range of college options and encourage them to explore them all so that they have better choices later. This strategy is similar to that of most middle-class students, who tend to apply to a larger number of schools to increase their chances of getting into the most prestigious institutions.

Unfortunately, most outreach staff observed did not outline for students strategies for applying to college such as applying to schools in different selectivity level tiers (i.e., highly selective, selective, less selective), a practice that is common among middle-class students. Thus, the advice students receive in some programs seemed formulaic and not always intentional in transmitting important educational knowledge and skills to students. After I interviewed numerous staff, it did not seem as though they themselves possessed this knowledge to pass on to their students, and that raises questions about how their programs train them for their professional positions.

I also did not hear much about the strategies outreach professionals use in assisting students with understanding and developing the academic skills needed for school success. This was evident in Sonia's comments about working with her College Prep students: "We hand-hold them throughout everything . . . sometimes you do have to do it for them, because they're not going to do it, or they forget, or they do it wrong, or they say, 'Okay, I'm going to do it,' but then they don't read the information, and they don't really know what they're filling out. I could email them a very detailed email about what's the next step, and then they'll text me back and say, 'Oh, so do I have to do this?'"

What is striking to me about Sonia's explanation of why students need hand-holding is that she assumed that her student did not read the information or forgot to do something because she is irresponsible rather than considering that perhaps the student is overwhelmed or intimidated by the educational process. It is fairly common for low-income minority students to disengage with school processes they are not familiar with and make them feel incompetent. Unlike the Pivotal Moment counselors and teachers described earlier, many academic outreach educators did not follow up their comments about hand-holding students with an explanation of why they need to positively affirm and guide students because the process is difficult for them.

Outreach staff also did not seem to be providing the type of guidance and counseling low-income minority students need when making their decision about where to attend college. In fact, some academic outreach professionals shared many characteristics with the counselors and teachers discussed earlier whose practices in working with students are more likely to reinforce school inequality rather than disrupt it. When one of Sonia's College Prep students received two college admissions offers and came to see her for advice on deciding whether to attend a less-selective public school or a highly selective private institution, she advised her, "'You know how when you go to CVS Pharmacy to buy Tylenol, there's the Tylenol brand, and there's the CVS brand? When you turn the box around, what do you read? The same thing, right? Well, same thing with schools.' I said, 'One you just pay more, one you pay less, it's the same kind of education.'"

As she further explained, Sonia told her student that her decision should be based solely on whether the school is a good "fit" for her: "Another thing educators need to know is that they need to route the student to go where they fit, not where people want them to fit because they want them to go to a school that has that name, but then they're miserable for the rest of the four years there. We need to tell them that when some people say, 'Why are you going to that public university?

You're better than that. Go to Stanford University,' they need to have that basic understanding of who they are as a person within the school." But this advice is problematic, because it assumes that the student knew the criteria to determine fit, and they usually do not.

The available research on college prestige and selectivity suggests that Sonia's advice is misguided and misinformed for another reason: not only do highly selective schools graduate first-generation college students at higher rates, but school prestige also plays a role in future labor market and graduate school options. This information was completely absent from Sonia's advice to her student, and, as a result, her student did not make an informed decision about her college choice. In this instance, Sonia did not transmit to her student the relevant educational knowledge she needed, and Sonia missed an opportunity to initiate a significant academic intervention. This example raises the question, Do outreach educators have the necessary college knowledge to pass on to their students, or do they just not see it as part of their program's mission?

One task a few outreach professionals did well was encouraging students to develop help-seeking behaviors. The staff who did this said it was one of the most important skills for students to have in navigating through the educational system. Megan, for example, said this skill is important to teach her College Prep students: "We really try to teach them about how to seek out resources—like if something is not going right how to take care of it, who to go to on campus. That's key for success. I really work hard to teach them how to seek out the resources, because I think that it is critical in college to be able to figure out who to go to, or what you need to do to pass some classes, or if you're struggling or having a problem with your roommate, you have to be able to figure it out. You can't just give up." Although Megan models many of these behaviors herself when counseling her students, she also said it is important to explicitly point them out to students for them to be aware of in the future.

Joanna also uses college visits to emphasize to her College Prep students the importance of being resourceful in educational contexts: "We try to schedule a presentation about student services, because I think being able to connect to student services on campus a lot of times will dictate how successful a student is because a student who doesn't understand what student services does, quite honestly, is not very success-ful because they don't understand who can help them when they run into problems once they get there." Joanna said that if students know where they can find help, they will always look for support and assis-tance, particularly at the college level, when the stakes for success are high for first-generation college students.

A few outreach professionals also did a good job of transmitting knowledge about language and communication as well as social net-working. Two staff members, who coincidentally work for the same program, provided examples of coaching a student on how to commu-nicate with a school official. They first explain to students what they should do, and then they follow up by explaining why it is important. Karla, coordinator of College Prep, said, "First I explain it to them, be-cause they're the ones that have to go to the teachers, they're the ones who have to advocate for themselves. Sometimes they try and come back to me and say, 'No they wouldn't do it.' So I ask, 'When did you try talking to him?' 'Oh, during class.' So I tell them, 'Well, then ask before or after class, or when he's not busy. Ask to set up an appoint-ment to talk to him. He'll see that you're responsible by asking for an appointment.' Teachers are going to see it more favorably."

In another example, Karla described her strategy for helping students learn how to develop and maintain relationships with key educators to enlist their support on educational endeavors: "I always advise them that every week they should be meeting with their teachers and their coun-selors, one-on-one, to get their grades up. And for seniors, they're going to need them to write letters of recommendation for scholarships and for college. I tell them that all the time. When they come to see me because their grade is falling, I ask them if they went to see their teacher. If they say no, I tell them to go talk to them first and then come to me." She explained why students need to understand how to communicate with educators: "I tell all my students, it's like a game, and they have to learn the rules of the game—they have to get people on their team, because these people are going to give them the skills to play the game better. I tell them they have to get to know people. I stress to them to shake hands with adults, because that always impresses me when a high school student shakes my hand. I coach them on how to introduce themselves.

I have everyone shake my hand, and I coach them on that too, to make sure it's firm and they're not shaking too much, and that they're saying 'Thank you, nice to meet you, it was wonderful to meet you,' and when they leave to make sure to say thank you."

Karla recognizes that her first-generation students need to acquire the skills to know how to play the game and navigate school. Joanna also helps and encourages her students to develop good communication and interpersonal skills with their instructors:

> One of the things that I emphasize is communicating with their instructors. I ask them, "Do you ever talk to your instructor?" A lot of them respond with "No." So a lot of times I'll make them get progress reports from their teachers even though they're doing well in their classes, because they have to go have a conversation with the instructor. I tell them, "When you're in college introduce yourself: 'Professor, my name is so-and-so, and I'm in your third period class.'" If they're not doing well they can say, "I'm really struggling to keep up," or just tell the professor, "I loved the lecture today" or "I'm really good at some of this stuff, but could use could use some help on other stuff."

Joanna explains why she teaches students how to talk to instructors: "I'm first generation myself, and no one ever told me, but it would've made all the difference. It matters if the professor knows your name. I don't think I ever went to office hours unless I had to, but I wish I had, because there's so much more I could've gotten out of my education." She said that this type of information and skill building should be imparted to students as early as possible to assist them with doing well long-term in the educational system.

Some outreach professionals are very intentional when they transmit knowledge to students. They explained that they actively seek out opportunities to assess what students are doing and suggest how they can make changes that will allow them to be more successful in school. Elva, director of College Prep, is one example. "If a student comes in late, this is a teachable moment for me to work with the student," she said. "I talk about being organized, knowing if they have something coming up. I approach it more as, 'Let me understand where you are with your time.'

Or, 'How do you think you manage time?' And maybe they don't realize that they do this." In this instance, Elva is teaching the student the technical skill of time management, which she knows will be helpful to her student in high school as well as when she goes to college. Interestingly, it is often during these "teachable moments" that staff establish strong bonds with their students, allowing them to build trust while simultaneously passing on knowledge and skills.

Academic outreach professionals are effective at building trust and rapport with students as well as providing encouragement and support. Working with students for this extended amount of time is an important factor in the trusting and caring connections they are able to develop with students. They hold tremendous potential for creating a multitude of Pivotal Moments for low-income minority students. Despite the amount of assistance provided by precollege outreach programs, many students still do not feel fully prepared to make the academic transition to college. This is because programs are not always effective in the task of transmitting academic knowledge and skills even though they often work with students for three to four years.

Unfortunately, most outreach professionals I interviewed were not like Elva but were more like Sonia, who employed practices that did not fully embrace the Pivotal Moment approach. Although outreach staff are actively doing two of the three components—building trust and mentoring or advocating—needed for a Pivotal Moment, they are deficient in the third requirement of transmitting academic and college knowledge and skills. Without this critical part, a transformative intervention that has the potential to interrupt school inequality for disadvantaged students cannot happen. The failure to launch a Pivotal Moment, as the result of not passing on academic information, raises the issue about whether outreach staff even have this knowledge in the first place. The danger in this situation is that these educators can end up reinforcing inequality rather than disrupting it for low-income minority students, a result that in principle runs counter to the purpose and goals of a precollege academic outreach program.

It is not a complete surprise, therefore, that the academic outcomes of students in government-funded academic outreach programs are not stellar. Most students are not attending highly selective colleges and universities. A majority of students (approximately 80 percent) attend less-selective public universities (California State Universities), 10 percent attend selective public universities (Universities of California), and the remaining 10 percent attend community colleges. Only a few programs reported students attending highly selective institutions such as Harvard, Columbia, and Stanford. The programs that get their students into the highly selective schools are also those that are more explicit in transmitting the knowledge to students on how to apply to those schools and how to be strategic in the application process to increase their competitiveness.

Something that struck me about academic outreach professionals is that none of them ever compared the educational process of their low-income students to that of middle-class students in terms of the types and amount of information and guidance they receive to prepare for and gain access to college. I was particularly surprised that none of the outreach staff explicitly aligned her strategies of working with students to the highly effective strategies of many middle-class families. This observation might suggest that most outreach professionals do not have access to that knowledge themselves. Thus, they cannot pass it on to their students in a concerted and intentional way.

9

TRANSMITTING COLLEGE KNOWLEDGE

Successes of Nonprofit Organizations
in Pivotal Moment Interventions

Within minutes after our conversation began, Harley Frankel recited the guiding principle of College Match, the nonprofit organization he had founded more than seven years before, to help low-income high school students get into college. He proudly stated, "We believe that smart low-income kids of color are just as capable as white middle-class and upper-class kids from wealthy families to get into great colleges if they get the same levels of support that middle-class and upper-class kids get." To him, the goal is fairly simple: "Identify low-income high school sophomores with strong academic records and provide each of them [on an individualized basis] an intensive array of services comparable to what affluent students receive at elite private prep schools."

According to the statistics of his program, there is no doubt it is successful. As he proudly articulated during our interview, 80 percent of his students go to highly selective private schools, and the other 20 percent go to top public universities. Of his 2011 graduating seniors, more than half (51 percent) were admitted to Ivy League institutions (Harvard, Yale, Princeton, Brown) or their equivalent (Stanford, MIT, Wellesley). Additionally, all of his 2011 seniors were admitted to at least one top-tier college.

It is clear from Frankel's program that nonprofit, community-based organizations hold tremendous promise and are beginning to play an important role in getting first-generation, low-income minority students to the best colleges and universities. There is much we can learn from the creative strategies they use to achieve such high college-going rates. This chapter provides a detailed look at nonprofit academic outreach programs and highlights some of the practices their staff use as effective Pivotal Moment educators.

Although building trust is not at the forefront of their agenda—as it is for government-funded outreach programs and public school educators—nonprofit programs do it adequately enough to mentor and advocate for students as well as efficiently transmit critical academic and college knowledge. As such, College Match has successfully institutionalized the educational Pivotal Moment approach to disrupt school inequality for the most disadvantaged students. The following section describes several nonprofit community-based academic outreach programs that are effective in working with low-income minority students.

NONPROFIT ACADEMIC OUTREACH PROGRAMS

It is during the transition between high school and college that many low-income minority students get lost in the educational system.[1] That is one of the most critical educational junctures where students and their families should receive assistance.[2] In 2002, the Bill & Melinda Gates Foundation began the Early College High School Initiative (ECHSI) to address two important goals: improving students' secondary and postsecondary experiences. Through this initiative, more than two hundred early college schools (ECSs) opened by fall 2009. All of the schools aim to provide underserved students access to college classes while in high school. The ECHSI targets students who are the first in their families to attend college, including students from minority backgrounds, English language learners, and low-income students of any background.[3] The philosophy of ECHSI is that even reluctant or discouraged high school students, who may be unengaged in traditional school settings, can be motivated at a relatively early age to view themselves as successful participants in the college experience.

Early college schools engage students in a comprehensive support system that develops academic and social skills as well as the behaviors and conditions necessary for college completion. Most schools offer formal academic or social support courses or seminars to assist students with skills such as literacy, research, and mathematics.[4] Examples include a required weekly noncredit advisory class to ensure that at least one adult in the school has a handle on the academic and emotional needs of each student. They also offer assistance to students undergoing this transition by providing support for college entrance exam preparation, college tours, and scholarship information sessions. Although these formal supports fit within a school's comprehensive system of services, early college schools also try to strike a balance between requiring students to attend support activities and teaching students to be self-advocates and find support on their own when they need assistance.[5]

Since the implementation of these programs, higher numbers of students from diverse racial, ethnic, and socioeconomic backgrounds are participating in college course work.[6] Although all early college schools have student academic and social support systems, there is variation in how formal and integrated the supports are. Some support activities have been found to be too informal or poorly attended to have dramatic impacts, and some schools put off setting up formal programs.[7] Recent increases in enrollment and funding levels have led more schools to put more supports into place.[8] By allowing high school students to take college-level classes for college credits, early college schools provide three primary benefits to students: the opportunity to earn free college credit, gain a taste of college, and increase students' confidence in their academic abilities.[9]

Gateway to Higher Education is a four-year secondary school program that has been implemented in New York City high schools. The program provides rigorous precollege academic preparation to underrepresented minority students who are interested in pursuing majors in science, technology, engineering, and medicine. Both the school day and the school year are extended for participants, who enroll in an additional period of math or science, participate in small group study and afterschool tutoring, and attend academic summer programs. Enrichment experiences include internships, social outings, campus visits, college fairs, and research experiences. Participants are expected to enroll in Advanced Placement courses and take college entrance exams.

Gateway students are more apt to graduate from high school, take the SAT at least once, and earn a higher combined SAT score than non-participant students. Gateway students also enroll in and graduate from college at high rates.[10]

The Quantum Opportunities Program was designed to determine whether community-based organizations could help increase the educational achievement and social competencies of highly disadvantaged youth. The program provides year-round services, assistance, and coaching to participants, beginning in ninth grade and continuing through high school. Program activities are designed to foster learning, community service, and development. Students are paired with caring adult mentors and receive small financial incentives for their participation. Higher percentages of program participants graduate from high school, enroll in two-year and four-year colleges, receive honors or awards, and participate in community service in comparison to similar students who do not participate in the program.[11]

Sponsor-A-Scholar is a college preparatory and college retention program administered by the nonprofit organization Philadelphia Futures. The program serves low-income students of color who have average grades, demonstrate motivation, and attend one of the participating public high schools in Philadelphia. Students are nominated for participation by school staff and must sign a Statement of Intent upon acceptance to the program. Participants are paired with volunteer adult mentors, who meet with them monthly from ninth grade through the first year after high school. In addition, program staff arrange academic enrichment opportunities, including tutoring, SAT preparation, study skills workshops, college visits, college selection assistance, and summer programs. Upon graduating from high school, participants receive a $6,000 scholarship that is donated by the mentor or an outside partner. The program has a positive impact on participation in college preparation activities and on college attendance during the first and second years after high school. The program's impact is largest for students who enter the program with the fewest resources and students who have strong relationships with their mentors.[12]

RTS was created by the nonprofit organization Roads To Success in 2004. It is an in-school, classroom-based guidance program designed to address the lack of systematic guidance offered to students and their lack of engagement with school. Initially, the RTS organization examined the theoretical and empirical research base for a career and education planning program. Based on this work, the RTS staff created a scope and sequence of thematic units and lesson plans.[13] The RTS program is implemented with whole-grade cohorts by specially trained facilitators. RTS consists of a comprehensive college and career planning curriculum that includes career exploration, education planning, and education and workplace skills. Key features include the use of engaging teaching methods, weekly delivery of curriculum, and attendance for three-quarters of an hour per week for six school years. The program runs from seventh grade through twelfth grade.[14]

There are many benefits of the various activities and program elements found in the nonprofit and community-based programs described. They provide support structures to students who may be inadequately prepared, academically and emotionally, for college-level work and learning.[15] However, similar to government-funded efforts, nonprofit and community-based programs also suffer from similar limitations. Some of these include high program dropout rates, inexplicit participant selection, underrepresentation of male students, inadequate records of participation levels, vague completion and retention rates, unsystemic, noncontinuous services, limited evidence of impact on academic achievement, little information about long-term outcomes such as degree completion, and spotty reporting of cost data.[16] Additionally, most programs do not have a major impact on increasing enrollment in selective colleges and universities but rather affect enrollment in community colleges and less-selective four-year institutions. One of the biggest challenges most academic outreach programs face is hiring and retaining effective staffs and sustaining funding.[17]

A NEW MODEL FOR ACADEMIC OUTREACH

Frankel's program works intensely with low-income minority students for two full years—the junior and senior years of high school—to guide them through the process of planning and preparing college applications. The program works with a select number of inner-city high schools to recruit students and serves approximately 150 students yearly. The programming they provide to students is multidimensional and well structured. The model of this nonprofit academic outreach program is to work collaboratively with schools and community volunteers to provide the needed support for students. Frankel said that it is most beneficial to students if everyone works together in this effort: "We have SAT teachers, we have a lot of volunteers, and the college counselors at each of the high schools work with us very collaboratively and very constructively. So they've become an adjunct to our program, we've become an adjunct to what they do, and it works out very nicely."

Frankel also invites high school counselors on college trips with the students. He sees this as a "win–win" situation that serves two purposes. First, he gets the free help of seasoned adults who are familiar with the students, something that benefits the program. Second, the counselors get exposure to the colleges and admissions staff at those universities, something that ultimately helps students when applying to those schools. He said that having connections at each of the schools his students apply to is very important, and so he makes a concerted effort to establish those networks during campus trips with his students.

Frankel also has a group of volunteers who are successful professionals. He assigns each volunteer a group of students to work closely with on their personal statements. He explained why these volunteers are so helpful: "I have about ten volunteers, all bright women, not surprisingly, who work with each kid. I give them somewhere between four and ten kids, depending on how much time they think they have, and they work with them on the supplemental essays . . . these women are really bright, many of whom are very, very successful and have gotten their kids into great colleges." In fact, it was after he went through the college application process with his own son that Frankel decided to start this program to help low-income youth who do not have the same resources:

> My son went to the best private high school in California, and he got into Williams College, Pomona College, and a few other great schools. At the end of it, when he graduated, he had two parents who had gone to Ivy League schools, we are well connected, we were willing to spend whatever it took to help him with SAT prep, with counselors, with es-

says, with whatever, which is what a lot of middle-class parents do. He had great college counselors, and, at the end of it, I was exhausted. It was like a full-time job. He got into a great school, but I was like, "Wow, that took a lot of work!" And I started thinking about all those kids who I used to be focused on back in Washington who didn't have parents who were well connected, who didn't have the financial resources to get SAT prep, or didn't have anyone to explain to them the intricacies of the college application process. And so it just occurred to me one day to start a program like that.

As noted in the beginning of this chapter, the philosophy of the program is that low-income students are just as capable as their middle-class peers of getting into prestigious colleges if they get the same guidance and support to assist them in that process. In comparison to the academic outreach educators in chapter 8, Frankel seems well aware of the differences in support that middle-class children get in comparison to their low-income counterparts. Thus, his actions are consistent with being an effective Pivotal Moment educator with his students. As a college-educated adult with very intimate knowledge of the educational system, he transmits information to students to prepare them for strategically navigating the college application process.

BUILDING TRUST

Unlike the academic outreach educators who prioritize connecting with students to provide support, the nonprofit organizations I observed had a slightly different model. They focused less effort on connecting with students, and more on the transmission of academic knowledge and skills. When I asked Frankel how well program staff connect with students, he cited an example: "It depends on the student. Some students we get to know very well, and some students we get to know somewhat well. Julie [the program's head college counselor] gets to know a few of them better than I do, because she's really involved with their essays and their personal stories more than I am. I get to know some of them because they reach out. It just really depends." Frankel does establish strong connections with various students in his program. For example, during a college trip bus ride, he walked up and down the bus aisle to chat with students. In his interactions, he asked them questions about their college aspirations and schools they were considering applying to. He also uses these field trip exchanges with students to share strategies about college applications.

Similar to the academic outreach professionals, nonprofit staff build trust with students by being easily accessible to them. Students know that the staff is available to them 24/7, especially during application season. Often this availability, as you learned earlier, creates a sense of caring that students respond to in positive ways. In addition to being accessible, staff noted that being honest and honoring commitments was important for establishing strong educator–student relationships. Frankel explained, "I just think that being true, meeting the commitments that you make to them, always being there for them is important. We're available twenty-four seven. They know they can call me anytime, they know they can email me anytime, same with Julie, same with Erica [the program's college counselor]. They also know they can confide in us." Sometimes students share very intimate details about personal and family issues and dilemmas, reflecting their level of trust in the staff and seeing them as adults whom they can count on for emotional and moral support.

Instilling a sense of belief among low-income minority students that they have the ability to go to college is foundational to getting them on the path to higher education. In addition to telling students repeatedly that they can go to college, students and parents need convincing that they will qualify for financial aid. Frankel noted that when he starts working with students as sophomores, most do not believe that expensive colleges will offer them financial aid if admitted. Educating parents about the availability of financial aid is also critical in convincing low-income students to see college as a possibility:

> You have to tell them over and over and over again that they're as good as any kids anywhere, and they are just as smart, just as capable, and they'll do just as well as long as they work hard and they're dedicated. The other thing that is really important is that they and their families need to know that the financial aid is there. None of them believe they can go because

they don't think they can afford it, because they don't understand how the system works. They don't understand that if they're low income, they're going to get more money . . . parents need to understand that the money will be there if they do well enough to get in. Those are the two messages you have to give them to start with.

The work that Frankel and his organization do is very different from the work of teachers and counselors who work primarily with upper-middle-class students. According to Richard, a counselor at an elite private preparatory school, his students are very prepared and knowl-edgeable about college: "Most of the students, by their sophomore year, already know where they want to go to college. They know a lot about the process." Whereas Frankel spends a lot of time trying to con-vince students and parents to apply to highly selective private schools, upper-middle-class students and their parents are having a different conversation with their counselors, as Richard explained: "Some of the meetings include conversations about connections they have at differ-ent schools. They ask questions like, 'What about if I make a donation of this amount—would this help?' So it was not so much about the ba-sics. It was more about negotiating in business."

MENTORING AND ADVOCATING FOR STUDENTS

Encouraging students to apply to highly selective schools and assuring them that the financial will be available is often followed with support to help students prepare for and navigate the college application process. In this effort, nonprofit programs take various steps to accomplish this goal, including sponsoring college trips, helping students write personal statements, and offering SAT preparation classes. Frankel notes that you must coach students through the various steps after you get them ex-cited about going to college. "Once they get interested, you have to give them the support along the way. 'Here's how you learn about schools, here's how you write essays, you should go visit some schools, the SATs are really important.'"

Similar to government-funded academic outreach agencies, non-profit organizations believe that exposing students to college campuses is important in getting low-income minority students to envision themselves in college. What was most striking about the College Match process is that unlike the outreach professionals, Frankel is very intentional and strategic about where he takes students. When I asked him to tell me what schools he takes his students to visit, he explained that College Match tries to show students a diverse set of schools:

> We try to expose our kids to the best colleges we can expose them to. The first trip was mostly New England, and then when we got larger, we started doing two trips. We started a southern trip and a northern trip. We see seven out of the eight Ivies, we see four or five of the top women's colleges, we see three or four of the best Jesuit schools, because a lot of these kids are Catholic and that's important to their parents. Then we see schools that we just think they're great, like Occidental College and the Claremont Colleges. The only UC we go to is UC Berkeley.

All the schools he listed are highly selective. Even during the three-day college trip my research assistant went on with them, they visited top schools like Stanford University, Santa Clara University, Mills College, and UC Berkeley. By the time students in Frankel's program are ready to apply to college, they will have seen at least twenty-five highly selective schools. He explains, "What I find is that they will not apply to schools they haven't seen." In fact, low-income minority students are consistently more likely to apply to schools that they have seen and where they have spent time on the campus.

Another key element is the extensive SAT prep that students receive every Saturday for two years. Overall, Frankel's students do one hundred hours of SAT prep, and, as a result, last year they raised the average SAT score by 350 points. A good portion of the budget is allocated for this purpose because of the test's importance in the college application process for highly selective schools: "We spend a lot of money on the SAT prep. We find individuals who are great teachers, and we pay them very well. They come every Saturday morning almost all year long from 8:30 a.m. to noon, and we teach SAT to our kids." He does this much SAT prep to coach students as best as he can through the exam so that they have good options for college.

Nonprofit outreach programs are extremely effective in providing support and guidance to students. Additionally, the guidance students receive is intentional and well planned. Although students are allowed to make their own choices, they are greatly influenced and guided by program staff: "We don't write the personal statements for kids, but we give them a lot of guidance," Frankel said. "We have them come in with drafts every two weeks. We meet with every kid for forty minutes, and we go over their essays, applications, lists of schools, and all the issues related to the application process . . . sometimes the essays take seven drafts, and we want to get them really good. We won't write them, but we'll constantly give them guidance so they come out good." He said that low-income minority students need consistent guidance and support because they often do not get it from school educators or their families.

According to Frankel, guidance includes step-by-step instructions on how to accomplish a task like writing a personal statement as well as affirmation of their ability to do it. In writing personal statements, for example, the biggest hurdle is convincing students that they have important stories to tell: "The real problem is these kids don't believe that they have anything to write about. Most of them have fascinating stories . . . but most of the kids will say, 'I have nothing to write about,' and Julie will say, 'Well, tell me about your life, tell me about your family life. What do you care about? What's been going on since junior high school?' And something will evolve that's worth writing about, and so framing those essays is really important."

Frankel is constantly assessing students' needs so that he can tailor how he advises them through the college process. He guides students by giving them all their options but then lets them make their own decisions: "We guide it, but we let them decide. I give them options to pick from, and they don't have to pick them, but if the kid's not so strong on the SATs—and there's some that just don't test well—they need to know there are about twenty great colleges around the country that don't require the SATs, including one of the Claremont Colleges and Smith College, for example." In this instance, Frankel is guiding and transmitting important knowledge that students can use to make their decisions about where to apply for college. Students who have high GPAs but low SATs need to know how to be strategic about where they apply to increase their likelihood of acceptance into top programs. This is very similar to the strategies middle-class students employ because they are better acquainted with the high-stakes process of college admissions.

The way Frankel's program is organized is very similar to how private college counselors structure their services for upper- and middle-class students. Jorge, an independent private college counselor, discussed the highly structured program he keeps his clients on during their junior and seniors years of high school:

> They start meeting with me in the junior year, so I develop the relationship then. I meet with them during the spring, usually once a month. In the fall, once they become seniors, naturally between two or three times a month. So I'm holding their hand through the process . . . I do everything from planning out an SAT schedule to helping them with summer plans, academic planning, a community service placement, and then their senior year, I help them with time management, GPA management. I obviously help them come up with a list of colleges, then talk to families, with the parents, and be a liaison between what parents want and what the student wants. Then I help them with their personal statements. I try to make them unique and distinct, because I think a lot of my students lack creativity. Not all of them, but a lot of them do, so I have to inject creativity into them. A lot of these kids also need help with interview skills, so I do a lot of that.

Even though Jorge works with students who come from very well educated, high-income families, they hire him to "hand-hold" their children through the college application process to maximize their chances of getting into highly selective schools. He helps his clients strategize about every part of the college process, from course preparation to college application.

In addition to providing information to students, Frankel recognizes that parents also need to have information about college, especially about financial aid. Because the cost of the schools to which he encourages his students to apply range from $50,000 to $60,000 a year, he must make sure parents know they will not be responsible for this burden and that students will qualify for the full amount. He knows that the highly selective schools with large endowments that have a "need blind" admissions policy will meet students' full financial need if admitted. Thus, he tries to pass this information on to parents so that they are informed about financial aid in higher education.

He even continues working with parents after students have decided where they are going to college, because he believes that parents who have not gone to college need to be informed about what to expect from their college-going children. Because many students are going to highly demanding and academically rigorous schools where they will live on campus, parents' understanding of that plays a part in their child's academic success and persistence. Like the college-level academic counselor introduced earlier, Frankel tries to educate parents on what will be expected of their children in college: "I want the parents to be involved in this and want them to understand all the issues, like, 'Don't call your daughter every day. Set up a time on Sunday afternoon when you can talk.' . . . 'Don't expect them to come home every weekend. She's not going to do that. If she does she's making a mistake.' So we do that. But we also get into serious issues, too, like academic issues, financial issues, social issues, what happens if you don't like your roommate, what resources are available on campus. And we get into personal health issues too." Frankel explicitly connects everything he does with college. For this reason, he constantly transmits Pivotal Moment–caliber knowledge to his students, as you will see in the following section.

TRANSMITTING ACADEMIC KNOWLEDGE AND SKILLS

The transmission of knowledge is the most critical component of an effective Pivotal Moment intervention. Frankel's program intertwines support with transmission of knowledge and skills in both formal and informal student activities, as shown in both the interview and the college trip we observed. Frankel advises students to be strategic when applying to college by picking schools based on their selectivity level:

> We tell them to do two or three "wish schools" (20 percent likely to get in), four or five "maybes" (50 percent likely to get in), and two or three "sure things," and we do that both with the University of California

schools and with the private schools. Now if I got a kid who's off the charts, I'll let him do four, five, or maybe even six wish schools, because it increases their chance of getting into one of them. If the kid's not off the charts, I'll let him do one or two wish schools, but I'm not going to waste an application on a wish school. And we guide them. We don't tell them what they have to pick, but we give them strong guidance about what makes sense in their particular case.

Again, students are getting "strong guidance" about how to pick schools they will apply to. Frankel doesn't assume that they know how to make that decision on their own. This strategy is very similar to one middle-class students might use to position themselves to get into the most competitive schools. Middle-class students often use this strategy so that they have more options when choosing a college. They also use college ranking resources such as *U.S. News and World Report* to make decisions about where to apply. For example, a middle-class doctoral student at a highly selective university I interviewed said this about her very early college planning: "The most distinct memory I have occurred in second grade. I read an article in *Time* magazine or *U.S. News and World Report* about the top-ranked U.S. universities, and Stanford University was ranked number one, and I decided then that I wanted to go to Stanford because it was the best."

Unlike government-funded academic outreach programs that encourage and require students to apply to a specific number of schools such as "four University of California schools and four California State University schools," Frankel's organization encourages students to apply to a larger number of schools and categorize them according to the likelihood of being accepted. Researchers who study college choice have found that students who apply to a higher number of schools usually have more knowledge about the college admissions process and make decisions based on that information.[18] Thus, students in this outreach program are being given the knowledge and strategies used by their middle-class peers, knowledge that will ultimately provide them with educational advantages.

Jorge, the private college counselor mentioned earlier, does something similar with his clients: "Something I try to convey is coming up with a well-balanced list of colleges." He highly encourages his students to "diversify" the schools where they apply to increase their chances of getting accepted. Initially, many of his students have the Ivies and University of California schools on their lists but are not well informed about private schools, specifically private liberal arts colleges. He explains, "They come in with certain schools . . . But a lot of what I do from the very beginning is say, 'Look, we need to diversify this. We cannot just have these schools because there's a chance your kid may not get into these, so we need to look beyond that.'" In his advising, Jorge insists that his students make a list of a range of schools to maximize their likelihood of being accepted.

Frankel has a lot of knowledge about the college application process, especially to highly selective institutions. By passing on this knowledge to his students, he teaches them to better navigate important school processes. Although the college application process can be confusing for all students, it is especially so when no one in the family has gone before. Understanding the process as a progression of steps and learning how one step is related to another allows students to keep moving forward toward higher education.[19]

Frankel is particularly knowledgeable and strategic about personal statements and other essays that private schools require in their applications:

> Most schools have two or three extra essays in addition to a common application, and they're really important. If you talk to the college admissions people they say, "If you want to know what's important to us, read the small supplemental essay questions, because those are the ones that we really care about." And if Columbia University says, "Why did you pick Columbia?" they don't want you to say because you're in New York City. They want you to say, "Because you've got this great professor of sociology or political science who I've heard about, read her work, and I'd like to study with her," or something like that.

He acquires this information by networking with college admissions staff to build relationships with them to advocate for his students. At every campus he and his students visit, he meets with someone from the admissions office. When they went to Stanford University during the college visit, he met with the dean of admissions while the students went on the campus tour. At UC Berkeley, he met with a university staff that had helped his students write their supplemental essays. His networking with the admissions staff gives him insight into admissions decisions that he is then able to use to help his students gain an advantage when applying to those schools. He has insider information about all the top schools his students apply to as he befriends the admissions counselors at each campus. They all seem to know him well. He said he often "takes them to dinner or ball games."

When appropriate, Frankel passes on the information not only to his students but also to his staff and the high school counselors who go on the college trips. On the bus during these trips, he builds rapport with his students while at the same time providing them with valuable college information and guidance. He often asks them about their test scores, advises them on what schools would accept that score, and tells them how to strategize if they do not. When a student said he wanted to go to Stanford after visiting the campus, he asked him what his SAT score was, and when the student said 2000 out of 2400 combined, he told him that he would be a great candidate even though his scores were a little low for Stanford. Then he told the student that he just needed a strategy for it and Frankel would consult with a former admissions counselor who was a "good friend." Frankel seems to have a lot of good friends at all the top schools.

Based on his insider knowledge about what colleges look for, he also advises students on which exams to take to strengthen their applications and give students every possible advantage: "We have them take the SAT three times in May, October, December, and we have them take the subject test in June and November. The reason we take it in November is because you can take Spanish listening in November, and 80 percent of my kids are Latino and they knock that one out of the park, so then they only need one good one after that. It's the only advantage they have so we take advantage of it." During the college trip he also advised counselors on things they could do to help students in the college application process. He told them to remind students not to list AP test scores on the transcript if they are not three or higher, because that places them at a disadvantage in the admissions process.

In addition to walking students through the college application process, Frankel counsels students through the decision-making process. He often must intervene when he feels students are not making decisions that are best for them in the long term. He explains a recent intervention:

> We do think there's value to leaving home and getting into a new culture, a new experience, and getting a better feel for themselves and how other people think. I have a kid this year who had a choice between going to Vassar College or going to what I would consider a low-level film school because he wanted to be a film person. In fact, my daughter's good friend is a Vassar graduate who was in the media program there. So I had her email all the things you can do at Vassar. And my daughter's former boyfriend (at the time) did a great email for me listing five wonderful film directors who had gone to Vassar. So we sent the email off to this kid. Plus, the film school wanted him to pay like $30,000 a year in loans, whereas Vassar was giving him a full ride. So in that case, we did intervene, and in the end after we gave him all the information, he did pick Vassar, thank God!

Frankel said that advising students in choosing which college to attend is just as important as advising them throughout the college application process. Unlike the academic outreach professional who let her student eventually choose the less-selective university because the student decided it was a good fit for her, Frankel convinced his student to attend the private liberal arts college instead of the less-prestigious film school.

Frankel also intervened with a student whose mother was pressuring her to pick a less-selective local school instead of going to Brown University, an Ivy League institution:

> She [an African American female] got into Brown University and she wanted to go. Her mother wanted her to go to a local school that's not as well respected as Brown. So we had a meeting at the college counselor's office with the college counselor who wanted her to go to Brown, with me, the kid, and the mother. The mother walks in, and before I even open my mouth she says, "Why are you telling my daughter that the

local school sucks?" . . . I said, "I never told her that." I told her that her daughter was incredibly capable, and for her not to go to Brown would be a tragedy.

In this case, he brought everyone together to advocate for the student and also let her mother know that not going Brown would be unfortunate and would impact the student's future opportunities. He explained that a degree from Brown University would be more prestigious and valuable than a college degree from a less-selective institution. He intervened because he understood the long-term consequences for the student if she attended a less-selective university.

In another instance, Frankel intervened by coaching a student on how to talk to her parents about her desire to go away for college rather than attend a college closer to home. Her parents wanted her to attend the college thirty-five minutes from home rather the school on the east coast.

I had a girl a few years ago—it's a wonderful story that was actually in the front page of the *LA Times* . . . A woman reporter followed this girl and her family around for, like, a month while she was making the decision of where to go to college. The kid wanted to go to Trinity College, and her father wanted her to go to Pitzer College because it was close by. She called me up and said, "What do I do? I want to go to Trinity, but my dad keeps saying Pitzer." I said, "Go in there and just tell them that you're a big girl now, you'll always love him, and you'll always have his back, but you want to go to Trinity." And she did . . . she was able to persuade her parents to let her do this.

Frankel also assists students in making their decisions by calling schools and negotiating for them to pay for their visit, even when it's last minute. He described one example:

I had a girl this year who was choosing between Dartmouth College and Wellesley College, up until the very last minute. Then three days before she decided, she wanted to go visit Brown University real quick, last minute. She hadn't bothered with Brown for the whole month of April. So I called the woman at Brown who's a good friend, and I said, "Can you send her?" Because the school pays for these trips. She goes, "No, it's too late, we can't do it because we lost that window to get the cheap ticket." I said, "Look, there's a decent chance she might want to go to Brown. She's a great kid, Latino girl, she's top of her class, she's really a top kid." She said, "Let me see if an alumni will pay for it," and she got an alumni to pay for it, flew the kid out, and the kid chose Brown.

He often uses his rich social networks to the benefit of his students. If he did not have these relationships with admissions offices at various universities, he would not be able to assist his students as well as he does in an advocacy capacity.

Tapping in to established connections with college admissions offices is typical of most nonprofit outreach programs. A spokesperson at another program said that the organization often calls admissions offices during the summers to reconnect with the staff and advocate for its upcoming seniors. Its strategy is similar to academic counselors at private high schools, who actively and intentionally develop relationships with college admissions staff. They do not hesitate to call their connections during college admissions season to advocate for their students. Richard, the counselor at a private preparatory high school, explained, "I think that's one of the advantages to being at this type of school, that there are strong personal connections between the counselor, the school, and the universities. So we knew like when colleges were going to be in committee making decisions. We would call X University and say, 'Hey, so-and-so, let's talk about my students,' and this happens at all private schools." The government-funded program outreach staff, unfortunately, did not have these types of relationships with college or university admissions offices, and thus they would not be able to accomplish the same things for their students.

Frankel's program continues working with students even after they go away to college. They stay in touch with students to know how students are adjusting to college life. If students are struggling, they do their best to help: "I do a survey every summer," Frankel said. "I hire some of our students to reach out to every one of the kids to see where they are, and if they have any needs to let us know. Most of them have these wonderful success stories. But every now and then you've got a

kid with a problem, so we work with the kid to try to solve the problem. We don't do extensive remedial work at the college level, but if
they have an academic problem, we try to give them the best advice on
how to deal with it." Sometimes he even contacts someone at the school
to get students assistance: "We usually contact the admissions office and
say, 'Remember Sally Jones? Well, see if you can get her some extra tutoring or something like that.' We try to intervene. We have good relations with most of these colleges. Most of them, to be honest, they really
like us because we're delivering a product to them that they can't get on
their own. We have very good relations with them. I can call up 80 percent of the schools we send our kids to and get a receptive person on the
other end of the line who is willing to work with us."

It is evident that much of the success of Frankel's program is dependent on his social connections to both admissions staff and his program
funders. In comparison to government-funded programs, Frankel's
serves a similar number of students but attains better educational outcomes in terms of the selectivity of the colleges his students are accepted to and attend. It is important to note that he does select the most
academically promising students to participate in his program. There
are, however, other nonprofit academic outreach programs I encoun-
tered that have similar results to College Match that work with students with all GPAs. As you learned earlier from Ms. Johnson and Mr.
Montes, even the high-achieving, top-ranked students that are first
generation need guidance with navigating the college process. It is pre-
mature to assume that just because low-income minority students have
high GPAs they will be fine on their own planning for and applying to
college. These students are probably in the greatest need of an academic
intervention to facilitate their path to higher education. Thus, it is important to highlight the structure and practices of nonprofit programs
like College Match as successful models for getting disadvantaged students to college. Frankel's program also illuminates the institutional-
ization of the educational Pivotal Moment approach.

It is not surprising that the success rate of this nonprofit academic
support program is outstanding. Not only does it get students accepted
to highly selective schools where they are more likely to graduate, but
students also often get full funding. The program claims that the to-

tal amount of the financial assistance their seniors receive represents a 2,000 percent return on their investment. Additionally, between 96 and 99 percent of the students who participate in the program graduate from college. The graduation rate is high because students are provided with all the necessary forms of support needed to excel in accessing and succeeding in higher education. The findings in this chapter highlight the great potential of nonprofit and community-based organizations in getting low-income minority students into highly selective colleges where they have highest likelihood of graduating and continuing on to graduate school.

PART IV

Implementing the Pivotal Moment Approach

10

BECOMING A PIVOTAL
MOMENT EDUCATOR

Qualities, Legacies, Training, Capacity

Utilizing the concept of Pivotal Moment educators, I set out to understand the ways in which K–16 educators help low-income and
minority students navigate the educational system to access and graduate from college. My interviews quickly revealed that first-generation
college students who are academically successful at the primary and secondary school levels have important stories to tell about their relationships with teachers, counselors, academic outreach professionals, and
professors. I learned that school success for these students was dependent
on establishing strong and trusting relationships with supportive educators. Their accounts provide useful insights about the characteristics of
effective educator practices that can help future disadvantaged students
be successful in school.

Conversations about practitioner influence on students have always
centered on the importance of educator–student interactions—but
only on the interactions, and not on the transfer of concrete academic
knowledge and resources—and that is why the educational Pivotal
Moment framework is particularly useful. It provides a deeper understanding of exactly how educator–student relationships develop, the
ways they facilitate the transmission of academic information, and how
newly acquired knowledge helps students overcome the social class and

racial or ethnic disadvantages they encounter in the educational system. It also illuminates the important role Pivotal Moment educators play in providing low-income minority students with knowledge about educational procedures and cultural norms necessary to function successfully in school.

QUALITIES OF PIVOTAL MOMENT EDUCATORS

Pivotal Moment educators possess academic and social resources and effectively use those resources to enhance students' educational success. They generally belong to multiple social networks and hold positions of authority. They are motivated, strategic, action-oriented, and resourceful. The combination of the desire to act and the know-how to do so makes these individuals extremely powerful.

Pivotal Moment educators are characterized by several distinct attributes. First, their efforts to support students go above and beyond their formal job descriptions. They are readily available and spend a purposeful amount of time with students. This is often in contrast to other educators, who make students feel rushed during interactions or are not easily accessible. Pivotal Moment educators are helpful in connecting students to academic and institutional resources, and make referrals to others on or off campus when they cannot assist students.

Second, Pivotal Moment educators are more likely to be connected to the school campus because of their involvement on campus beyond their formal job titles, such as being a club or student organization adviser. Through these roles they impart greater knowledge about the campus environment and provide students with information about opportunities or activities on and off campus. They also have well-developed relationships with influential school agents on their school campuses—relationships that they use to advocate for students.

Third, Pivotal Moment educators challenge and empower their students to promote personal growth. They provide students with direction in a firm manner, strongly suggest a course of action, and assertively guide the student in a positive way. They confront students' assumptions and perceptions and push them to engage in activities or thinking beyond their comfort zone. They hold students accountable for their actions and their word by consistently reminding them about obligations or promises made to themselves or others. They confer power on students to make their own decisions and give them the tools and confidence to draw their own conclusions. They affirm students' thinking by confirming that their actions and thought processes are following the correct path.

Fourth, Pivotal Moment educators are described by students as "real life people," because they display a greater sense of sympathy and caring for students, such as taking a general interest in students' personal and family lives and overall well-being. These educators are perceived as being nonjudgmental of students' thoughts, behaviors, or actions and understanding of students' needs. They display a sense of openness toward students, are candid, and allow students to speak freely about their lives. Pivotal Moments educators are perceived as trustworthy and honest. They often share personal stories about their upbringing and educational experiences with students, a practice that creates a sense of camaraderie. They also display enjoyment and enthusiasm for their job, in contrast to educators who complain about their work or have a poor attitude when working with students.

Finally, Pivotal Moment educators are valued for providing students with educational support and information related to academic, financial, and personal matters. Academic matters include sharing academic success strategies, helping students with course planning, and encouraging future aspirations. Financial matters include dealing with financial aid, applying for scholarships, and paying for school and other related expenses. Personal matters include helping students develop appropriate behavior on campus and in the community and improving their quality of life in a way that relates to the student's overall school success.

Overall, individuals who are Pivotal Moment educators demonstrate "authentic caring" through concrete actions.[1] Authentic caring is expressed both affectively and instrumentally. Pivotal Moment educators can reduce informational and cultural barriers for students by supporting them in three critical ways: by building trust, serving as a mentor and advocate, and most importantly, transmitting valuable educational knowledge and skills. They not only provide students with valuable translations of bureaucratic and academic requirements, but they also play a role in providing encouragement and support. As a result, students build their academic confidence and aspirations for postsecondary education. The difference between someone who is a Pivotal Moment educator and someone who is not can be more fully appreciated by referring to the examples in chapters 5 through 7 that describe educators whose practices reinforce inequality, such as using a generic approach to help students, holding low expectations, lacking empathy for students, and blaming parents for their children's academic difficulties rather than recognizing the socioeconomic constraints they face.

PIVOTAL MOMENT LEGACIES

Just as poor educational practices can reinforce inequality, Pivotal Moments can breed more educators who initiate transformative interventions with their own students—proving they have a legacy, too. Pivotal Moment educators differed from other educators not only in their teaching and counseling practices but also in their self-reflection about their own educational histories. Two remarkable similarities that all Pivotal Moment educators shared was having been the first in their family to graduate from college and having also experienced a Pivotal Moment intervention during their own schooling. Often without prompting, most of them described in great detail the efforts educators made to reach out to them when they were students. The question during the interview that most often elicited a description of their Pivotal Moment was when I asked them why they had decided to become educators.

For Ms. Johnson, her first Pivotal Moment educator was her third-grade teacher, Mrs. Ramsey. She remembered that Mrs. Ramsey was the first teacher who told her, "You can be someone!" She vividly described how Mrs. Ramsey was able to win her trust and subsequently have a major impact on her: "She would get down on our level and make us feel comfortable. She had a way about herself that attracted me to her, and it was more of, 'I'm open, I'm honest, I'm giving, but yet I can stand my ground and the things I'm going to provide you are going to be solid, you can trust it, you can trust in me.' I'll never forget it. She was the one that made the difference."

Ms. Johnson's high school counselor, Mr. Byron, was the reason she ultimately became a counselor herself. He did everything for her that a Pivotal Moment educator does, including most of the things she now does for her students:

> In tenth grade, I went to my counselor, Mr. Byron, who's a black male, and I told him, "I want to graduate early," and he said, "What do you want to graduate early for? You're going to college." I didn't know I could go . . . I didn't think college was an option for me. He helped me, sat down with me, and we did an application for Grambling State University in Louisiana. He actually gave me the money to file my application. He even went as far as to pay my dorm fee, the $250 for the deposit. From that moment, it's been one thing after the next, my master's degree and all that, but it was because of those pivotal moments, those people that were there, the teachers and the counselors.

Ms. Pineda also noted that most of the ninth- and tenth-grade counselors at her high school were first-generation college graduates like herself. She described them as "Latinos who feel that we need to empower students from an early age so they can make those education decisions to get on the right track and keep all those doors open for themselves." Like Ms. Johnson, Ms. Pineda credits a teacher for setting her on a path to educational advancement and success. In her case, it was a high school English teacher who took a chance on her and allowed her to stay in the Honors class even though she was ineligible to enroll because she was still designated an English language learner. In fact, Ms. Pineda's work as a counselor is driven by her own lack of support and guidance during her high school years. She does not want to leave students' educational opportunities to chance but rather chooses to intentionally guide them. She explained, "I personally feel I got lucky. Nobody ever reached out, nobody called, nobody invited my mom, nobody sent anything. I just happened to get lucky the day I walked into the library and somebody was there filling out college applications. So we don't want to leave it to luck."

A big influence on Ms. Reyes's decision to become a counselor was the support she received from an academic support counselor during her first year in college. Like many students I interviewed, she did not drop out because the counselor intervened and helped her raise her grades and stay in school. "I was ready to leave, and the counselor was awesome. He had a really large impact on my life and just made me feel like I could do it. He listened. I could cry with him. He made it a safe place for me, and that's what I learned from him, to have that safe space for my kids."

Similarly, one of the reasons Professor Lopez is so committed to helping her students is that she experienced a Pivotal Moment with a professor when she was a community college student: "The person that really inspired me to do political science was Professor Lynch at Los Angeles City College. She was great. She would spend a lot of time with us outside of class . . . she told me, 'You need to continue in school.' Those things stayed with me. I was exceptionally impressionable, and I think she took care of me so she's probably the greatest mentor that I had. She talked to me a lot about the transfer process, pointing me to the transfer center." These case studies demonstrate the urgency to train more educators on how to create Pivotal Moments.

TRAINING PIVOTAL MOMENT EDUCATORS

The educational Pivotal Moment framework gives educators the tools to disrupt the sorting process of schools and stop the reinforcement of inequality. The practice of creating Pivotal Moments can be powerful and transformative if implemented in an intentional and systematic way. The big question is, How do educators become motivated to change the practices and policies in which they are embedded to become Pivotal Moment educators?

Although this book presents the interventions of individual Pivotal Moment educators, it is important that schools also play a part in implementing the Pivotal Moment approach to effectively work with disadvantaged students. This can be done through well-planned professional development workshops with educators to explain the importance of all three components of a Pivotal Moment intervention: building trust, mentoring and advocating, and transmitting academic knowledge and skills. A follow-up workshop should educate staff on the most recent college and financial aid information. School leaders should make sure that all staff who have direct contact with students are well acquainted with information about higher education so that they can pass on that knowledge to students they interact with. As you learned earlier, educators need to have the right knowledge before they can transmit it to students. In addition to professional development workshops, Pivotal Moment information can be incorporated in teacher preparation and credential course work as well as counseling program course work and practicum.

There are several key steps that educators who wish to create Pivotal Moments for low-income students should take. First, it is important that educators understand the unique social and economic obstacles students face that interfere with their academic performance and transition to higher education. Second, educators should be conscious of the critical role they play in students' lives as life changers. This insight will allow educators to compensate for the shortcomings of the public school system, particularly by offering a more comprehensive approach to college access. Educators should understand how mentors play an important supportive role in helping low-income minority students overcome educational obstacles.

Third, educators should make sure that they are well versed in the academic knowledge and skills that low-income minority students need and are capable of transmitting it to them in various ways. This information includes knowing about the importance of a college degree for first-generation students. Educators should also know about academic outreach programs, internship opportunities, support services, and college admissions. Table 10.1 provides a summary of the information that Pivotal Moment educators should know before they begin working with students.

Once an educator understands the socioeconomic circumstances of low-income students and gains insight on the influence they can have in passing on knowledge about educational processes, they can begin to implement a variety of strategies to transmit it. First, educators should intervene as early as possible by adopting a proactive and assertive approach to student advising, including meeting with students several times per semester, continually tracking student performance, assessing student progress, and making referrals as needed.

Second, educators should help students prepare academically by encouraging them to enroll in rigorous courses and prepare for college

TABLE 10.1

Background information Pivotal Moment educators should know

Obstacles students face

- Social challenges, economic constraints, difficult transition between high school and college.

Critical role of educators

- Pivotal Moment educators compensate for the shortcomings of the educational system by providing comprehensive support for student success and access to college.
- Mentors and advocates can play a key supportive role in helping low-income students overcome challenges and obstacles to enroll in college.

Academic and college knowledge

- Inform parents about the importance of college degree for first-generation college students.
- Provide students with knowledge about college admissions, academic outreach programs, internship opportunities, and other academic resources.

entrance exams. Educators should also help students develop key academic behaviors, contextual skills, cognitive strategies, and content knowledge. Third, educators should make efforts to develop trust with students so that they are receptive to academic advice and support. They should also raise student aspirations for college by exposing them to cultural events and activities and helping them become independent self-advocates who can recognize when they need assistance and whom to call on to get the support.

Fourth, educators should involve and encourage parents by teaching parents how to support their children's education and providing college information. Fifth, educators should help students navigate the college admissions process by starting early, meeting often, and holding them to high standards. Sixth, educators should provide comprehensive, long-term support to help students learn about the demands of college work and the expectations that colleges hold for undergraduate students. They should also help ease the initial transition and adjustment to the college environment by staying in contact with students and serving as a supportive resource.

Seventh, educators should encourage systemic reform. One example is advocating to establish partnerships between secondary schools and postsecondary institutions to ensure that students complete college entrance requirements. Eighth, educators should provide students with information and assistance in applying for financial aid. Finally, educators in college and university settings should facilitate students' connections with peers and college personnel and encourage students to participate in research to develop their interest in pursuing graduate studies. Table 10.2 provides a summary of the various strategies educators can use to create educational Pivotal Moments for low-income minority students.

To provide all educators with the knowledge and effective strategies to become Pivotal Moment educators, schools and their leaders should gather the appropriate content and implement training procedures. Training content should include resources for educators, such as examples of effective Pivotal Moment practices, and a list of student resources such as tutoring, mentoring, and academic enrichment programs. Training procedures and content delivery can include holding professional development workshops, offering information during department meetings, providing all educators with a handbook, manual, or reference guide of critical college information they should know and tools for transmitting it to students. Training and resources should also be provided to preservice counselors and teachers in their credential and training curriculum. Figure 10.1 summarizes the entire process of becoming an effective Pivotal Moment educator.

BUILDING INSTITUTIONAL CAPACITY

The No Child Left Behind Act (NCLB) mandates that in order to receive federal funding, school districts must employ "highly qualified" teachers. Title IX of the federal law defines a highly qualified teacher as one who possess a bachelor's degree, has obtained full state certification as a teacher or passed the state licensing examination, and holds a license to teach in the respective state.[2] It is clear that the government's expectation is for teachers to demonstrate competency based on paper credentials, including a teaching certificate, a passing score on an exam, and a degree. According to Walsh and colleagues, "The 'highly

TABLE 10.2

How to become an effective Pivotal Moment educator

Intervene early

- Adopt an active and intrusive approach to advising students that includes meeting several times per semester, continually tracking student performance, checking student progress, and making referrals as necessary.

Help students prepare academically

- Encourage students to enroll in Advanced Placement courses and take college entrance exams.
- Help students develop key academic behaviors, contextual skills, cognitive strategies, and content knowledge for school success.

Provide academic advice and social support

- Develop trust to allow students to be receptive to information and support.
- Raise aspirations for college.
- Expose students to cultural events and activities, and explain their importance.
- Help students become independent self-advocates who can recognize when they need assistance and where to go to find the support they need.

Involve and encourage parents/family

- Involve parents and other family members by providing college information and teaching them how to support their children's education.

Help students navigate the college admissions process

- Start early, and meet often with students, holding them to high expectations.

Provide comprehensive, long-term support

- Help students learn about the demands of college work and the expectations that colleges hold for undergraduate students.
- Help to ease the initial transition to college; help students adjust to college environment.

Encourage systemic reform

- Advocate to establish partnerships between secondary schools and postsecondary institutions that can help students complete college entrance requirements.

Provide financial assistance

- Provide students with information and assist them in applying for financial aid and scholarships.

Higher education Pivotal Moment educators

- Facilitate connections with peers and college personnel.
- Encourage students to participate in research to develop camaraderie and pursue graduate school.

qualified' standard turns on education, certification, and demonstrated competence."[3] Under NCLB, a candidate's academic background is the primary, if not the only, consideration in determining the individual's teaching qualifications.[4] Some observers have argued that this heavy emphasis on educational background and testing will result in universities graduating academic technicians rather than professional educators committed to social responsibility and school transformation.[5]

FIGURE 10.1

Steps to become a Pivotal Moment educator

Necessary background information to create a Pivotal Moment
- Obstacles students face
- Critical role of educators
- Academic and college knowledge

How to create a Pivotal Moment
- Intervene early
- Help students prepare academically
- Provide academic advice and social support
- Involve and encourage parents/family
- Help students navigate the educational process
- Provide comprehensive, long-term support
- Encourage systemic reform

Information to train others on how to create a Pivotal Moment
- Use examples of effective Pivotal Moment practices
- Develop/provide a list of academic resources available to students

Pivotal Moment training format
- Professional development workshops
- Department meetings
- Handbook/reference guide
- Incorporate content in teacher and counselor preservice curriculum

As Pivotal Moment educators demonstrate, many attributes of effective teachers cannot be measured by a test or a person's ability to earn a degree. Good teaching should equate not only to knowledge of a list of techniques but also to proficiency in human relationships.[6] Relationships make up the basic fabric of human life and should not be pushed to the periphery of educational considerations.[7] Although the staid empiricism of NCLB suggests that highly qualified teachers in all schools who are themselves well prepared will eventually teach all students to meet high standards, the complexity of learning communities is conspicuously absent from the code.[8] The definition of teacher quality under NCLB is limited, because it focuses on relatively narrow content knowledge at the expense of determining many other qualities needed for effective teaching.[9] For instance, caring, patience, social and emotional intelligence, and other attributes are not measured under the current system. In view of the enactment of this federal accountability system, which in many ways influences teacher selection at the school district level, it is important to consider what constitutes effective teaching and to be mindful of a broader spectrum of competencies.

Most effective teachers, like Pivotal Moment educators, possess technical skills and nurturing behaviors.[10] Nurturing behavior is evidenced by the "teacher's personal attention," which is demonstrated by a humanistic interest in the learners. Technical skills are "pedagogical techniques" designed to keep the student engaged in the learning. Nurturing behavior and an ethnic of caring have been found to be very important in the work that teachers are expected to do.[11] For example, most preservice teachers endorse "student-centeredness" as a characteristic of effective teachers in primary and secondary classroom schools.[12] It is especially important to have teachers with the qualities and attributes necessary for positive social change in demographically challenged areas, such as regions of the country typically populated by higher numbers of minorities and economically disadvantaged students.[13]

Latino students, similar to their white and African American peers, consider student-centeredness to be an extremely important characteristic of effective instruction for teachers at the elementary and secondary levels. According to Latino college students, the characteristics of effective elementary school teachers include patience, caring, knowledgeable, positive attitude, understanding, teaches well, loving, creative, organized, fun, passion for the job, communication, service, involving, uses different modalities, flexibility, disciplinarian, motivating, builds relationships, and friendly. Of these themes, patience receives the highest endorsement, followed by caring. Being an enthusiastic, empathetic, and communicative teacher is also important to Latino students.

These qualities represent what the American Association of School Administrators (AASA) refers to as effective teacher characteristics.[14] These have also been mentioned among "nonmeasurable" skills that effective teachers possess, "measurable" skills being knowledge of subject matter, effective and efficient use of time, clear communication, and organization.[15] Competent teachers are also effective in developing and nurturing student–teacher relationships because a solid student–teacher relationship is conducive to a positive classroom climate.[16] Caring and patience are important to cultivating student skills necessary for effective advocacy for social justice.[17] According to college students, student-centeredness should also be prioritized for college instructors to be more effective.[18]

Educational institutions have the ultimate control when it comes to creating developmental experiences for their staff to gain the skills to become a Pivotal Moment educator. Although professional development programs may be in place at the institution, there are some key components that must accompany such a program. First, learning experiences must be created for educators to develop and display the characteristics of being student-centered and going above and beyond the call of duty.

Second, the professional development experiences to nurture these skills must not be delivered via a one-time, haphazard approach.[19] These developmental programs must be ongoing and allow for educators to constantly link activities, programs, workshops, and on-the-job experiences to developing and implementing the Pivotal Moment approach. This would require educational institutions to create professional development programs that are long term and specific to the educator and experiences that fit directly with the educator's role on campus. For example, the interactions that teachers or professors have with students in the classroom are very different from the experiences of counselors and academic outreach professionals. Schools and programs must create ways in which all educators can exude the attributes of Pivotal Moment educators despite their different roles on campus.

Motivating educators to change a behavior or learn a new characteristic may be a significant challenge, because ultimately it is up to the individual to control and modify his own behavior. Before a professional development training plan to socialize educators into a Pivotal Moment educator philosophy can be implemented, the campus environment should be assessed to determine to what extent it is conducive to change.[20] Schools should utilize the existing research regarding institutional change in order to establish an environment that is open to the Pivotal Moment approach. Without creating an environment that is supportive to such a change, it is difficult for school staff to buy in to becoming Pivotal Moment educators.

Finally, schools should provide continuous support for educators when change is to occur and the Pivotal Moment educator philosophy is to be embraced and acquired through training. Providing a formal reward system, promotion plan, and continuous feedback mechanism may be necessary to create a comprehensive professional development plan to promote Pivotal Moment educator characteristics and attributes.[21] If a school provides the training and has willing staff but does not constantly support the process for development, then the loop is not complete and the desire for an institution of Pivotal Moment educators will be lost. Schools therefore must not forget the final key component of organizational change, which is to continuously support educators as they develop and implement new behaviors.

Becoming a Pivotal Moment educator places a number of responsibilities on school staff that they may not see as desirable. For instance, some may not see themselves as the appropriate person to transmit certain information outside their level of expertise. Academic information is an area that teachers and faculty feel most comfortable with, because it falls within their realm of knowledge. Teachers and faculty may even be resistant to learning other educational information that is critical for first-generation students to acquire, because it falls outside their formal job title or might infringe on the curriculum and class time that they have previously planned. These are definitely challenges to the implementation of a Pivotal Moment educator ethos, but as you have seen in this book, there are teachers and faculty that commit themselves to learning new knowledge outside their formal roles and embed this new information into their class curricula.

The implementation of a Pivotal Moment educator professional development program is complex and may take time and valuable resources. It may require the evaluation of each individual employee to discover the particular areas in which they need enhancement as well as an individualized plan of how to go about improving in those areas. There may be difficulties acquiring buy-in from the faculty and staff as to the program's role in first-generation student success. It might be more difficult to deal with the individuals who may not appreciate hearing that they need to change some of their characteristics and attributes, or that their behavior is not the best way to work with students. This is why the buy-in from key personnel and administrators is important in the implementation of such a program, because they need to communicate with employees about how these measures can help first-generation students to become successful in their higher education pursuits.

For a Pivotal Moment approach to be established at a school campus, educators must desire to learn about the process of possibly modifying their current behaviors and actions to be more in line with those of Pivotal Moment educators. Schools must also work to establish an environment that is conducive to such a change by providing ongoing professional development and training opportunities. Thus, schools and educators must work together in collaboration for a Pivotal Moment curriculum to be successfully implemented in a systematic way. The following section provides strategies for educators to begin the process of becoming a Pivotal Moment educator.

BECOMING A PIVOTAL MOMENT EDUCATOR

Educators who want to create Pivotal Moments for low-income minority students not only need to learn about the specific challenges they face but also need to reflect on and assess their own practices. Table 10.3 provides a checklist of Pivotal Moment behaviors for educators to gauge their own efforts. How many can you check off? Have you ever created a Pivotal Moment for a low-income or minority student?

TABLE 10.3

Pivotal Moment educator checklist

As an educator, think about the ways in which you support first-generation college students. Check off the Pivotal Moment practices and actions you have engaged in with your students in the past.

Building trust

☐ Share details about personal struggles in the educational system.

☐ Ask students about their personal/family lives outside school.

☐ Find a way to personalize interactions, such as addressing students by first name.

☐ Provide a safe space for students to express their opinions and concerns.

☐ Show sympathy and care toward students' dilemmas and struggles.

☐ Make yourself accessible to all students.

Mentoring and advocating

☐ Constantly encourage students to do their best in school.

☐ Provide emotional and moral support.

☐ Employ highly proactive and intentional advising and guidance.

☐ Assess students' needs and identify resources to address them.

☐ Learn about available academic and institutional resources and how to access them.

☐ Continually track and assess student progress and performance.

☐ Hold all students to high expectations and standards of academic excellence.

☐ Raise aspirations for college and graduate school, and instill the possibility students can attend.

☐ Encourage students to enroll in rigorous courses and take college and graduate school entrance exams.

☐ Help students research and gather college and graduate school information.

☐ Develop relationships with important and influential school personnel to advocate for students.

☐ Promote and protect students' interests at all times.

☐ Involve parents and families in supporting their children's education.

☐ Question the educational system, and envision alternative ways to ensure student success.

☐ Work with colleagues to establish partnerships between secondary and postsecondary institutions.

☐ Advocate for systemic school reform.

Transmitting academic knowledge and skills

☐ Advise and guide students in making a concrete plan to prepare for college and graduate school, including course planning, extracurricular activities, and deadlines for taking entrance exams.

☐ Provide students with extensive information about educational and occupational options.

☐ Expose and explain to students the value of cultural events and activities.

☐ Teach students to utilize academic and institutional resources effectively.

☐ Help students become independent self-advocates and to develop help-seeking behaviors.

☐ Teach students effective communication skills, and coach them on networking with educators and other adults.

☐ Using a step-by-step approach, teach students how to navigate school processes such as selecting colleges and graduate schools, filling out applications, and applying for financial aid and scholarships.

☐ Promote and guide effective problem solving and decision making.

☐ Help students learn about the expectations that colleges and graduate schools hold for undergraduate and graduate students.

Finally, table 10.4 provides a list of questions to help educators undertake meaningful introspection and begin to develop a plan of action to create educational Pivotal Moments. The questions are not intended to produce specific answers but rather to provoke a self-analysis of educational practices, which will vary from person to person and from situation to situation. My intent is to help educators think about educational opportunity and inequality in their own classrooms and schools. I hope educators find these questions useful as they work to transform their practices to support students who are potentially the first in their family to attend college. Unless more educators initiate Pivotal Moments for low-income and minority students, we will continue to witness significant disparities in educational outcomes. The questions presented here challenge all those who work in the educational system to become Pivotal Moment educators.

TABLE 10.4

Questions to guide self-reflection on how to become a Pivotal Moment educator

Building trust

1. Do you feel that your students trust you?

2. What strategies have you found to be effective in gaining students' trust?

3. Do you make yourself available to students? If so, how?

4. Do students consider you approachable? Why or why not?

5. Are you sympathetic and caring toward your students? If so, how?

6. How do you show your students you care about them?

7. What can you do in the future to build trust with your students to initiate Pivotal Moments?

Mentoring and advocating

1. In what ways do you mentor low-income minority students?

2. In what ways do you advocate for low-income minority students?

3. How do you respond when students are hesitant about following academic or educational advice? Do you insist that they reconsider? If so, how?

4. What institutional connections and resources have you used to support students?

5. How do you develop and utilize your networks and resources on behalf of students?

6. What resources and networks can you draw upon to increase your support of students at your institution?

7. In what ways can you go beyond your school to act as a cultural guide for low-income minority students?

8. What can you do in the future to become a mentor and advocate for your students to initiate Pivotal Moments?

Transmitting academic knowledge and skills

1. In what ways do you advise and guide students in advancing their educations?

2. What knowledge do you have about what it takes to be successful in the educational system?

3. What skills do you feel are the most important for students to possess to do well in school?

4. What information about the educational system have you shared with students in the past?

5. What school processes do you talk to students about most frequently? Why?

6. What academic and institutional resources do you mention to students most often? Why?

7. Are you well informed about what it takes to successfully get to college? Are there things you do not know? Have you ever struggled to provide students with the information they need?

8. What can you do in the future to transmit academic knowledge and skills to students to initiate Pivotal Moments?

CONCLUSION

Social historian David Labaree has described the educational system of the United States as one of unlimited possibilities and limited probabilities.[1] Because of a distinctly American mix of political ideals and economic imperatives, the door never closes on the hopes of individuals wishing to better themselves through education. Low-income minority students who are the first in their family to attend college face a variety of challenges that limit the likelihood that they will enjoy the possibilities afforded to them by a college education. They lack models of educational success in their families and are often told in subtle and indirect ways that they are not "college material."[2] There are few educators who realize the critical importance of relationships between themselves and students, and consequently, when connections do occur, they happen haphazardly or accidentally. Educators who authentically connect with students engage in a variety of practices to support them that include helping them navigate complicated academic requirements and application procedures, validating their educational aspirations, and dispelling their fears that they do not belong. Without structured interventions and active educator involvement, students who do succeed need to be in the right place at the right time to connect with trusted advisers who can assist them.

Low-income students receive less parental support in preparing for and gaining access to college compared to students with college-educated parents.[3] Although their parents encourage and support education, low-income students are more likely to seek advice about schooling from peers because their parents do not have college degrees and are not familiar with educational processes.[4] Although the academic intensity and the quality of high school curriculum are crucial for academic success and a smooth transition to college, other factors, such as educators—teachers, guidance counselors, academic advisers, professors—facilitate students' transition from high school to college, and can predict adjustment more than student background characteristics.[5]

This book attempts to broaden our understanding of the theory and practice behind academic interventions for low-income minority students that help them succeed academically and gain access to higher education. The concept of educational Pivotal Moments offers a new and novel approach that can be put into practice to help students achieve high levels of educational success. By analyzing the accounts of students' schooling experiences, I identified key academic interventions that significantly changed the course of their educational trajectories by triggering the accumulation of academic knowledge and skills that facilitate school success and advancement. The findings highlight the critical role of Pivotal Moment educators when they make efforts to gain students' trust, serve as mentors and advocates, and transmit academic knowledge and skills to increase students' educational and life opportunities in extremely positive and enduring ways.

Most studies on educational success and college access are quantitative, drawing on national databases and regression analysis. Given the complex nature of students' decisions, experiences, and outcomes, qualitative work, like the one presented in this book, is particularly well suited to understand the educational experiences of low-income minority students. Qualitative research focuses on context and meaning, and it is uniquely suited to illuminate the ways in which educational institutions and student agency work together to produce distinct academic outcomes.[6]

CURVING EDUCATIONAL TRENDS FOR LOW-INCOME STUDENTS

The long-term health of the United States depends on the existence of social mobility and a widely shared confidence that students from racial and ethnic minority and poor families have a real opportunity to move ahead. A consistent and sobering finding in the research literature is that high schools provide few students with the skills, content, and credentials needed for access to four-year colleges and for success there once students are enrolled. This is particularly disturbing given that many of these students begin high school with relatively high achievement test scores and manage to graduate from high school despite high dropout rates and low high school achievement. Their lack of access to higher education is not solely the result of students entering high school poorly prepared.[7]

Nationally, Latinos have a lower overall level of educational attainment than African Americans and whites.[8] Increasing the educational attainment of this target group must be a high priority if we are to improve the overall educational attainment levels in the United States and reduce disparities related to race and ethnicity. One trend specific to Latinos is the high proportion of this group that initially enrolls in two-year colleges.[9] Latino students are particularly disadvantaged because few of their parents have any college experience.[10] Although Latino students now come from more-educated families than they did in the 1970s, they remain the racial or ethnic group with the lowest parental education attainment levels in the nation.[11]

Whereas students from high-income college-educated families have experienced an increase in college completion rates in the past three decades, alarmingly, the opposite is true for low-income, first-generation students. For example, the college completion rate for students from high-income college-educated families increased from 60 percent in 1972 to 68 percent in 1992. In comparison, for students from low-income families and parents who have less than a college education, the college completion rate decreased from 12 percent in 1972 to 10 percent in 1992. Currently, 13 percent of twenty-six-year-olds whose parents have no college education had a college degree, compared to 50 percent of those whose parents have at least a college education. Taking both income and parental education into account, 81 percent of students from high-income families and at least one degreed parent earned a bachelor's degree by age twenty-six, compared with just 47 percent of those from low-income families where neither parent had a college degree. The trend is also not encouraging for ethnic minority students, particularly males. Even after controlling for SAT scores, high school GPA, and family income, black males are 6 percent less likely, and Latino males are 7 percent less likely, to graduate in six years compared to white males.[12]

Another alarming trend among low-income and racial or ethnic minority students is that many well-qualified students end up at institutions that are less selective than the ones for which they are qualified. Fewer than half of those from academically advanced programs end up enrolling in colleges that match their qualifications. In most cases, mismatches are due to lack of information and a simple lack of college planning. In a recent study, undermatching was 64 percent for students with nondegreed parents, compared to 41 percent of students with parents who had at least a bachelor's degree. Of the students who undermatched, 64 percent did not even apply to a matching school, and 28 percent chose to attend a less-selective institution. The six-year graduation rate for the 66 percent of low-income students who undermatched was 66 percent, compared to 81 percent for those who attended a highly selective matching school.

In another recent study of Chicago public schools, Latino students were significantly less likely than other racial or ethnic groups to enroll in a college whose selectivity level matched or exceeded their level of qualifications. Overall, 44 percent of Latino students enrolled in colleges whose selectivity levels were far below match, compared to 28 percent for African American high school graduates. Even among students who worked hard throughout high school and earned the GPAs and ACT scores that give them access to very selective colleges, fewer than 30 percent of Latino graduates enrolled in such a college, compared to 40 percent of African American and white or other ethnic graduates with similar qualifications. Factors that lead to so much undermatching among Latino students include financial concerns compounded by the difficulty of completing complicated financial aid forms; problems in the application process, including lack of information and proper guidance; failure to understand the importance of applying to more than one "match" school; and lack of a "college-going culture" in high school.

An encouraging trend is that students attending more-selective institutions graduate at higher rates and in less time than do "observationally equivalent" students attending less-selective institutions. Unfortunately, most first-generation students enroll at less-selective colleges and universities. The overall graduation rate for first-generation students was 69 percent at highly selective public universities, compared to only 57 percent at the less-selective public universities.

The relative graduation rate advantage associated with going to a more-selective university is even more pronounced for African American men at the lower end of the high school grade distribution than it was for students with better high school records. For Latino students, the more selective the institution was that they attended, the higher their graduation rates. In fact, the positive association between graduation rates and institutional selectivity is even stronger for Latinos than it is for African Americans. In considering ways to increase the number of students from low-income families who earn bachelor's degrees, these findings suggest that in general, students are well advised to enroll at the most challenging university that will accept them, because low-income students do much better at highly selective private colleges and universities.[13]

Higher graduation rates at highly selective universities is driven principally by five broad sets of factors: peer effects, expectations, access to excellent educational resources, financial aid, and student work opportunities as well as other unobservable selection effects. Because students learn from each other, being surrounded by highly capable classmates improves the learning environment and promotes positive educational outcomes of all kinds, including timely graduation. The high overall graduation rates at the most selective public universities unquestionably create a climate in which graduating, and doing so with one's incoming class, are compelling norms. Students feel a great pressure to keep pace with their classmates. Highly selective universities also have superior faculty and distinctly above-average library and laboratory resources. These factors improve learning environments for students because they are able to more easily identify stimulating faculty mentors, take graduate-level courses, and benefit from having exceptionally able graduate students as teaching assistants. In general, students at highly selective universities, especially those who are members of racial or ethnic minority groups, are likely to have access to more generous financial aid than other students. Also, research grants and contracts obtained by faculty members provide attractive on-campus work opportunities, especially in the sciences and engineering, that foster engagement with the academic process and facilitate degree completion. Finally, there may be some modest association between enrollment at the most selective universities and unobservable characteristics of entering students, such as ambition and drive.[14]

High schools must both increase their capacity to facilitate the matching process and help students understand that "college does not mean just any college."[15] The overall extent of undermatching and the prevalence of undermatching among students from low-socioeconomic groups is both disturbing and an opportunity for high schools, colleges, and nonprofit community-based organizations to collaborate to improve the sorting process. There is a considerable opportunity to increase the social mobility of low-income students and augment the nation's human capital. The key is to find more-effective ways of informing high-achieving students and their parents of the educational options that are open to them, and the benefits they can derive from taking advantage of these opportunities. We need to find better ways to help these students navigate the process of gaining access to the strongest academic programs possible.[16]

The U.S. educational system harbors huge disparities in educational outcomes, especially as measured by graduation rates that are systematically related to race or ethnicity, socioeconomic status, and gender. Moreover, these disparities appear to be growing rather than narrowing. This pattern is unacceptable because of its implications for social mobility and access to opportunity as well as because of what it says about our collective failure to take full advantage of pools of latent talent. The only way to substantially improve overall levels of educational attainment is by improving graduation rates for underrepresented students generally (with ethnic minority men requiring special attention) and for students from low socioeconomic backgrounds.[17]

As the title of this book suggests, educational Pivotal Moments can compensate for the social class and racial or ethnic disadvantages low-income minority youth experience in school. Early Pivotal Moments are particularly critical, because they help develop, at an early age, the necessary psychological dispositions and high aspiration orientations to succeed in school. The findings strongly suggest that early academic interventions are very effective in getting students through the educational pipeline and into higher education. The timing of Pivotal Moments, therefore, is significant because those who have experienced early Pivotal Moments have more time to develop higher stocks of academic knowledge and skills compared to students who have later ones.

The findings imply that teachers, counselors, and other school personnel need to be mindful of how they can serve as Pivotal Moment educators. Most low-income ethnic minority students are unable to accumulate sufficient educational knowledge and skills from their parents. Although this knowledge is vital to their academic achievement, these students receive mostly emotional and moral support. As a consequence, they are dependent on individuals and programs within the schools to accumulate additional academic information and resources. For the students I studied, it was the accumulation of large amounts of these educational resources from various individuals and programs that expanded their educational opportunities and pathway to higher education.

As the composition of our nation's school-age population becomes more racially, ethnically, and socioeconomically diverse, we will see an increasing number of students who could be the first generation in their families to enter higher education.[18] However, low-income students are less likely to attend college and more likely to attend less-selective institutions.[19] Furthermore, they are less likely to persist and attend graduate school. Despite these findings and calls for research on social class differences, scholars often control for social class rather than focus on how those differences may shape students' outcomes. Understanding such differences can help inform education policies in the future.

Although there is a host of structural and financial factors that produces inequalities in educational outcomes that merit attention, examining the ways in which the acquisition and use of academic knowledge and skills are mediated by social interaction is an important step in understanding the contextual factors that affect educational success and postsecondary transition for low-income and minority students. Sociocultural factors such as race or ethnicity and socioeconomic characteristics of families as well as schools interact in the transmission of academic knowledge and skills, but the role educators play in students' educational outcomes is frequently overlooked.[20] Instead, most research correlates educational success with students' characteristics and their self-reported experiences, behaviors, and accomplishments. Rarely are teachers, counselors, academic outreach professionals, and university faculty given attention in terms of how they may or may not contribute to student success.[21] I do not mean to suggest that educators should be targeted or blamed for poor student outcomes. Rather, I believe that educators are an important part of the educational social context, and they can make a tremendous difference in closing the equity gap in educational access.

THE INFLUENCE OF NONPARENTAL ADULTS

Most parents want their children to go to college, but students from college-educated families start with some undeniable educational advantages—among them, that their parents typically have experience planning for college. Well-educated, affluent families often invest considerable energy in helping their children look at different colleges and accumulating the needed financial resources. For some, college planning is a major parental enterprise that can begin from the moment a child is born. It pays off as students whose parents have a four-year degree are much more likely to be successful when they enter a four-year college or university.[22]

Thus, parental income and education level are strongly correlated with student success in completing a college degree, but nationwide, more than half of public school students are from families in which neither parent has completed college. Among students who complete a two- or four-year degree or certificate, about half say that when they were living at home, their family had money left over at the end of the month, and nearly seven in ten say their parents had at least some college education. Among those who fail to finish college, 56 percent come from families that just barely made ends meet or had trouble getting by, and almost half have parents whose highest degree is a high school diploma or less.[23]

For young people from less-well-educated, lower-income families, the ability to know and talk to adults who are familiar with the higher education system can be essential. The vast majority of lower-income and less-well-educated parents have high educational aspirations for their children, but they do not have enough in-depth, practical knowledge about how the school system works to give their children the best advice. In such cases, access to an attentive and knowledgeable guidance counselor can be crucial. Unfortunately, high school counselors are viewed by students as less helpful than teachers.[24] Students who get perfunctory counseling in school are more likely to delay college and make more-questionable higher education choices. The dismal ratings students give their high school counselors would be disturbing under any circumstances, but the fact that they typically give their teachers and mentors better ratings suggests that, at least as students see it, a malfunctioning counseling system is a particularly conspicuous gap.

In education, we tend to think of the ideal student as an autonomous and self-motivated individual who exemplifies commitment, engagement, self-regulation, and goal orientation.[25] A distinctive feature of this perspective is that success is understood as an outcome of individual efforts, assuming that all students are free to make independent choices about what college to attend, what goals to pursue, what activities to become involved in, and with whom to spend time. The underlying explanation of student success is that the greater the academic effort students make, the greater the likelihood of their school success. The common assumption characterizes the student as the agent of success, which is a matter of whether she exerts the effort to participate in educationally purposeful activities or engages in behaviors that represent commitment, self-discipline, and the integration of desirable academic values and norms.[26]

Practitioners as well as researchers assume that institutional support systems are already in place and that motivated students will take advantage of them.[27] However, some students may not know how to become engaged or may not feel entitled to be engaged—particularly if it involves requests for help—and may shun activities that signify engagement to avoid failure or the risk of rejection. In predominantly white college campuses, minority students may consciously decide not to speak in class or not attempt a conversation with a faculty member outside class for fear of being stereotyped.[28] African American students perceive the college environment and their relationships with faculty more negatively than other groups and believe that faculty do not take their academic ability seriously, even when they are high achieving.[29] Minority students' perceptions of the quality of their relationships with college faculty as remote, discouraging, and unsympathetic, or approachable, helpful, understanding, and encouraging has been found to be a strong predictor of learning for minority students.[30] Research on sense of belonging, validation, and stereotype threat points to the significance of practitioners in the educational outcomes of minority students.[31]

In general, nearly all adults identify a nonparental adult who made an important difference in their lives during adolescence.[32] Most high school students report having a nonparental adult who played a "very important" role in their lives, but few of these adults were teachers.[33] Importantly, among young adults from diverse racial or ethnic backgrounds, the majority report that they had a teacher who really took an interest in them personally and encouraged them to go to college. Most say that they had a teacher or coach who really inspired them and motivated them to do their best.[34] At the college level, more than half of students give their college advisers positive ratings for helping them decide what classes to take. The numbers are somewhat less positive for helping them understand how to get loans and scholarships.[35] Those who identify an important nonparental adult in their lives tend to report better psychological well-being, academic success, and higher school completion.[36]

Although nonparental adults play an increasingly important role in students' lives, access to empowering nonparental adults for low-income adolescents has not been well addressed. Even though they can make positive contributions to the development of youths, nonparental adults may not have the knowledge and skills to truly alter a low-income student's social mobility. Low-income nonparental adults may inculcate particular aspirations, values, and norms, but they may not have the capacity to guide educational processes.[37]

Pivotal Moment educators give students a sense of belonging, validate their knowledge and personal experiences, and help them muster the confidence and courage to pursue a college education.[38] During the processes of academic identity formation, students become deeply influenced by perceptions and evaluation of teachers as well as classroom peers.[39] In time, such appraisals are internalized and become reflected in students' view of themselves, as well as their educational aspirations. These internalized appraisals and aspirations—together with the academic encouragement provided by teachers—drive individual effort engagement and degree of investment in school, factors that in turn largely determine educational attainment.[40] Teacher–student relationships and teacher encouragement are critical "resources" for motivating African American and Latino students.[41] Minority students, especially African Americans, identify teacher encouragement as a "very important" reason for working "really hard" in school.[42]

IMPLICATIONS FOR EDUCATIONAL PRACTICE

Toward the end of his career, French social theorist Pierre Bourdieu reported that he came to believe that one of the main vectors of inequality reinforcement in the French educational system was the absence of explicit mediations between knowledge and learners. He characterized such mediation as an "invisible pedagogy" accessible only to students from privileged social backgrounds.[43] He saw the need for continuous and systematic clarification of educational expectations, content, and methods by teachers as a way of reducing the communication gap between teachers and working-class students and thereby limiting their disadvantage relative to their middle-class peers.

There is a need in our educational system for a universal pedagogy in which the implied necessary knowledge is taught to all students no matter their racial, ethnic, or socioeconomic background. In many ways, Pivotal Moment educators implement this type of universal pedagogy in their efforts to play a significant role in the educational experiences of low-income minority students, because they are able to provide such students with the type of knowledge and resources found in the social networks of the middle and upper classes.[44] These educators seem to have special predispositions that motivate their student advocacy. They seem to be directed by an inner ethical compass to use their expertise for the good of promising students who otherwise might be overlooked.[45]

Discussions about improving student success and retention focus mostly on enrollment and course-taking patterns, the economic consequences of changing demographics, incentive funding for institutions and students, standards of accountability, and new regulations. Student success is viewed almost exclusively as a function of background characteristics that have been found to correlate with persistence and graduation. The role of practitioners is almost always absent from the dialogue. When scholars translate their findings into recommendations for action, practitioners are rarely the target of change or intervention.[46] The role of practitioners in students' educational experiences is not always considered, even though they are the most consistent point of contact with students.[47] Surveys typically ask only a few cursory questions regarding student relationships with educators. Although student success models place a great emphasis on the benefit of educator–student interaction, there is almost no research on the value of informal communication between educators and students.[48]

The findings presented in this book have important implications for practice. They highlight the importance of early academic interventions in the educational trajectories of students from disadvantaged social class and racial or ethnic backgrounds. Based on these results, I suggest we facilitate teacher and counselor capacity to initiate Pivotal Moments and develop more programs that prompt early academic interventions for low-income minority students. The only way to continue the effort of narrowing the academic achievement gap and getting students to college is to give students chances for early academic interventions. The findings also suggest that institutions of higher education should develop and implement programs to encourage faculty and staff to provide mentoring, apprenticeship, and informal social interaction opportunities for students to acquire the skills needed to succeed academically, complete college, and increase their pursuit of graduate studies.

Lack of specialized knowledge about racial or ethnic minorities may prevent educators from seeing that behavior patterns that seem to suggest low motivation or indifference are often learned coping strategies. Consequently, when minority students do not perform well academically nor exhibit the behaviors and attitudes of the archetypical student, practitioners who lack knowledge of students' history and cultural lives are likely to attribute poor outcomes to lack of integration, involvement, engagement, and effort. When practitioners lack knowledge of their students' cultural lives, they are severely limited in their capacity to adapt their actions and be responsive to their students' unique experiences.[49] For example, they may not realize that low-income minority students sometimes avoid desirable practices of academic engagement because of embarrassment, fear of being judged incompetent, or concern about reinforcing negative stereotypes.[50] These circumstances can make first-generation, low-income, and minority students feel as if they are invisible and undeserving in their instructors' eyes.

Individual and school-level action is not a substitute for state policy initiatives to improve academic achievement and college access for low-income and minority students, but individual and school-level change certainly is a powerful force to encourage and support state policy actions and initiatives to provide examples to educators of how achievement and college access can be increased. Pivotal Moment practices of individual educators, schools, and school districts can serve as evidence to which state policy makers can refer when considering instituting systemic solutions that can make educational success a reality for all low-income and minority students.[51]

NEXT STEPS

A trend that needs to be explored further is the referral of students to Pivotal Moment educators by their peers. Although it was mentioned on various occasions by students as well as educators, I did not explore this process extensively. Generally, first-generation and ethnic minority students are more likely to go to peers, as opposed to educators, when they need educational support. The referral of peers to Pivotal Moment educators when they need further guidance highlights the role of peers in student success. For some first-generation minority students, peer social networks may be what they use to initially identify a Pivotal Moment educator. Whether through peers, taking a class, being an advisee, or participating in an academic outreach program with a Pivotal Moment educator, students became connected with a person at their school. The student then begins to develop a sense of trust with their educator and utilizes the provided educational information to produce some academic benefit for themselves. The student continues to return to his Pivotal Moment educator, who eventually becomes deeply embedded in his social network. Educational institutions must take an active role in creating these social network opportunities between first-generation minority students and Pivotal Moment educators by creating an environment that is conducive to such relationships and by educating school staff on the importance of such interactions.

If we wish to produce knowledge to improve student success, we cannot ignore the significant role practitioners play in that effort. More specifically, if our goal is to make a difference in the lives of students whom higher education has been least successful in educating (e.g., racially marginalized groups and the poor), we must expand the scholarship on student success and take into account the positive and negative influence of practitioners. If we continue to concentrate only on what students accomplished or failed to accomplish when they were in high school and what they fail to do once they enter college, our understanding of academic achievement will be incomplete.

Even though economically and educationally challenged students face significant structural impediments, there are still many low-income and minority students who do manage to surmount the barriers and make decisions that result in persistence and attainment. As educators, we must learn from the successful students to minimize future obstacles and assist students with their decisions all along the educational pipeline.[52] If educators and schools identify the characteristics and attributes of Pivotal Moment educators, incorporate them into an intentional professional development training program—particularly focusing on educators who have direct contact with students—then they will have the means for transmitting academic information to first-generation, low-income minority college students. Schools cannot overlook the importance of educational knowledge and skills transmission in the exchanges between first-generation minority students and educators, because it is important for students to acquire this information, and educators need to be more holistic in passing on this information.

Additionally, schools need to be more intentional in training educators on the importance of providing educational knowledge and skills in conjunction with other academic information such as career, financial, and personal connections that most first-generation minority students do not have. Although they may not be intentionally withholding from students, educators need to be more purposeful in providing the information to help students in more-deliberate ways. These efforts are crucial for educators who look to enhance the school success of first-generation minority students. By implementing a comprehensive Pivotal Moment educator approach to create an atmosphere that is focused on the transmission of educational knowledge and skills to first-generation minority students, the function of reinforcing inequality that is so often associated with schools can be significantly decreased.

NOTES

Introduction

1. J. L. Hochschild, *Facing Up to the American Dream: Race, Class, and the Soul of the Nation* (Princeton, NJ: Princeton University Press, 1995); J. L. Hochschild and N. Scovronick, *The American Dream and the Public Schools* (New York: Oxford University Press, 2003); J. Oakes, *Multiplying Inequalities* (Santa Monica, CA: RAND Corporation, 1990).

2. E. Ladd, "Thinking About America," *Public Perspective* 4, no. 5 (1993): 19–34.

3. R. Espinoza, "The Good Daughter Dilemma: Latinas Managing Family and School Demands," *Journal of Hispanic Higher Education*, 9, no. 4 (2010): 317–330.

4. C. Jencks, S. Bartlett, M. Corcoran, J. Cruse, et al., *Who Gets Ahead? The Determinants of Economic Success in America* (New York: Basic Books, 1979); P. W. Kingston, *The Classless Society* (Stanford, CA: Stanford University Press, 2000).

5. P. Bourdieu, "The Forms of Capital," in *Handbook of Theory for Research in the Sociology of Education,* ed. J. E. Richardson (Westport, CT: Greenwood Press, 1986).

6. M. Fetler, "Television Viewing and School Achievement," *Journal of Communication* 34, no. 2 (1984): 104–118; V. Rideout, D. Roberts, and U. Foehr, *Generation M: Media in the Lives of 8–18 Year Olds* (Menlo Park, CA: Kaiser Family Foundation, 2005).

7. S. Brice Heath, *Ways with Words* (Cambridge, UK: Cambridge University Press, 1983).

8. M. Hout, "More Universalism, Less Structural Mobility: The American Occupational Structure in the 1980s," *American Journal of Sociology* 93, no. 3 (1988): 1358–1400; L. Mishel, J. Bernstein, and J. Schmitt, *The State of Working America 1998–99* (Ithaca, NY: Cornell University Press, 1999).

9. S. Aronowitz, "Against Schooling: Education and Social Class," *Social Text* 22, no. 2 (2004): 13–35.

10. U.S. Department of Education, *The Condition of Education, 1995* (Washington, DC: National Center for Educational Statistics, 1995).

11. D. R. Entwisle, K. L. Alexander, and L. S. Olson, *Children, Schools, and Inequality* (Boulder, CO: Westview, 1997).

12. C. Jencks and M. Phillips, *The Black–White Test Score Gap* (Washington, DC: Brookings Institute, 1998).

13. Bourdieu, "Forms of Capital."

14. J. Oakes, *Keeping Track: How Schools Structure Inequality* (New Haven, CT: Yale University Press, 1985); L. I. Rendon, "Eyes on the Prize: Students of Color and the Bachelor's Degree," *Community College Review* 21, no. 2 (1992): 3–13; R. R. Skemp, "Relational Understanding and Instrumental Understanding," *Arithmetic Teacher* 26, no. 3 (1978): 9–15.

15. W. G. Bowen, M. M. Chingos, and M. S. McPherson, *Crossing the Finish Line: Completing College at America's Public Universities* (Princeton, NJ: Princeton University Press, 2009).

16. Bowen et al., *Crossing the Finish Line.*

Chapter 1

1. S. Bowles and H. Gintis, *Schooling in Capitalist America* (New York: Basic Books, 1976); P. Bourdieu, "Cultural Reproduction and Social Reproduction," in *Power and Ideology in Education*, ed. J. Karabel and A. H. Hasley (New York: Oxford University Press, 1977); B. Bernstein, "Social Class, Language, and Socialization," in *Power and Ideology in Education*, ed. Karabel and Hasley; Paul E. Willis, *Learning to Labour: How Working Class Kids Get Working Class Jobs* (Farnborough, U.K.: Saxon House, 1977); S. Brice Heath, *Ways With Words* (Cambridge, U.K.: Cambridge University Press, 1983); H. A. Giroux, "Theories of Reproduction and Resistance in the New Sociology of Education," *Harvard Educational Review* 53 (1983): 257–293; J. MacLeod, *Ain't No Makin' It: Aspirations and Attainment in a Low-Income Neighborhood* (Boulder, CO: Westview, 1987).

2. R. D. Stanton-Salazar, *Manufacturing Hope and Despair: The School and Kin Support Networks of U.S.-Mexican Youth* (New York: Teachers College Press, 2001).

3. Stanton-Salazar, *Manufacturing Hope and Despair.*

4. C. Jencks, *Rethinking Social Policy: Race, Poverty, and the Underclass* (New York: Harper Perennial, 1993).

5. R. D. Stanton-Salazar, "A Social Capital Framework for Understanding the Socialization of Racial Minority Children and Youths," *Harvard Educational Review* 67 (1997): 1–40.

6. M. Ceja, "Understanding the Role of Parents and Siblings as Information Sources in the College Choice Process of Chicana Students," *Journal of College Student Development* 47, no. 1 (2006): 87–104; R. L. Farmer-Hinton and T. L. Adams, "Social Capital and College Preparation: Exploring the Role of Counselors in a College Prep School for Black Students," *Negro Educational Review* 57, no. 1–2 (2006): 101–116; P. Gandara, "Building Bridges to College," *Educational Leadership* 62, no. 3 (2004): 56–60; K. Gonzalez, C. Stoner, and J. Jovel, "Examining the Role of Social Capital in Access to College for Latinas," *Journal of Hispanic Higher Education* 2 (2003): 146–170; R. J. Noeth and G. L. Wimberly, *Creating Seamless Educational Transitions for Urban African American and Hispanic Students: ACT Policy Report (No. ED475197)* (Iowa City, IA: ACT, 2002); Stanton-Salazar, "A Social Capital Framework"; G. L. Wimberly and R. J. Noeth, *Schools Involving Parents in Early Postsecondary Planning* (Iowa City, IA: ACT, 2004).

7. Gonzalez et al., "Examining the Role of Social Capital."

8. Farmer-Hinton and Adams, "Social Capital and College Preparation."

9. McDonough, *Choosing Colleges*.

10. Stanton-Salazar, *Manufacturing Hope and Despair*.

11. Stanton-Salazar, *Manufacturing Hope and Despair*.

12. V. E. Lee and R. C. Croninger, *Elements of Social Capital in the Context of Six High Schools* (Washington, DC: Office of Educational Research and Improvement, 1999); V. E. Lee, B. A. Smerdon, C. Alfred-Liro, and S. L. Brown, "Inside Small and Large High Schools: Curriculum and Social Relations," *Educational Evaluation and Policy Analysis* 22, no. 2 (2000): 147–171.

13. R. Fry, *The High Schools Hispanics Attend: Size and Other Key Characteristics* (Washington, DC: Pew Hispanic Center, 2005); U.S. Department of Education, *The Condition of Education, 1995* (Washington, DC: National Center for Educational Statistics, 2003).

14. Ceja, "Understanding the Role of Parents and Siblings"; Z. B. Corwin, K. M. Venegas, P. Oliverez, and J. E. Colyar, "School Counsel: How Appropriate Guidance Affects Educational Equity," *Urban Education* 39, no. 4 (2004): 442–457; Gonzalez et al., "Examining the Role of Social Capital"; V. E. Lee and R. B. Ekstrom, "Student Access to Guidance Counseling in High School," *American Educational Research Journal* 24, no. 2 (1987): 287–310.

15. Ceja, "Understanding the Role of Parents and Siblings"; Corwin et al., "School Counsel."

16. Stanton-Salazar, *Manufacturing Hope and Despair*.

17. Stanton-Salazar, "A Social Capital Framework."

18. Bourdieu, "Cultural Reproduction and Social Reproduction."

19. Unless otherwise noted, quoted material from interviews in this book is from personal interviews conducted by the author. The names are pseudonyms.

20. McDonough, *Choosing Colleges*.

21. C. Adelman, *The Toolbox Revisited: Paths to Degree Completion from High School Through College* (Washington, DC: U.S. Department of Education, 2006); K. Akerhielm, J. Berger, M. Hooker, and D. Wise, *Factors Related to College Enrollment: Final Report* (Washington, DC: U.S. Department of Education, 1998); A. F. Cabrera and S. M. La Nasa, "Overcoming the Tasks on the Path to College for America's Disadvantaged," *New Directions for Institutional Research* 107 (2000): 31–44; I. Martin, J. Karabel, and S. W. Jaquez, "High School Segregation and Access to the University of California," *Educational Policy* 19, no. 2 (2005): 308–330; Jennie Oakes, *Keeping Track: How Schools Structure Inequality* (New Haven, CT: Yale University Press, 1985); Laura Perna, "Differences in the Decision to Attend College Among African Americans, Hispanics, and Whites," *Journal of Higher Education* 71 (2000): 117–141; P. Terenzini, A. Cabrera, and E. Bernal, *Swimming Against the Tide: The Poor in American Higher Education* (No. 2001-01) (New York: College Entrance Examination Board, 2001).

22. A. V. Cicourel and J. I. Kitsuse, *The Educational Decision Makers* (Indianapolis: Bobbs-Merrill, 1963); J. Gaskell, "Course Enrollment in the High School: The

Perspective of Working-Class Females," *Sociology of Education* 58 (1985): 48–59; MacLeod, *Ain't No Makin' It*; Willis, *Learning to Labour*.

23. Cabrera and La Nasa, "Overcoming the Tasks"; S. P. Choy, L. J. Horn, A. M. Nunez, and X. Chen, "Transition to College: What Helps At-Risk Students and Students Whose Parents Did Not Attend College," *New Directions for Institutional Research* 107 (2000): 45–63; K. Freeman, "Increasing African Americans' Participation in Higher Education: African American High-School Students' Perspectives," *Journal of Higher Education* 68 (1997): 523–550; K. Freeman, "The Race Factor in African Americans' College Choice," *Urban Education* 34, no. 1 (1999): 4–25; E. M. Horvat, "The Interactive Effects of Race and Class in Educational Research: Theoretical Insights from the Work of Pierre Bourdieu," *Penn GSE Perspectives on Urban Education* 2, no. 1 (2003), http://www.urbanedjournal.org/archive/index.html; K. Lynch and C. O'Riordan, "Inequality in Higher Education: A Study of Class Barriers," *British Journal of Sociology of Education* 19, no. 4 (1998): 445–478; Martin et al., "High School Segregation and Access"; McDonough, *Choosing Colleges*; Terenzini et al., *Swimming Against the Tide*; M. Walpole, P. M. McDonough, C. J. Bauer, C. Gibson, et al., "This Test Is Unfair: Urban African American and Latino High School Students' Perceptions of Standardized College Admission Tests," *Urban Education* 40, no. 3 (2005): 321–349.

24. Akerhielm et al., *Factors Related to College Enrollment*; K. Freeman, "Increasing African Americans' Participation in Higher Education"; K. Freeman, "The Race Factor in African Americans' College Choice"; MacLeod, *Ain't No Makin' It*; L. Tett, "Mature Working-Class Students in an 'Elite' University: Discourses of Risk, Choice, and Exclusion," *Studies in the Education of Adults* 36, no. 2 (2004): 252–264; Willis, *Learning to Labour*.

25. P. Bourdieu and J. C. Passeron, *Reproduction in Education, Society, and Culture* (London: Sage, 1977)

26. Akerhielm et al., *Factors Related to College Enrollment*; K. Freeman, "Increasing African Americans' Participation in Higher Education"; K. Freeman, "The Race Factor in African Americans' College Choice"; MacLeod, *Ain't No Makin' It*; L. Tett, "Mature Working-Class Students in an 'Elite' University: Discourses of Risk, Choice, and Exclusion."

27. D. Swartz, *Culture and Power: The Sociology of Pierre Bourdieu* (Chicago: University of Chicago Press, 1997).

28. K. Lynch and C. O'Neill, "The Colonisation of Social Class in Education," *British Journal of Sociology of Education* 15 (1994): 307–324.

29. Julie Bettie, *Women Without Class: Girls, Race, and Identity* (Berkeley: University of California Press, 2003).

30. Bourdieu and Passeron, *Reproduction in Education, Society, and Culture*; Lynch and O'Neill, "The Colonisation of Social Class."

31. These skills and knowledge are often referred to in the research literature as *educational cultural capital*.

Chapter 2

1. D. Hossler, J. Schmidt, and N. Vesper, *Going to College: How Social, Economic, and Educational Factors Influence the Decisions Students Make* (Baltimore: Johns Hopkins University Press, 1999); J. MacLeod, *Ain't No Makin' It: Aspirations and Attainment in a Low-Income Neighborhood* (Boulder, CO: Westview, 1987); P. McDonough, *Choosing Colleges: How Social Class and Schools Structure Opportunity* (Albany: State University of New York Press, 1997).

2. J. S. Coleman, "Social Capital in the Creation of Human Capital," *American Journal of Sociology* 94 (1988): S95–S120; G. L. Wimberly, "Links Between Social Capital and Educational Attainment Among African American Adolescents" (UMI No. 9965178), *Dissertation Abstracts International* 61, no. 2 (2000): 1172.

3. R. D. Stanton-Salazar, *Manufacturing Hope and Despair: The School and Kin Support Networks of U.S.-Mexican Youth* (New York: Teachers College Press, 2001).

4. Stanton-Salazar, *Manufacturing Hope and Despair.*

5. W. G. Tierney, T. Bailey, J. Constantine, N. Finkelstein, et al., *Helping Students Navigate the Path to College: What High Schools Can Do* (NCEE No. 2009-4066) (Washington, DC: National Center for Education Evaluation and Regional Assistance, Institute of Education Sciences, U. S. Department of Education, 2009).

6. A. W. Johnson, *An Evaluation of the Long-Term Impacts of the Sponsor-A-Scholar Program on Student Achievement* (Princeton, NJ: Mathematica Policy Research, 1998).

7. A. Schirm, E. Stuart, and A. McKie, *The Quantum Opportunity Program Demonstration: Final Impacts* (Princeton, NJ: Mathematica Policy Research, 2006); Johnson, *An Evaluation of the Long-Term Impacts.*

8. M. Ceja, "Understanding the Role of Parents and Siblings as Information Sources in the College Choice Process of Chicana Students," *Journal of College Student Development* 47, no. 1 (2006): 87–104; K. Gonzalez, C. Stoner, and J. Jovel, "Examining the Role of Social Capital in Access to College for Latinas," *Journal of Hispanic Higher Education* 2 (2003): 146–170.

9. Ceja, "Understanding the Role of Parents and Siblings."

10. P. A. Pérez and P. M. McDonough, "Understanding Latina and Latino College Choice: A Social Capital and Chain Migration Analysis," *Journal of Hispanic Higher Education* 7 (2008): 249–265.

11. Gonzalez et al., "Examining the Role of Social Capital."

12. Ceja, "Understanding the Role of Parents and Siblings."

13. G. L. Wimberly, *School Relationships Foster Success for African American Students* (Iowa City, IA: ACT, 2002).

14. C. Casteel, "Attitudes of African American and Caucasian Eighth Grade Students," *Elementary School Guidance and Counseling,* 34, no. 4 (1997): 262–272.

15. R. J. Noeth and G. L. Wimberly, *Creating Seamless Educational Transitions for Urban African American and Hispanic Students: ACT Policy Report* (No. ED475197) (Iowa City, IA: ACT, 2002); R. D. Stanton-Salazar, "A Social Capital Framework for

Understanding the Socialization of Racial Minority Children and Youths," *Harvard Educational Review* 67 (1997): 1–40.

16. C. A. Grant and C. E. Sleeter, "Race, Class, and Gender and Abandoned Dreams," *Teachers College Record* 90, no. 1 (1988): 19–40; F. A. Hrabowski, K. I. Maton, and G. L. Greif, *Beating the Odds: Raising Academically Successful African American Males* (New York: Oxford University Press, 1998); C. O'Connor, "Dreamkeeping in the Inner City: Diminishing the Divide Between Aspirations and Expectations," in *Coping With Poverty: The Social Contexts of Neighborhood, Work, and Family in the African-American Community*, ed. S. Danziger and A.C. Lin (Ann Arbor: The University of Michigan Press, 2000), 105–140.

Chapter 4

1. A. Lareau, *Unequal Childhoods: Class, Race, and Family Life* (Berkeley: University of California Press, 2003).

2. P. Bourdieu, "Cultural Reproduction and Social Reproduction," in *Power and Ideology in Education*, ed. J. Karabel and A. H. Hasley (New York: Oxford University Press, 1977).

Chapter 5

1. L. Horn and L. Bobbitt, *Mapping the Road to College: First-Generation Students' Math Track, Planning Strategies, and Context of Support* (Washington, DC: National Center for Education Statistics, 2000); P. M. McDonough, J. Korn, and E. Yamasaki, "Admissions Advantage for Sale: Private College Counselors and Students Who Use Them," *Review of Higher Education* 20 (1997): 297–317; P. Terenzini, L. Springer, P. Yaeger, E. Pascarella, et al., "First Generation College Students: Characteristics, Experiences, and Cognitive Development," *Research in Higher Education* 37 (1996): 1–22.

2. T. Howard, "'A Tug of War for Our Minds': African American High School Students' Perceptions of Their Academic Identities and College Aspirations," *High School Journal* 87 (2003): 4–17.

3. A. W. Astin and L. Oseguera, "The Declining 'Equity' of American Higher Education," *Review of Higher Education* 27, no. 3 (2004): 321–341; A. E. Cabrera, K. R. Burkum, and S. M. La Nasa, "Pathways to a Four-Year Degree: Determinants of Transfer and Degree Completion," in *College Student Retention: A Formula for Student Success*, ed. A. Seidman (Westport, CT: ACE/Praeger, 2005); A. F. Cabrera and S. M. La Nasa, "Overcoming the Tasks on the Path to College for America's Disadvantaged," *New Directions for Institutional Research* 107 (2000): 31–44; S. P. Choy, L. J. Horn, A. M. Nunez, and X. Chen, "Transition to College: What Helps At-Risk Students and Students Whose Parents Did Not Attend College," *New Directions for Institutional Research* 107 (2000): 45–63; K. Freeman, "Increasing African Americans' Participation in Higher Education: African American High-School Students' Perspectives," *Journal of Higher Education* 68 (1997): 523–550; K. Freeman, "The Race Factor in African Americans' College Choice," *Urban Education* 34, no. 1 (1999): 4–25; J. C. Hearn, "Pathways to

Attendance at the Elite Colleges," in *The High Status Track: Studies of Elite Schools and Stratification,* ed. P. W. Kingston and L. S. Lewis (Albany: State University of New York Press, 1990); J. C. Hearn, "Academic and Nonacademic Influences on the College Destinations of 1980 High School Graduates," *Sociology of Education* 64 (1991): 158–171; E. M. Horvat, "The Interactive Effects of Race and Class in Educational Research: Theoretical Insights from the Work of Pierre Bourdieu," *Penn GSE Perspectives on Urban Education* 2, no. 1 (2003), http://www.urbanedjournal.org/archive/index.html; J. Karabel and A. W. Astin, "Social Class, Academic Ability, and College Quality," *Social Forces* 53, no. 3 (1975): 381–398; D. Karen, "The Politics of Class, Race, and Gender: Access to Higher Education in the United States, 1960–1986," *American Journal of Education* 99, no. 2 (1991): 208–237; K. Lynch and C. O'Riordan, "Inequality in Higher Education: A Study of Class Barriers," *British Journal of Sociology of Education* 19, no. 4 (1998): 445–478; I. Martin, J. Karabel, and S. W. Jaquez, "High School Segregation and Access to the University of California," *Educational Policy* 19, no. 2 (2005): 308–330; P. McDonough, *Choosing Colleges: How Social Class and Schools Structure Opportunity* (Albany: State University of New York Press, 1997); P. Terenzini, A. Cabrera, and E. Bernal, *Swimming Against the Tide: The Poor in American Higher Education* (New York: College Entrance Examination Board, 2001); V. Tinto, "Research and Practice of Student Retention: What's Next?" *Journal of College Student Retention* 8, no. 1 (2006): 1–19; M. A. Titus, "No College Student Left Behind: The Influence of Financial Aspects of a State's Higher Education Policy on College Completion," *Review of Higher Education* 29, no. 3 (2006): 293–317; M. Walpole, P. M. McDonough, C. J. Bauer, C. Gibson, et al., "This Test Is Unfair: Urban African American and Latino High School Students' Perceptions of Standardized College Admission Tests," *Urban Education* 40, no. 3 (2005): 321–349.

4. Astin and Oseguera, "Declining 'Equity,'"; L. E. Gladieux and W. S. Swail, *Financial Aid Is Not Enough: Improving the Odds of College Success* (Princeton, NJ: College Board, 1998); M. S. McPherson and M. O. Schapiro, *Keeping College Affordable: Government and Educational Opportunity* (Washington, DC: Brookings Institute, 1991).

5. C. Adelman, *The Toolbox Revisited: Paths to Degree Completion from High School Through College* (Washington, DC: U.S. Department of Education, 2006); K. Akerhielm, J. Berger, M. Hooker, and D. Wise, *Factors Related to College Enrollment: Final Report* (Washington, DC: U.S. Department of Education, 1998).

6. M. Walpole, "Social Mobility and College: Low SES Students' Experiences and Outcomes of College," *Review of Higher Education* 27, no. 1 (2003): 45–73.

7. H. G. Segal, D. K. DeMeis, G. A. Wood, and H. L. Smith, "Assessing Future Possible Selves by Gender and Socioeconomic Status Using the Anticipated Life History Measure," *Journal of Personality* 69, no. 1 (2001): 57–87.

8. E. T. Pascarella, C. T. Pierson, G. C. Wolniak, and P. T. Terenzini, "First-Generation College Students: Additional Evidence on College Experiences and Outcomes," *Journal of Higher Education* 75, no. 3 (2004): 249–284; M. B. Paulsen and E. P. St. John, "Social Class and College Costs: Examining the Financial Nexus Between College

Choice and Persistence," *Journal of Higher Education* 73, no. 2 (2002): 189–236; G. R. Pike and G. D. Kuh, "First- and Second-Generation College Students: A Comparison of Their Engagement and Intellectual Development," *Journal of Higher Education* 76 (2005): 276–300.

9. Gladieux and Swail, *Financial Aid Is Not Enough*; K. A. Goyette and A. L. Mullen, "Who Studies the Arts and Sciences? Social Background and the Choice and Consequences of Undergraduate Field of Study," *Journal of Higher Education* 77, no. 3 (2006): 497–538. ; Paulsen and St. John, "Social Class and College Costs"; W. S. Swail, A. F. Cabrera, and C. Lee, *Latino Youth and the Pathway to College* (Washington, DC: Pew Hispanic Center, 2004); Terenzini, Cabrera, and Bernal, *Swimming Against the Tide*; Tinto, "Research and Practice of Student Retention"; Titus, "No College Student Left Behind"; Walpole, "Social Mobility and College."

10. A. Masten, "Ordinary Magic: Resilience Processes in Development," *American Psychologist* 56, no. 3 (2001): 227–238; F. Redl, "Adolescents—Just How Do They React?" in *Adolescence: Psychosocial Perspectives,* ed. G. Caplan and S. Lebovici (New York: Basic Books, 1969), 79–99.

11. S. Alva, "Academic Invulnerability Among Mexican American Students: The Importance of Protective Resources and Appraisals," in *Hispanic Psychology: Critical Issues in Theory and Research,* ed. A. Padilla (Thousand Oaks, CA: Sage, 1995), 288–302.

12. R. D. Stanton-Salazar and S. U. Spina, "The Network Orientations of Highly Resilient Urban Minority Youth: A Network-Analytic Account of Minority Socialization and Its Educational Implications," *Urban Review* 32, no. 3 (2000): 227–261.

13. J. Garbarino, N. Dubrow, K. Kostelny, and C. Pardo, *Children in Danger: Coping With the Consequences of Community Violence* (San Francisco: Jossey-Bass, 1992).

14. M. Rutter, "Psychosocial Adversity: Risk, Resilience and Recovery," in *The Context of Youth Violence: Resilience, Risk and Protection,* ed. J. Richman and M. Fraser (Westport, CT: Praeger, 2001), 13–41; E. Werner and R. Smith, *Overcoming the Odds: High-risk Children from Birth to Adulthood* (Ithaca, NY: Cornell University Press, 1992).

15. C. Bassani, "Five Dimensions of Social Capital Theory as They Pertain to Youth Studies," *Journal of Youth Studies* 10, no. 1 (2007): 17–34; R. D. Stanton-Salazar and S. U. Spina, "Adolescent Peer Networks as a Context for Social and Emotional Support," *Youth & Society* 36, no. 4 (2005): 379–417; J. L. Terrion, "Building Social Capital in Vulnerable Families: Success Markers of a School-Based Intervention Program," *Youth & Society* 38, no. 2 (2006): 155–176.

16. R. Lapan and K. Harrington, *Paving the Road to College: How School Counselors Help Students Succeed* (Amherst, MA: Center for School Counseling Outcome Research, 2010).

17. F. A. Rowe, "College Students' Perceptions of High School Counselors," *School Counselor* 36 (1989): 260–264.

18. M. M. Gibbons, L. D. Borders, M. E. Wiles, J. B. Stephan, et al., "Career and College Planning Needs of Ninth Graders—as Reported by Ninth Graders," *Professional School Counseling* 10, no. 2 (2006): 168–178; A. Venezia and M. W. Kirst, "Ineq-

uitable Opportunities: How Current Education Systems and Policies Undermine the Chances for Student Persistence and Success in College," *Educational Policy* 19, no. 2 (2005): 283–307.

19. E. R. Matthay, "A Critical Study of the College Selection Process," *School Counselor* 36 (1989): 359–370.

20. P. M. McDonough, "Counseling Matters," in *Preparing for College: Nine Elements of Effective Outreach,* ed. W. G. Tierney, Z. B. Corwin, and J. Colyar (New York: State University of New York Press, 2005), 69–88; L. W. Perna, H. T. Rowan-Kenyon, S. L. Thomas, A. Bell, et al., "The Role of College Counseling in Shaping College Opportunity: Variations Across High Schools," *Review of Higher Education* 31 (2008): 131–159.

21. Lapan and Harrington, *Paving the Road to College.*

22. A. M. Nuñez and S. Cuccaro-Alamin, *First-Generation Students: Undergraduates Whose Parents Never Enrolled in College* (Washington, DC: National Center for Education Statistics, 1998); V. B. Saenz, S. Hurtado, D. Barrera, D. Wolf, et al., *First in My Family: A Profile of First-Generation College Students at Four-Year Institutions Since 1971* (Los Angeles: UCLA Higher Education Research Institute, 2007).

23. J. Oakes, J. Rogers, D. Silver, S. Valladares, et al., *Removing the Roadblocks: Fair College Opportunities for All California Students* (Los Angeles: UC All Campus Consortium for Research on Diversity and UCLA IDEA, 2006); P. A. Pérez and P. M. McDonough, "Understanding Latina and Latino College Choice: A Social Capital and Chain Migration Analysis," *Journal of Hispanic Higher Education* 7 (2008): 249–265.

24. L. D. Hill, "School Strategies and the 'College-Linking' Process: Reconsidering the Effects of High Schools on College Enrollment," *Sociology of Education* 81 (2008): 53–76; McDonough, "Counseling Matters."

25. American School Counselor Association, *K–12 Student to School Counselor Ratios: 2005–2006* (Alexandria, VA: ASCA, 2008); W. R. Fitzsimmons, "Risky Business," *Harvard* (1991): 23–29.

26. Pérez and McDonough, "Understanding Latina and Latino College Choice."

27. American School Counselor Association, *The ASCA National Model: A Framework for School Counseling Programs* (Washington, DC: ASCA, 2003); Education Trust, *Challenging the Myths: Rethinking the Role of School Counselors,* 2003, http://www2.edtrust.org/NR/rdonlyres/0EF57A7F-B336-46A8-898D-981018AFBF11/0/counseling_train_broch.pdf.

28. J. Lewis, M. S. Arnold, R. House, and R. L. Toporek, *ACA Advocacy Competencies* (Alexandria, VA: American Counseling Association, 2003).

29. D. Brown and J. Trusty, "Advocacy Competencies and the Advocacy Process," in *Designing and Leading Comprehensive School Counseling Programs: Promoting Student Competence and Meeting Student Needs,* ed. D. Brown and J. Trusty (Belmont, CA: Thomson Brooks/Cole J., 2005), 264–285.

30. R. Perusse, G. E. Goodnough, J. Donegan, and C. Jones, "Perceptions of School Counselors and School Principals About the National Standards for School Counseling

Programs and the Transforming School Counseling Initiative," *Professional School Counseling* 7, no. 3 (2004): 152–161.

31. C. A. Grant and C. E. Sleeter, "Race, Class, and Gender and Abandoned Dreams," *Teachers College Record* 90, no. 1 (1988): 19–40; F. A. Hrabowski, K. I. Maton, and G. L. Greif, *Beating the Odds: Raising Academically Successful African American Males* (New York: Oxford University Press, 1998); C. O'Connor, "Dreamkeeping in the Inner City: Diminishing the Divide Between Aspirations and Expectations," in *Coping with Poverty: The Social Contexts of Neighborhood, Work, and Family in the African-American Community*, ed. S. Danziger and A. C. Lin (Ann Arbor: University of Michigan Press, 2000), 105–140.

32. J. J. Irvine and R. W. Irvine, "Black Youth in School: Individual Achievement and Institutional Cultural Perspectives," in *African American Youth: Their Social and Economic Status in the United States* ed. R. Taylor (Westport, CT: Praeger, 1995); J. J. Irvine, *Black Students and School Failure: Policies, Practices, and Prescriptions* (Westport, CT: Greenwood Press, 1990); V. C. Polite, "Combating Educational Neglect in Suburbia: African American Males and Mathematics," in *African American Males in School and Society*, ed. V. C. Polite and J. E. Davis (New York: Teachers College Press, 1999), 97–107.

33. A. W. Astin, *Four Critical Years: Effects of College on Beliefs, Attitudes, and Knowledge* (San Francisco: Jossey-Bass, 1977); A. W. Astin, *What Matters in College? Four Critical Years Revisited* (San Francisco: Jossey-Bass, 1993); A. F. Cabrera, C. L. Colbeck, and P. T. Terenzini, "Developing Performance Indicators for Assessing Classroom Teaching Practices and Student Learning: The Case of Engineering," *Research in Higher Education* 42, no. 3 (2001): 327–352; T. A. Campbell and D. E. Campbell, "Faculty/Student Mentor Program: Effects on Academic Performance and Retention," *Research in Higher Education* 38, no. 6 (1997): 727–742; J. Endo and R. Harpel, "The Effect of Student–Faculty Interaction on Students' Educational Outcomes," *Research in Higher Education* 16, no. 2 (1982): 115–138; J. Ishiyama, "Does Early Participation in Undergraduate Research Benefit Social Science and Humanities Students?" *College Student Journal* 36 (2002): 380–386; G. D. Kuh, "The Other Curriculum: Out-Of-Class Experiences Associated with Student Learning and Personal Development," *Journal of Higher Education* 66, no. 2 (1995): 123–155; G. D. Kuh and S. Hu, "The Effects of Student–Faculty Interaction in the 1990s," *Review of Higher Education* 24, no. 3 (2001): 309–332; M. A. Lamport, "Student–Faculty Informal Interaction and the Effect on College Student Outcomes: A Review of the Literature," *Adolescence* 28 (1993): 971–990; E. T. Pascarella, "Student–Faculty Informal Contact and College Outcomes," *Review of Educational Research* 50, no. 4 (1980): 545–595; E. T. Pascarella, "Students' Affective Development Within the College Environment," *Journal of Higher Education* 56, no. 6 (1985): 640–663; E. T. Pascarella and P. T. Terenzini, "Informal Interaction with Faculty and Freshman Ratings of Academic and Nonacademic Experience of College," *Journal of Educational Research* 70 (1976): 35–41; L. C. Strauss and P. T. Terenzini, "The Effects of Students' In- and Out-Of-Class Experiences on Their Analytical

and Group Skills: A Study of Engineering Education," *Research in Higher Education* 48, no. 8 (2007): 967–992; P. T. Terenzini, E. T. Pascarella, and G. S. Blimling, "Students' Out-Of-Class Experiences and Their Influence on Learning and Cognitive Development: A Literature Review," *Journal of College Student Development* 40 (1999): 610–622; M. D. Thompson, "Informal Student–Faculty Interaction: Its Relationship to Educational Gains in Science and Mathematics Among Community College Students," *Community College Review* 29, no. 1 (2001): 35–57; J. F. Volkwein, M. C. King, and P. T. Terenzini, "Student–Faculty Relationships and Intellectual Growth Among Transfer Students," *Journal of Higher Education* 57, no. 4 (1986): 413–430.

34. Pascarella, "Student–Faculty Informal Contact."

35. E. T. Pascarella and P. T. Terenzini, *How College Affects Students, Vol. 2: A Third Decade of Research* (San Francisco: Jossey-Bass, 2005).

36. C. A. Lundberg and L. A. Schreiner, "Quality and Frequency of Faculty–Student Interaction as Predictors of Learning: An Analysis of Student Race/Ethnicity," *Journal of College Student Development* 45, no. 5 (2004): 549–565; J. Chang, "Faculty–Student Interaction at the Community College: A Focus on Students of Color," *Research in Higher Education* 46, no. 7 (2005): 769–802; D. Cole, "Do Interracial Interactions Matter? An Examination of Student–Faculty Contact and Intellectual Self-Concept," *Journal of Higher Education* 78, no. 3 (2006): 249–281; Kuh and Hu, "Effects of Student–Faculty Interaction."

37. Y. K. Kim and L. J. Sax, "Student–Faculty Interaction in Research Universities: Differences by Student Gender, Race, Social Class, and First-Generation Status," *Research in Higher Education* 50 (2009): 437–459.

38. Kim and Sax, "Student–Faculty Interaction in Research Universities."

39. B. W. Packard, "Student Training Promotes Mentoring Awareness and Action," *Career Development Quarterly* 51, no. 4 (2003): 335–345; D. Pulsford, K. Boit, and S. Owen, "Are Mentors Ready to Make a Difference? A Survey of Mentors' Attitudes Towards Nurse Education," *Nurse Education Today* 22, no. 6 (2002): 439–446.

40. T. Beyene, M. Anglin, W. Sanchez, and M. Ballou, "Mentoring and Relational Mutuality: Proteges' Perspectives," *Journal of Humanistic Counseling, Education and Development* 41, no. 1 (2002): 87–102; W. Lee, "Striving Toward Effective Retention: The Effect of Race on Mentoring African American Students," *Peabody Journal of Education* 74, no. 2 (1999): 27–43.

41. B. Smith, "Accessing Social Capital Through the Academic Mentoring Process," *Equity & Excellence in Education* 40, no. 1 (2007): 36–46.

42. C. Hudley, R. Moschetti, A. Gonzalez, S. Cho, et al., "College Freshmen's Perceptions of Their High School Experiences," *Journal of Advanced Academics* 20, no. 3 (2009): 438–471.

43. Adelman, *Toolbox Revisited*; M. Martinez and S. Klopott, *The Link Between High School Reform and College Access and Success for Low-Income and Minority Youth* (Washington, DC: American Youth Policy Forum and Pathways to College Network, 2005);

R. J. Noeth and G. L. Wimberly, *Creating Seamless Educational Transitions for Urban African American and Hispanic Students: ACT Policy Report* (No. ED475197) (Iowa City, IA: ACT, 2002).

44. M. J. Reid and J. L. Moore, "College Readiness and Academic Preparation for Postsecondary Education: Oral Histories of First-Generation Urban College Students," *Urban Education* 43, no. 2 (2008): 240–261.

Chapter 6

1. C. A. Grant and C. E. Sleeter, "Race, Class, and Gender and Abandoned Dreams," *Teachers College Record* 90, no. 1 (1988): 19–40; F. A. Hrabowski, K. I. Maton, and G. L. Greif, *Beating the Odds: Raising Academically Successful African American Males* (New York: Oxford University Press, 1998); C. O'Connor, "Dreamkeeping in the Inner City: Diminishing the Divide Between Aspirations and Expectations," in *Coping with Poverty: The Social Contexts of Neighborhood, Work, and Family in the African-American Community*, ed. S. Danziger and A. C. Lin (Ann Arbor: University of Michigan Press, 2000), 105–140

2. National Association of Secondary School Principals, *Breaking Ranks: Changing an American Institution* (Reston, VA: NASSA, 1996); National Association of Secondary School Principals, *What the Research Shows: Breaking Ranks in Action* (Reston, VA: NASSA, 2002).

3. National Association of Secondary School Principals, *Breaking Ranks*; National Association of Secondary School Principals, *What the Research Shows.*

4. R. J. Noeth and G. L. Wimberly, *Creating Seamless Educational Transitions for Urban African American and Hispanic Students: ACT Policy Report* (No. ED475197) (Iowa City, IA: ACT, 2002).

5. National Association of Secondary School Principals, *What the Research Shows.*

6. P. Bourdieu, "The Forms of Capital," in *Handbook of Theory for Research in the Sociology of Education,* ed. J. E. Richardson (Westport, CT: Greenwood Press, 1986).

7. S. Sutton, "Advocacy and Social Scaffolding: A Paradigm for Motivating Underachieving Students" (Dissertation, Claremont Graduate University and San Diego State University, 1998).

8. D. F. Bailey, Y. Q. Getch, and S. F. Chen-Hayes, "Professional School Counselors as Social and Academic Advocates," in *Transforming the School Counseling Profession*, ed. B. T. Erford (Upper Saddle River, NJ: Merrill Education/Prentice, 2003), 411–434; F. Bemak and R. C. Chung, "Advocacy as a Critical Role for Urban School Counselors: Working Toward Equity and Social Justice," *Professional School Counseling* 8, no. 3 (2005): 196–202; R. M. House and R. L. Hayes, "School Counselors: Becoming Key Players in School Reform," *Professional School Counseling* 5, no. 4 (2002): 249–256; R. M. House and P. J. Martin, "Advocating for Better Futures for All Students: A New Vision for School Counselors," *Education* 119, no. 2 (1998): 284.

9. K. Schaeffer, P. Akos, and J. Barrow, "A Phenomenological Study of High School Counselor Advocacy as It Relates to the College Access of Underrepresented Stu-

dents," *Journal of School Counseling* 8, no. 2 (2010), http://www.jsc.montana.edu/articles/v8n2.pdf.

10. Schaeffer, Akos, and Barrow, "Phenomenological Study."

11. J. E. Rosenbaum, *Beyond College for All* (New York: Russell Sage, 2001).

12. Schaeffer, Akos, and Barrow, "Phenomenological Study."

13. Bemak and Chung, "Advocacy as a Critical Role"; House and Martin, "Advocating for Better Futures."

14. J. E. Field and S. Baker, "Defining and Examining School Counselor Advocacy," *Professional School Counseling* 8, no. 1 (2004): 56–63.

15. R. Perusse, G. E. Goodnough, J. Donegan, and C. Jones, "Perceptions of School Counselors and School Principals About the National Standards for School Counseling Programs and the Transforming School Counseling Initiative," *Professional School Counseling* 7, no. 3 (2004): 152–161.

16. F. Bemak and R. C. Chung, "New Professional Roles and Advocacy Strategies for School Counselors: A Multicultural/Social Justice Perspective to Move Beyond the Nice Counselor Syndrome," *Journal of Counseling & Development* 86, no. 3 (2008): 372–382.

Chapter 7

1. P. McDonough, *Choosing Colleges: How Social Class and Schools Structure Opportunity* (Albany: State University of New York Press, 1997); R. J. Noeth and G. L. Wimberly, *Creating Seamless Educational Transitions for Urban African American and Hispanic Students: ACT Policy Report* (No. ED475197) (Iowa City, IA: ACT, 2002).

2. W. G. Tierney, T. Bailey, J. Constantine, N. Finkelstein, et al., *Helping Students Navigate the Path to College: What High Schools Can Do* (NCEE No. 2009-4066) (Washington, DC: National Center for Education Evaluation and Regional Assistance, Institute of Education Sciences, U. S. Department of Education, 2009).

3. R. D. Stanton-Salazar, *Manufacturing Hope and Despair: The School and Kin Support Networks of U.S.-Mexican Youth* (New York: Teachers College Press, 2001).

4. R. D. Hahn and D. Price, *Promise Lost: College-Qualified Students Who Don't Enroll in College* (Washington, DC: Institute for Higher Education Policy, 2008); P. M. McDonough, "Counseling Matters," in *Preparing for College: Nine Elements of Effective Outreach,* ed. W. G. Tierney, Z. B. Corwin, and J. Colyar (New York: State University of New York Press, 2005), 69–88.

5. Hahn and Price, *Promise Lost.*

6. A. Levine and J. Nidiffer, *Beating the Odds: How the Poor Get to College* (San Francisco: Jossey-Bass, 1996).

7. M. Walpole, "Social Mobility and College: Low SES Students' Experiences and Outcomes of College," *Review of Higher Education* 27, no. 1 (2003): 45–73.

8. M. J. Reid and J. L. Moore, "College Readiness and Academic Preparation for Postsecondary Education: Oral Histories of First-Generation Urban College Students," *Urban Education* 43, no. 2 (2008): 240–261.

Chapter 8

1. P. Gandara and D. Bial, *Paving the Way to Postsecondary Education: K–12 Intervention Programs for Underrepresented Youth* (Washington, DC: U.S. Department of Education, 2001); L. W. Perna, "Precollege Outreach Programs: Characteristics of Programs Serving Historically Underrepresented Groups of Students," *Journal of College Student Development* 43 (2002): 64–83.

2. W. S. Swail and L. W. Perna, *Outreach Program Handbook* (Washington, DC: College Board, 2001).

3. T. Domina, "What Works in College Outreach: Assessing Targeted and School-wide Interventions for Disadvantaged Students," *Educational Evaluation and Policy Analysis* 31, no. 2 (2009): 127–152.

4. For minority students, see B. Macy, *From Rusty Wire Fences to Wrought-Iron Gates: How the Poor Succeed in Getting to and Through College* (Washington, DC: The College Board, 2000); Gandara and Bial, *Paving the Way*; J. H. Vargas, *College Knowledge: Addressing Information Barriers to College* (Boston: Education Resources Institute, 2004). For at-risk students, see L. Horn and X. Chen, *Toward Resiliency: At-Risk Students Who Make It to College* (Washington, DC: U.S. Department of Education, 1998).

5. J. L. Schultz and D. Mueller, *Effectiveness of Programs to Improve Postsecondary Education Enrollment and Success of Underrepresented Youth: A Literature Review* (St. Paul, MN: Wilder Research, 2006).

6. L. W. Perna and W. S. Swail, "Pre-College Outreach and Early Intervention Programs," in *Condition of Access: Higher Education for Lower Income Students,* ed. D. E. Heller (Westport, CT: American Council on Education and Praeger Publishers, 2002), 97–112; W. S. Swail, *Educational Opportunity and the Role of Pre-College Outreach Programs: College Board Outreach Program Handbook* (Washington, DC: Educational Policy Institute, 2001), http://www.educationalpolicy.org/pdf/OutreachHandbookEssays.pdf.

7. J. Groutt, "Milestones of TRIO History: Part I," *Opportunity Outlook: The Journal of the Council for Opportunity in Education, TRIO History Short Papers* (Washington, DC: National TRIO Clearinghouse, 2003), http://www.pellinstitute.org/Clearinghouse/shared/2_Grout_Article.pdf.

8. Gandara and Bial, *Paving the Way*; Schultz and Mueller, *Effectiveness of Programs.*

9. Perna, "Precollege Outreach Programs: Characteristics."

10. S. Burd, "Programs for Disadvantaged Students Feud over Their Futures," *Chronicle of Higher Education* 49, no. 27 (2003): A21–A22; J. H. Blake, "The Full Circle: TRIO Programs, Higher Education and the American Future: Toward a New Vision of Democracy," *Journal of Negro Education* 67, no. 4 (1998): 329–332; R. H. Fenske, C. A. Geranios, J. E. Keller, and D. E. Moore, "Early Intervention Programs: Opening the Door to Higher Education," *ASHE-ERIC Higher Education Report* 25, no. 6 (1997); A. Laguardia, "A Survey of School/College Partnerships for Minority and Disadvantaged Students," *Urban Review* 30, no. 2 (1998): 167–186; E. J. McElroy and M. Armesto, "Trio and Upward Bound: History, Programs, and Issues—Past, Pres-

ent, and Future," *Journal of Negro Education* 67, no. 4 (1999): 373–380; L. W. Perna and W. S. Swail, "Pre-College Outreach and Early Intervention Programs: An Approach to Achieving Equal Educational Opportunity," *Thought and Action* 17, no. 1 (2001): 99–110; W. S. Swail, "Preparing America's Disadvantaged for College: Programs That Increase College Opportunity," *New Directions for Institutional Research* 107 (2000): 85–102; W. G. Tierney and A. Jun, "A University Helps Prepare Low Income Youths for College: Tracking School Success," *Journal of Higher Education* 72 (2001): 205–225.

11. E. J. Balz and M. R. Esten, "Fulfilling Private Dreams, Serving Public Priorities: An Analysis of TRIO Students' Success at Independent Colleges and Universities," *Journal of Negro Education* 67, no. 4 (1998): 333–345; G. T. McLure and R. L. Child, "Upward Bound Students Compared to Other College-Bound Students: Profiles of Nonacademic Characteristics and Academic Achievement," *Journal of Negro Education* 67, no. 4 (1998): 346–363.

12. Fenske et al., "Early Intervention Programs"; E. P. Bettinger and B. T Long, "Addressing the Needs of Under-Prepared Students in Higher Education: Does College Remediation Work?" *Journal of Human Resources* 44, no. 3 (2009).

13. T. Domina, "Higher Education Policy as Secondary School Reform: Texas Public High Schools After Hopwood," *Educational Evaluation and Policy Analysis* 29 (2007): 200–217; Gandara and Bial, *Paving the Way*.

14. W. Rhodes, L. Truitt, and A. Martinez, *A National Evaluation of the "I Have A Dream" Program* (Cambridge, MA: Abt Associates, 2006).

15. J. D. Fitts, *A Comparison of Locus of Control and Achievement Among Remedial Summer Bridge and Non-Bridge Students in Community Colleges in New Jersey* (Trenton: New Jersey Department of Higher Education, 1989), ERIC Document Reproduction Service No. ED315102; C. R. Logan, J. Salisbury-Glennon, and L. D. Spence, "The Learning Edge Academic Program: Toward a Community of Learners," *Journal of the First-Year Experience and Students in Transition* 12, no. 1 (2000): 77–104; Perna and Swail, "Pre-College Outreach and Early Intervention Programs," in *Condition of Access*; Perna and Swail, "Pre-College Outreach and Early Intervention: An Approach"; M. Valeri-Gold, M. P. Deming, and K. Stone, "The Bridge: A Summer Enrichment Program to Retain African-American Collegians," *Journal of the First-Year Experience and Students in Transition* 4, no. 2 (1992): 101–117.

16. P. Garcia, "Summer Bridge: Improving Retention Rates for Underprepared Students," *Journal of the First-Year Experience and Students in Transition* 3, no. 2 (1991): 91–105; R. Evans, "A Comparison of Success Indicators for Program and Nonprogram Participants in a Community College Summer Bridge Program for Minority Students," *Visions* 2, no. 2 (1999): 6–14; M. Obler, K. Francis, and R. Wishengrad, "Combining of Traditional Counseling, Instruction, and Mentoring Functions with Academically Deficient College Freshmen," *Journal of Educational Research* 70, no. 3 (2001): 142–147; E. T. Pascarella and P. T. Terenzini, *How College Affects Students, Vol. 2: A Third Decade of Research* (San Francisco: Jossey-Bass, 2005).

17. S. P. Ackermann, "The Benefits of Summer Bridge Programs for Underrepresented and Low-Income Students," *College and University* 66, no. 4 (1991): 201–208; Fitts, *Comparison of Locus of Control*.

18. Ackermann, "Benefits of Summer Bridge"; Garcia, "Summer Bridge: Improving Retention"; McLure and Child, "Upward Bound Students"; J. Suhr, *Study of the 1978 Summer Step: The Summer "Bridge" Program at the Learning Skills Center, University of California, Davis* (Davis: University of California, Office of Student Affairs Research and Evaluation, 1980), Eric Document Reproduction Service No. ED256275.

19. Fitts, *Comparison of Locus of Control*.

20. Gandara and Bial, *Paving the Way*.

21. Horn and Chen, *Toward Resiliency*.

22. Domina, "What Works in College Outreach."

23. Schultz and Mueller, *Effectiveness of Programs*.

24. Gandara and Bial, *Paving the Way*.

25. M. Martinez and S. Klopott, *The Link Between High School Reform and College Access and Success for Low-Income and Minority Youth* (Washington, DC: American Youth Policy Forum and Pathways to College Network, 2005).

26. L. Perna, "Differences in the Decision to Attend College Among African Americans, Hispanics, and Whites," *Journal of Higher Education* 71 (2000): 117–141.

27. A. F. Cabrera and S. M. La Nasa, "On the Path to College: Three Critical Tasks Facing America's Disadvantaged," *Research in Higher Education* 42, no. 2 (2001): 119–149.

28. D. Hossler, J. Schmidt, and N. Vesper, *Going to College: How Social, Economic, and Educational Factors Influence the Decisions Students Make* (Baltimore: Johns Hopkins University Press, 1999).

29. A. Levine and J. Nidiffer, *Beating the Odds: How the Poor Get to College* (San Francisco: Jossey-Bass, 1996).

30. Schultz and Mueller, *Effectiveness of Programs*.

31. Schultz and Mueller, *Effectiveness of Programs*.

32. Z. B. Corwin, J. E. Colyar, and W. G. Tierney, "Introduction: Engaging Research and Practice—Extracurricular and Curricular Influences on College Access," in *Preparing for College: Nine Elements of Effective Outreach*, ed. W. G. Tierney, Z. B. Corwin, and J. E. Colyar (Albany: State University of New York Press, 2005), 1–9; Levine and Nidiffer, *Beating the Odds*; Perna, "Precollege Outreach Programs: Characteristics."

33. Cabrera and La Nasa, "On the Path to College"; Perna and Swail, "Pre-College Outreach and Early Intervention," in *Condition of Access*.

34. Gandara and Bial, *Paving the Way*.

35. Schultz and Mueller, *Effectiveness of Programs*.

36. Perna, "Precollege Outreach Programs: Characteristics"; Corwin and Colyar, *Preparing for College*; W. S. Swail and L. W. Perna, "Pre-College Outreach Programs: A National Perspective," in *Increasing Access to College*, ed. W. G. Tierney and L. S. Hagedorn (Albany: State University of New York Press, 2002), 15–34.

37. Gandara and Bial, *Paving the Way*.

38. Martinez and Klopott, *Link Between High School Reform*.

39. Gandara and Bial, *Paving the Way*.

40. Schultz and Mueller, *Effectiveness of Programs*.

41. J. Engle, A. Bermeo, and C. O'Brien, *Straight from the Source: What Works for First-Generation College Students* (Washington, DC: Pell Institute for the Study of Opportunity in Higher Education, 2006).

42. All outreach programs discussed in this chapter have been given pseudonyms.

43. Engle et al., *Straight from the Source*.

44. Engle et al., *Straight from the Source*.

Chapter 9

1. M. W. Kirst, "The High School/College Disconnect," *Education Leadership* 62, no. 3 (2004): 51–55.

2. M. Kirst, A. L. Antonio, and A. C. Bueschel, "Improving the Transition from High School to Postsecondary Education" (working paper, series 04-1, Policy Analysis for California Education, University of California, Berkeley, 2004), http://gse.berkeley.edu/research/pace/reports/WP.04 1.pdf.

3. A. Berger, N. Adelman, and S. Cole, "The Early College High School Initiative: An Overview of Five Evaluation Years," *Peabody Journal Of Education* 85 (2010): 333–347.

4. American Institutes for Research and SRI International, *Fifth Annual Early College High School Initiative Evaluation Synthesis Report: Six Years and Counting: The ECHSI Matures* (Washington, DC: American Institutes for Research, 2009).

5. Berger et al., "Early College High School Initiative."

6. J. E. Kim and E. A. Barnett, *2006–07 MCNC Early College High School Students: Participation and Performance in College Coursework* (New York: National Center for Restructuring Schools, Education, and Teaching, Teachers College, Columbia University, 2008).

7. American Institutes for Research and SRI International, *Early College High School Initiative Evaluation Year-End Report: 2003–2004* (Washington, DC: American Institutes for Research, 2005).

8. Berger et al., "Early College High School Initiative."

9. K. L. Hughes, M. M. Karp, B. J. Fermin, and T. R. Bailey, *Pathways to College Access and Success* (Washington, DC: U.S. Department of Education, Office of Vocational and Adult Education, 2005).

10. P. B. Campbell, E. Wahl, M. Slater, E. Iler, et al., "Paths to Success: An Evaluation of the Gateway to Higher Education Program," *Journal of Women and Minorities in Science and Engineering* 4, no. 2–3 (1998): 297–308.

11. A. Hahn, T. Leavitt, and P. Aaron, *Evaluation of the Quantum Opportunities Program (QOP): Did the Program Work? A Report on the Postsecondary Outcomes and Cost-Effectiveness of the QOP Program (1989–1993)* (Waltham, MA: Brandeis University, Heller Graduate School, 1994), http://eric.ed.gov/ERICDocs/data/ericdocs2sql/content_storage_01/0000019b/80/14/1b/89.pdf.

12. A. W. Johnson, *An Evaluation of the Long-Term Impacts of the Sponsor-a-Scholar Program on Student Achievement* (Princeton, NJ: Mathematica Policy Research, 1998).

13. D. Chaplin, M. Bleeker, and C. Smither, *Rigorous Evaluation of Roads to Success: Design Report* (Washington, DC: Mathematica Policy Research, 2009).

14. D. Chaplin, M. Bleeker, and K. Booker, *Roads to Success: Estimated Impacts of an Education and Career Planning Program During Middle School* (Washington, DC: Mathematica Policy Research, 2010).

15. J. E. Howell, "Especially for High School Teachers," *Journal of Chemical Education* 78, no. 12 (2001): 1569.

16. P. Gandara and D. Bial, *Paving the Way to Postsecondary Education: K–12 Intervention Programs for Underrepresented Youth* (Washington, DC: U.S. Department of Education, 2001); J. H. Vargas, *College Knowledge: Addressing Information Barriers to College* (Boston: The Education Resources Institute, 2004).

17. W. S. Swail and L. W. Perna, *Outreach Program Handbook* (Washington, DC: College Board, 2001).

18. D. Karen, "The Politics of Race, Class, and Gender: Access to Higher Education in the United States, 1960–1986," *American Journal of Education* 99, no. 2 (1991): 208–237.

19. J. Engle, A. Bermeo, and C. O'Brien, *Straight from the Source: What Works for First-Generation College Students* (Washington, DC: Pell Institute for the Study of Opportunity in Higher Education, 2006).

Chapter 10

1. A. Valenzuela, *Subtractive Schooling: U.S.-Mexican Youth and the Politics of Caring* (Albany: State University of New York Press, 1999).

2. The No Child Left Behind Act, 2001, Title IX, 9191 {23} A-C.

3. J. Walsh, F. Kemerer, and L. Maniotis, *The Educator's Guide to Texas School Law* (Austin: University of Texas Press, 2005).

4. P. M. Earley, "Searching for the Common Good in Federal Policy: The Missing Essence in NCLB and HEA, Title II," in *Teacher Education for Democracy and Social Justice,* ed. N. M. Michelli and D. L. Keiser (New York: Routledge, 2005), 57–76.

5. Earley, "Searching for the Common Good."

6. J. Cummins, *Negotiating Identities: Education for Empowerment in a Diverse Society* (Los Angeles: CABE, 1996).

7. C. M. Shields, "Dialogic Leadership: Overcoming Pathologies of Silence," *Educational Administration Quarterly* 40 (2004): 109–132.

8. D. L. Keiser, "Learners Not Widgets: Teacher Education for Social Justice During Transformational Times," in *Teacher Education for Democracy and Social Justice,* ed. N. M. Michelli and D. L. Keiser (New York: Routledge, 2005), 31–56.

9. N. M. Michelli, "Education for Democracy: What Can It Be?" in *Teacher Education for Democracy and Social Justice,* ed. N. M. Michelli and D. L. Keiser (New York: Routledge, 2005), 57–76.

10. J. Goodlad, *A Place Called School: Prospects for the Future* (New York: McGraw-Hill, 1984).

11. K. Cotton, *The Schooling Practices That Matter Most* (Portland, OR: Northwest Regional Educational Laboratory, and Alexandria, VA: Association for Supervision and Curriculum Development, 2000); T. L. Good and J. E. Brophy, *Looking into Classrooms* (New York: Allyn and Bacon, 2003); Goodlad, *Place Called School*; L. C. Minor, A. J. Onwuegbuzie, A. E. Witcher, and T. L. James, "Pre-service Teachers' Educational Beliefs and Their Perceptions of Characteristics of Effective Teachers," *Journal of Educational Research* 96 (2002): 116–127; N. Noddings, *The Challenge of Care in Schools: An Alternative Approach to Education* (New York: Teachers College Press, 1992); N. A. Peart and F. A. Campbell, "At-Risk Students' Perceptions of Teacher Effectiveness," *Journal for a Just and Caring Education* 5 (1999): 269–284; A. E. Witcher, A. J. Onwuegbuzie, and L. Minor, "Characteristics of Effective Teachers: Perceptions of Pre-Service Teachers," *Research in the Schools* 8, no. 2 (2001): 45–57.

12. Minor et al., "Pre-service Teachers' Educational Beliefs."

13. G. R. Lopez, M. L. Gonzalez, and E. Fierro, "Educational Leadership Along the U.S. Mexico Border: Crossing Borders/Embracing Hybridity/Building Bridges," in *Leadership for Social Justice: Making Revolutions in Education,* ed. C. Marshall and M. Oliva (New York: Pearson, 2006), 279–306; Texas Education Agency, *Academic Excellence Indicator Report (AEIS)* (Austin, TX: TEA, 2006), http://www.tea.state.tx.us/perfreport/aeis/2006/index.html.

14. D. Deman-Burger, *Effective Teaching: Observations from Research* (Arlington, VA: American Association of School Administrators, 1986), ERIC Document Reproduction Service No. ED274087.

15. A. J. Reed and V. E. Bergemann, *In the Classroom: An Introduction to Education* (Guilford, CT: Dushkin, 1992).

16. T. Wubbels, I. Levy, and M. Brekelmans, "Paying Attention to Relationships," *Educational Leadership* 54, no. 7 (1997): 82–86.

17. Lopez et al., "Educational Leadership Along the U.S. Mexico Border"; B. C. Rubin and B. Justice, "Preparing Social Studies Teachers to Be Just and Democratic: Problems and Possibilities," in *Teacher Education for Democracy and Social Justice,* ed. N. M. Michelli and D. L. Keiser (New York: Routledge, 2005), 57–86.

18. A. J. Onwuegbuzie, A. E. Witcher, K. M. Collins, J. D. Filer, et al., "Students' Perceptions of Characteristics of Effective College Teachers: A Validity Study of a Teaching Evaluation Form Using a Mixed-Methods Analysis," *American Educational Research Journal* 44 (2007): 113–160.

19. D. V. Day, "Leadership Development: A Review in Context," *Leadership Quarterly* 11 (2000): 581–613.

20. W. G. Tierney, "Organizational Culture in Higher Education," *Journal of Higher Education* 59 (1988): 2–21.

21. C. D. McCauley, "Leaders Training and Development," in *The Nature of Leadership Development,* ed. S. J. Zaccaro and R. J. Klimoski (San Francisco: Jossey Bass, 2001).

Conclusion

1. D. F. Labaree, *How to Succeed in School Without Really Learning: The Credentials Race in American Education* (New Haven, CT: Yale University Press, 1997).

2. J. Pak, E. M. Bensimon, L. Malcom, A. Marquez, et al., *The Life Histories of Ten Individuals Who Crossed the Border Between Community Colleges and Selective Four-Year Colleges* (Los Angeles: University of Southern California, 2006).

3. P. Terenzini, L. Springer, P. Yaeger, E. Pascarella, et al., "First Generation College Students: Characteristics, Experiences, and Cognitive Development," *Research in Higher Education* 37 (1996): 1–22.

4. A. Yazedjian, K. E. Purswell, T. Sevin, and M. L. Toews, "Adjusting to the First Year of College: Perceptions of the Importance of Parental, Peer, and Institutional Support," *Journal of the First-Year Experience and Students in Transition* 19, no. 2 (2007): 29–46.

5. C. Adelman, "The Relationship Between Urbanicity and Educational Outcomes," in *Increasing Access to College: Extending Possibilities for All Students,* ed. W. G. Tierney and L. S. Hagedorn (Albany: State University of New York Press, 2002), 35–64; L. Attinasi, "Mexican Americans' Perceptions of University Attendance and the Implications for Freshman Year Persistence," *Journal of Higher Education* 60 (1989): 247–277; A. F. Cabrera and S. M. La Nasa, "Overcoming the Tasks on the Path to College for America's Disadvantaged," *New Directions for Institutional Research* 107 (2000); D. Hossler, J. Schmidt, and N. Vesper, *Going to College: How Social, Economic, and Educational Factors Influence the Decisions Students Make* (Baltimore: Johns Hopkins University Press, 1999); S. Hurtado, "The Study of College Impact," in *Sociology of Higher Education,* ed. P. J. Gumport (Baltimore: Johns Hopkins University Press, 2007), 94–112; S. Hurtado, D. Carter, and A. Spuler, "Latino Student Transition to College: Assessing Difficulties and Factors in Successful College Adjustment," *Research in Higher Education* 37 (1996): 135–157; J. R. Keup and B. O. Barefoot, "Learning How to Be a Successful Student: Exploring the Impact of First-Year Seminars on Student Outcomes," *Journal of the First-Year Experience and Students in Transition* 17, no. 1 (2005): 11–47; M. Saunders and I. Serna, "Making College Happen: The College Experiences of First-Generation Latino Students," *Journal of Hispanic Higher Education* 3 (2004): 146–163; W. G. Tierney, Z. B. Corwin, and J. E. Colyar, *Preparing for College: Nine Elements of Effective Outreach* (Albany: State University of New York Press, 2005).

6. R. C. Bogdan and S. K. Biklen, *Qualitative Research for Education: An Introduction to Theories and Methods* (Boston: Pearson Education Inc., 2007); M. Walpole, "Economically and Educationally Challenged Students in Higher Education: Access to Outcomes," *ASHE Higher Education Repository* 33, no. 3 (2007).

7. W. G. Bowen, M. M. Chingos, and M. S. McPherson, *Crossing the Finish Line: Completing College at America's Public Universities* (Princeton, NJ: Princeton University Press, 2009).

8. Some 11 percent of Latinos aged 25–29 had a college degree or more compared to 17 percent of African Americans and 32 percent of whites.

9. In fall 2000, 58 percent of Latinos enrolled in college were attending two-year institutions compared to 42 percent of blacks and 36 percent of whites.

10. Approximately 60 percent of Latino high school seniors state that their mother has no formal schooling beyond high school.

11. Hurtado et al., "Latino Student Transition."

12. Bowen et al., *Crossing the Finish Line.*

13. Bowen et al., *Crossing the Finish Line.*

14. Bowen et al., *Crossing the Finish Line.*

15. Bowen et al., *Crossing the Finish Line.*

16. Bowen et al., *Crossing the Finish Line.*

17. Bowen et al., *Crossing the Finish Line.*

18. C. Adelman, *The Toolbox Revisited: Paths to Degree Completion from High School Through College* (Washington, DC: U.S. Department of Education, 2006); E. T. Pascarella, C. T. Pierson, G. C. Wolniak, and P. T. Terenzini, "First-Generation College Students: Additional Evidence on College Experiences and Outcomes," *Journal of Higher Education* 75, no. 3 (2004): 249–284.

19. A. W. Astin, *Preventing Students from Dropping Out* (San Francisco: Jossey-Bass, 1975); A. W. Astin, *What Matters in College? Four Critical Years Revisited* (San Francisco: Jossey-Bass, 1993); J. C. Hearn, "The Relative Roles of Academic, Ascribed, and Socioeconomic Characteristics in College Destinations," *Sociology of Education* 57, no. 1 (1984): 22–30; J. C. Hearn, "Pathways to Attendance at the Elite Colleges," in *The High Status Track: Studies of Elite Schools and Stratification,* ed. P. W. Kingston and L. S. Lewis (Albany: State University of New York Press, 1990); Hossler et al., *Going to College*; J. Karabel, "Community College and Social Stratification," *Harvard Educational Review* 41 (1972): 521–562; P. McDonough, *Choosing Colleges: How Social Class and Schools Structure Opportunity* (Albany: State University of New York Press, 1997); M. B. Paulsen and E. P. St. John, "Social Class and College Costs: Examining the Financial Nexus Between College Choice and Persistence," *Journal of Higher Education* 73, no. 2 (2002): 189–236; V. Tinto, *Leaving College: Rethinking the Causes and Curses of Student Attrition* (Chicago: University of Chicago Press, 1987).

20. A. Lareau and E. M. Horvat, "Moments of Social Inclusion and Exclusion: Race, Class, and Cultural Capital in Family–School Relations," *Sociology of Education* 72 (1999): 37–53.

21. E. M. Bensimon, "The Underestimated Significance of Practitioner Knowledge in the Scholarship on Student Success," *Review of Higher Education* 30, no. 4 (2007): 441–469.

22. J. Johnson, J. Rochkind, A. N. Ott, and S. DuPont, *Can I Get a Little Advice Here? How an Overstretched High School Guidance System Is Undermining Students' College Aspirations* (San Francisco: Public Agenda, 2010).

23. Johnson et al., *Can I Get a Little Advice.*

24. Johnson et al., *Can I Get a Little Advice.*

25. A. W. Astin, "Expanding the Quantity and Quality of Educational Opportunities," in *Achieving Educational Excellence*, ed. A. W. Astin (San Francisco: Jossey-Bass, 1985); G. D. Kuh, J. Kinzie, J. Schuh, and E. J. Whitt, *Assessing Conditions to Enhance Educational Effectiveness: The Inventory of Students Engagement and Success* (San Francisco: Jossey-Bass, 2005); G. D. Kuh, J. Kinzie, T. Cruce, R. Shoup, et al., *Connecting the Dots: Multi-Faceted Analyses of the Relationships Between Student Engagement Results from the NSSE, and the Institutional Practices and Conditions That Foster Student Success* (Bloomington: Center for Postsecondary Research, Indiana University, 2006); E. T. Pascarella and P. T. Terenzini, *How College Affects Students, Vol. 2: A Third Decade of Research* (San Francisco: Jossey-Bass, 2005).

26. Kuh et al., *Connecting the Dots*.

27. R. D. Stanton-Salazar, *Manufacturing Hope and Despair: The School and Kin Support Networks of U.S.-Mexican Youth* (New York: Teachers College Press, 2001).

28. E. V. Peña, E. M. Bensimon, and J. Colyar, "Contextual Problem Defining: Learning to Think and Act from the Standpoint of Equity," *Liberal Education* 92, no. 2 (2006): 48–55; C. M. Steele, "A Threat in the Air: How Stereotypes Shape the Intellectual Identities and Performance of Women and African-Americans," *American Psychologist* 52 (1997): 613–629.

29. J. R. Ancis, W. E. Sedlacek, and J. J. Mohr, "Student Perceptions of Campus Cultural Climate by Race," *Journal of Counseling and Development* 78 (2000): 180–185; C. A. Lundberg and L. A. Schreiner, "Quality and Frequency of Faculty–Student Interaction as Predictors of Learning: An Analysis of Student Race/Ethnicity," *Journal of College Student Development* 45, no. 5 (2004): 549–565.

30. Lundberg and Schreiner, "Quality and Frequency."

31. Hurtado et al., "Latino Student Transition"; A. Nora, E. Barlow, and G. Crisp, "Student Persistence and Degree Attainment Beyond the First Year in College: The Need for Research," in *College Student Retention: Formula for Student Success*, ed. A. Seidman (Westport, CT: Praeger, 2005), 130–153; L. I. Rendón, "Validating Culturally Diverse Students: Toward a New Model of Learning and Student Development," *Innovative Higher Education* 19, no. 1 (1994): 23–32; Steele, "A Threat in the Air."

32. D. L. DuBois and N. Silverthorn, "Natural Mentoring Relationships and Adolescent Health: Evidence from a National Study," *American Journal of Public Health* 95, no. 3 (2005): 518–524.

33. M. R. Beam, C. Chen, and E. Greenberger, "The Nature of Adolescents' Relationship with Their 'Very Important' Nonparental Adults," *American Journal of Community Psychology* 30, no. 2 (2002): 305–325.

34. Johnson et al., *Can I Get a Little Advice*.

35. Johnson et al., *Can I Get a Little Advice*.

36. A. L. Bryant and M. A. Zimmerman, "Role Models and Psychosocial Outcomes Among African American Adolescents," *Journal of Adolescent Research* 18 (2003): 36–67; DuBois and Silverthorn, "Natural Mentoring Relationships"; E. Greenberger, C.

Chen, and M. R. Beam, "The Role of 'Very Important' Nonparental Adults in Adolescent Development," *Journal of Youth and Adolescence* 27 (1998): 321–343; S. McDonald, L. D. Erickson, K. Johnson, and G. H. Elder, "Informal Mentoring and Young Adult Employment," *Social Science Research* 36 (2007): 1328–1347; J. E. Rhodes, L. Ebert, and K. Fischer, "Natural Mentors: Overlooked Resources in the Social Networks of Youth African American Mothers," *American Journal of Community Psychology* 20 (1992): 445–461; M. A. Zimmerman, J. B. Bingenheimer, and P. C. Notaro, "Natural Mentors and Adolescent Resiliency: A Study of Urban Youth," *American Journal of Community Psychology* 30 (2002): 221–243.

37. F. Ianni, *The Search for Structure: A Report on American Youth Today* (New York: Free Press, 1989); A. Lareau, *Unequal Childhoods: Class, Race, and Family Life* (Berkeley: University of California Press, 2003).

38. Bensimon, "Underestimated Significance."

39. W. H. Sewell and R. M. Hauser, "The Wisconsin Longitudinal Study of Social and Psychological Factors in Aspirations and Achievements," *Research in Sociology of Education and Socialization* 1 (1980): 59–99.

40. Sewell and Hauser, "Wisconsin Longitudinal Study."

41. A. Valenzuela, *Subtractive Schooling: U.S.-Mexican Youth and the Politics of Caring* (Albany: State University of New York Press, 1999).

42. R. F. Ferguson, *What Doesn't Meet the Eye: Understanding and Addressing Racial Disparities in High-Achieving Suburban Schools* (North Central Regional Educational Laboratory, 2002), http://www.ncrel.org.

43. B. Bernstein, "Social Class, Language, and Socialization," in *Power and Ideology in Education*, ed. J. Karabel and A. H. Hasley (New York: Oxford University Press, 1977).

44. Stanton-Salazar, *Manufacturing Hope and Despair.*

45. Bensimon, "Underestimated Significance."

46. Bensimon, "Underestimated Significance."

47. F. K. Stage and S. Hubbard, "Teaching Latino, African American and Native American Undergraduates: Faculty Attitudes, Conditions, and Practices," in *Interdisciplinary Approaches to Understanding Minority-Serving Institutions,* ed. M. Gasman, B. Baez, and C. Turner (Albany, NY: SUNY Press, 2007).

48. A. M. Martínez-Alemán, "The Nature of the Gift: Accountability and the Professor–Student Relationship," *Educational Philosophy and Theory* 39, no. 6 (2007), DOI [Digital Object Identifier] 10.1111/j.1469-5812.2007.00307.x.

49. D. E. Polkinghorne, *Practice and the Human Sciences: The Case for a Judgment-Based Practice of Care* (Albany: State University of New York Press, 2004).

50. Peña et al., "Contextual Problem Defining."

51. D. T. Conley, C. McGaughy, J. Kirtner, A. van der Valk, et al., *College Readiness Practices at 38 High Schools and the Development of the College Career Ready School Diagnostic Tool* (Eugene, OR: Educational Policy Improvement Center, 2010).

52. Walpole, "Economically and Educationally Challenged."

ABOUT THE AUTHOR

Roberta Espinoza is assistant professor of sociology at California State University, Fullerton. She received her BA from Pomona College and her PhD in sociology from the University of California, Berkeley. She has worked at various research institutes, including the University of California, Berkeley Center for Working Families; the University of California, Los Angeles Center for Research on Evaluation, Standards, and Student Testing; and the Tomás Rivera Policy Institute. She has written articles on minority and working-class students' access to college, women of color in doctoral education, and Latino undocumented students. Her research on Latina doctoral students was featured in the *Hispanic Outlook in Higher Education Magazine*. She speaks annually for academic outreach programs and teaches in college programs that aim to increase the number of underrepresented students in higher education. She also consults with schools and districts concerning the pathways to college for working-class minority students.

INDEX